NATIVE AMERICAN
RELIGIOUS IDENTITY

NATIVE AMERICAN RELIGIOUS IDENTITY

UNFORGOTTEN GODS

edited by

Jace Weaver

ORBIS BOOKS

Maryknoll, New York 10545

The Catholic Foreign Mission Society of America (Maryknoll) recruits and trains people for overseas missionary service. Through Orbis Books, Maryknoll aims to foster the international dialogue that is essential to mission. The books published, however, reflect the opinions of their authors and are not meant to represent the official position of the society.

Manufactured in the United States of America

Manuscript editing and typesetting by Joan Weber Laflamme

Library of Congress Cataloging-in-Publication Data

Native American Religious Identity : Unforgotten gods
    / edited by Jace Weaver.
          p. cm.
     Includes bibliographical references.
     ISBN 1-57075-181-1 (paper)
       1. Indians of North America–Religion.   2. Indians of
 North America–Missions.   3. Missions–North America.   I. Weaver, Jace,
 1957-   .
 E98.R3U58   1998
 299'.7–dc21   97-35474
                                                                        CIP

Who can say that the desert does not live? Or that the dark, serrated ridges conceal no spirit? Who can love the lost places yet believe himself truly alone in the silent hills? How can we be sure the ancient ones were wrong when they believed each rock, each tree, each stream or mountain possessed an active spirit? Are the gods of those vanished peoples truly dead, or do they wait among the shadows for some touch of respect, the ritual or sacrifice that can again give them life?

It is written in the memories of the ancient peoples that one who chooses the desert as an enemy has chosen a bitter foe, but he who accepts it as a friend, who will seek to understand its moods and whims, shall drink deeply of its hidden waters, and the treasures of its rocks shall be opened before him. Where one may walk in freedom and find water in the arid places, another may gasp out his last breath under the desert sun and mark the sands with the bones of his ending.

Louis L'Amour
"The Lonesome Gods"

Despite desires and assurances to the contrary, Indians did not vanish. In spite of the efforts of both Church and State, through coercive evangelization and promulgation of regulations like the Religious Crimes Codes that sought to ban indigenous religious traditions, suppression of Native religions could not be complete. The gods of Native North America have never left themselves without witnesses.

Jace Weaver

Contents

Preface

Each one possessed a stick of wood. Their dying fire was in need of logs.

It was a freezing night.

The first held his back, for in the faces around the fire, he noticed one was black.

The next one saw that one of the group was not of his church. He couldn't bring himself to throw in his and warm that man.

The third, a poor man, his clothes in tatters, held his thin coat close to his body. Why should he put his only log to use to warm the idle rich?

The rich man sat quietly, thinking of how to keep the wealth he accumulated from the shiftless poor.

The face of the next among them spoke of revenge. The fire was dying away. Why should he throw on his log when the others would not? He wanted to spite them.

The sixth man in the forlorn group did nothing except for gain. He too would not throw his log on the fire until another did.

The seventh log you hold. The choice is now yours. The others, their logs held tight in death's still grasp, were proof of human sin. They didn't die from the cold without. They died from the cold within.

Cherokee Folktale[1]

Jack Forbes (Powhatan/Lenape/Saponi), in his book *Columbus and Other Cannibals,* observes of religion:

"Religion" is, in reality, "living." Our "religion" is not what we profess, or what we say, or what we proclaim; our "religion" is what we do, what we desire, what we seek, what we dream about, what we fantasize, what we think—all of these things—twenty-four hours a day. One's religion, then, is one's life, not merely the ideal life but life as it is actually lived.

"Religion" is not prayer, it is not a church, it is not "theistic," it is not "atheistic," it has little to do with what white people call "religion." It is our every act. If we tromp on a bug, that is our religion; if we experiment on living animals, that is our religion;

if we cheat at cards, that is our religion; if we dream of being famous, that is our religion; if we gossip maliciously, that is our religion; if we are rude and aggressive, that is our religion. All that we do, and are, is our religion.[2]

In so speaking, Forbes reflects a traditional Native American view that, as I discuss in one of the essays that follows, recognizes no sharp distinction between sacred and profane spheres of existence. Native cultures and religious traditions are in many ways synonymous and coextensive. As Charles Eastman (Sioux) states, "Every act of [an Indian's] life is, in a very real sense, a religious act."[3] It is this intricately intimate relationship between culture and religious tradition that makes the question of religious identity a vital inquiry. It also means that some of the pieces contained herein—which may on their face have very little to do with "religion" as commonly conceived—are nonetheless profoundly religious in their implications.

The dominant culture has always sought to homogenize and essentialize Native Americans. It has tried to determine those things that are "Indian." What do Natives believe about "God," for instance? What are the elements of *the* Native worldview? No universalized essence can encompass the six hundred different tribal traditions, eight major language families, and probably three distinct racial strains lumped together under the collective construct *Native American* or *American Indian.* Often these different traditions differ one from another as radically as the cultures of France and Tibet differ from each other. Their religious systems and beliefs are often as radically divergent as Christianity is from Buddhism or Hinduism is from Judaism.

Nevertheless, it may seem to the reader that writers in this volume engage in a kind of essentialism when they speak about, for instance, *the* Apache teachings about *usen* or concerning *the* beliefs about the Sun Dance. On some level this may be true. It is necessary to essentialize in order to speak about a group's, as opposed to a given individual's, beliefs—in order to say *something* rather than *nothing.* This is what might be called strategic essentialism in speaking of religious identity. As Gayatri Spivak writes, "Identity is a very different word from essence. We 'write' a running biography with life-language rather than only word-language in order to 'be.' Call this identity! Deconstruction, whatever it may be, is not most valuably an exposure of error, certainly not other people's error, other people's essentialism. The most serious critique in deconstruction is the critique of things that are extremely useful, things without which we cannot live on, take chances; like our running self-identikit. That should be the approach to how we are essentialists." Thus we must run "the risk of essence," the "*strategic* use of a positivist essentialism in a scrupulously visible political interest."[4]

On another level, however, discussion of, let us say, *Cherokee beliefs* about X is not to engage in essentialism in a critical theory sense. To view it as such is to misunderstand the fundamental differences between Native and Western cultures. Central to a Native's sense of self is the individual's sense of how he or she fits into Native community. Anthropologist Clifford Geertz states that "the Western conception of the person as a bounded, unique, more or less integrated motivational and cognitive universe, a dynamic center of awareness, emotion, judgement, and action organized into a distinctive whole and set contrastively both against other such wholes and against its social and natural background, is . . . a rather peculiar idea within the context of the world's cultures." Native societies are *synecdochic* (part-to-whole) rather than the more Western conception that is *metanymic* (part-to-part). As Donald Fixico (Shawnee/ Sac and Fox/Muscogee/Seminole) notes, Native persons tend to see themselves in terms of "self in society" rather than "self and society." It is an "enlarged sense of self."[5] One is thus able to speak more broadly about commonly shared attitudes and beliefs within a given grouping than is possible in discussing Western cultures.

Red Jacket (Seneca) told an early Christian missionary, "We also have a religion which was given to our forefathers, and has been handed down to us their children. It teaches us to be thankful, to be united, to love one another! We never quarrel about religion."[6] Indigenous religious traditions are not, like Christianity or Islam, proselytizing faiths. Rather, one tribe has its instructions from the Creator and respects that others have their own instructions as well. One group sees no need to convert another to its religious system. As long as both tribes fulfill their responsibilities, all will be well. It is not necessary for sparrows to want to be eagles. This religious pluralism is one factor in Natives' easy initial acceptance of European invaders. They were simply one more set of people with different gods and different ways of organizing themselves.

The impact of the conquest and five hundred years of ongoing missionization and colonialism has created a different kind of religious pluralism among Natives. Today there are practitioners of indigenous religious traditions, Native Christians, and adherents of syncretic religions that blend elements of both Christianity and traditional practice. The pieces in this volume reflect this diversity of religious expression. They also reflect the inevitable tensions that such variety creates.

No effort has been made to disguise our differences. Readers must understand, however, that what they are experiencing is an ongoing dialogue on the issues central to this volume. They are privileged to glimpse, as it were, a snippet of a discussion already in progress. It may seem, for example, that I am highly critical of George Tinker. Critique, however, is not dismissal. And our communities arrive at an approximation of truth and right action as they always have, through honest sharing, discussion, and consensus. Today the seventh log is in our hands. Will we opt for cooperation and unity, however tenuous and uneasy, or with-hold our fuel and let the fire die?

The essays in this volume grew out of discussions concerning Native American religious identity in a post-Christian age. We live today in a world where *post* is attached, often too casually, to a great many modes of existence—*post-colonial, postmodern, post-Christian.* I address the question of the post-colonial in my introductory essay, "From I-Hermeneutics to We-Hermeneutics." Steven Charleston seeks a post-modern vision. *Post-Christian,* however, requires some explanation. Just as the post-co-lonial may be said to commence at the moment of colonization and continue to the present, so post-Christian could be said to begin at the first moment of Christian/Native encounter, an encounter that altered Native American lives forever. Some of the authors herein interpret the term in such a manner. Perhaps more fundamentally, though, the age in which we live might be described as post-Christian in that Christianity is no longer considered normative, no longer the all-encompassing force it may once have been. In this sense, post-Christian means something akin to post-Christendom.

Before closing, a couple of further words about terminology are nec-essary. For non-Natives, the issue of what is the preferred term for American indigenes has been a source of no minor confusion. The terms *American Indian, Native American, Native,* or *First Nations* are all inad-equate (once again homogenizing diverse traditions and groupings) yet widely in use. Rather than impose a standard vocabulary, I have re-spected individual authors' choices in this matter and have, in fact, used the terms more or less interchangeably myself. The same is true of terminology regarding White non-Natives. The most common appella-tion is Euro-American, but I (and, in this, George Tinker follows me) have opted for the use of the term of John Joseph Mathews (Osage), *Amer-European,* as more adequately reflecting the relationship of the progeny of colonizers to the American land.[7]

This volume contains pieces dealing with aspects of life throughout North America. This reflects the many commonalities shared by indi-genes in all parts of the hemisphere and is necessary to begin to get some picture, however partial, of Native post-Christian experience here. Many of the contributions are overtly autobiographical (e.g., Freda McDonald's, Donald Grinde's). People telling their own stories repre-sent a kind of modern ethnography. Other articles may seem more "detached" and "scholarly" in a Western, academic sense. When one speaks of religious identity, however, one is dealing with something intimately consequential for Native peoples; thus, even those articles that seem more strictly academic contain an element of autobiography (e.g., those by Leana Hicks or George Tinker). Stories such as those of McDonald or Craig Womack are intensely painful to read, but their voices must be heard. They, and the other contributions in this volume, reflect the way, to quote Simon Ortiz (Acoma Pueblo) "this America [or this Canada, or this Mexico] has been a burden" to Native peoples.[8]

Finally, this is a work about community, and any Native scholarship, ultimately, must be communal. In addition to the authors, thanks must go to the following persons who participated in the birthing of this project but who, for a variety of reasons, are not represented by contributions: Elizabeth Cook-Lynn (Sicangu Dakota), Laura Donaldson (Cherokee), Joe Iron Eye Dudley (Yankton Sioux), Christopher Jocks (Mohawk), Thomas King (Cherokee), Paul Ojibway (Anishinaabe), Stan McKay (Cree), Anne Marshall (Muscogee), Inés Talamantez (Mescalero Apache), Sammy Toineeta (Lakota), Gerald Vizenor (Anishinaabe), Robert Warrior (Osage). Finally, thanks to *Wicazo Sa Review,* in which a version of my essay "Indian Presence with No Indians Present" appeared prior to publication, and to *Semeia,* which published a version of "From I-Hermeneutics to We-Hermeneutics."

Notes

[1] "The Seventh Log: The Choice Is Yours," *Native Journal* (February/March 1993), p. 19.

[2] Jack D. Forbes, *Columbus and Other Cannibals: The Wétiko Disease of Exploitation, Imperialism, and Terrorism* (Brooklyn: Autonomedia, 1979), pp. 26-27.

[3] Charles Alexander Eastman, *The Soul of the Indian* (Boston: Houghton Mifflin Company, 1911), p. 47.

[4] Gayatri Chakravorty Spivak, *Outside in the Teaching Machine* (New York: Routledge, 1993), pp. 3-7.

[5] Jace Weaver, *That the People Might Live: Native American Literatures and Native American Community* (New York: Oxford University Press, forthcoming), pp. 77-79 (manuscript).

[6] Eastman, p. ix.

[7] Weaver, *That the People Might Live,* pp. 15-16 (manuscript).

[8] Simon J. Ortiz, *From Sand Creek* (New York: Thunder's Mouth, 1981), p. 2.

1.

From I-Hermeneutics to We-Hermeneutics

Native Americans and the Post-Colonial[1]

JACE WEAVER

IRONIC HISTORIES: NATIVES AND CHRISTIANITY

Vignette No. 1: In 1782, Christian Delawares left their homes and their already planted fields in Gnadenhutten and moved into a new "praying town" organized by Moravian missionary David Zeisberger at Sandusky. The move was voluntary, to avoid conflict with Amer-European farmers. When the Natives returned to harvest their crops, however, they were confronted by a patrol of one hundred militia from Fort Pitt. The peaceful band surrendered and explained their presence. The colonel in command ordered them bound and—in order to save ammunition—clubbed, scalped, and burned. According to eyewitness reports, the unresisting Natives sang hymns and prayed as the soldiers went about their grisly work. Twenty-nine men, twenty-seven women, and thirty-four children were killed.[2]

Vignette No. 2: In 1838, in one of the best remembered incidents of the Removal of Natives from the American Southeast, sixteen thousand Cherokees were forcibly marched 900 miles from Georgia to present-day Oklahoma. One-fourth of the Cherokee Nation died en route along what came to be called the Trail of Tears. As they walked, Christian Indians among them sang Christian hymns in their own language. The best known of these was an atonement hymn, "One Drop of Blood," which asks, "Jesus, what must I do for you to save me?" The reply is, "It only takes one drop of blood to wash away our sins. You are King of Kings, the Creator of all things." The Cherokee translation of "Guide Me, O Thou Great Jehovah," also sung on the trail, is equally poignant:

Take me and guide me, Jehovah, as I am walking
    through this barren land.
I am weak, but thou art mighty.
Ever help us.

Open unto us thy healing waters.
Let the fiery cloud go before us
and continue thy help.

Help us when we come to the Jordan River
and we shall sing thy praise eternally.[3]

Christian Choctaws, enduring a similar trek, sang too. Theirs, a song of Christian hope, promised that Jesus would save them and stated, "For each of you the heavenly place where you shall dwell is there for you. Follow Jesus to the heavenly place. You will see joy such as you have never seen."[4] Oklahoma proved a heavenly place for neither nation.

Vignette No. 3: In 1862, 303 Sioux were sentenced to die for their roles in an uprising against their brutal treatment led by Little Crow, an Episcopalian. President Abraham Lincoln demanded to review personally the records of the entire proceedings. In the end, he authorized the hanging of 39 men. On the day after Christmas, in Mankato, Minnesota, 38 men (one having received a reprieve) quietly followed the provost marshal to the scaffold. They showed no fear and stood calmly as the nooses were placed around their necks. Then they broke into song. Contemporary newspaper accounts reported that they had sung their Sioux death chant. In reality, a good many were Christian. They were singing the hymn "Many and Great, O God." As the trap dropped, they grabbed for each others' hands and sang, saying "I'm here! I'm here!" It was the greatest mass execution in United States history.[5]

Vignette No. 4: In his book *Custer Died for Your Sins,* Vine Deloria, Jr. (Standing Rock Sioux) describes an encounter in 1967 with the Presbyterian minister in charge of that denomination's Indian missions. Deloria listened to the clergyman describe missionary work among the Shinnecocks of New York's Long Island and then asked how long his church intended to continue such work among a tribe that had lived as Christians for more than 350 years. The impassive reply was, "Until the job is done."[6]

Vignette No. 5: From 1845 to 1848 it was a criminal offense in the Creek Nation to profess Christianity. The penalty for infraction was thirty-nine lashes from a cowhide whip. When less than twenty years old, Samuel Checote was so punished. According to one account, "While blood flowed to his ankles, he was asked 'Will you give up Christ?' He replied 'You may kill me but you cannot separate me from my Lord

Christ.'" He later served as chief of the Nation and as a clergyman. He was instrumental in having the ban on Christianity lifted. Out of respect for his people, he never admitted having suffered at the whipping post for his Christian confession.[7]

These five brief vignettes, which could be replicated many times over, attest to what Marie Therese Archambault (Hunkpapa Lakota), herself a Catholic nun, describes as the "terrible irony" of being both Native and Christian.[8] During the eighteenth and early nineteenth centuries, by necessity, Natives in the eastern United States made great efforts to adapt to and accommodate the Amer-European culture that had engulfed them. Many converted to Christianity, the borrowed religion of the foreign invader. They thought that these things would protect them from further depredations. They were wrong. The attempts at acculturation did not matter. The profession of Christianity did not matter. In the end, it only mattered that they were Indian. Their continued occupation of their homelands served as both a rankling reminder of a brutal conquest not yet complete and an impediment to its final completion. In the process by which Natives were dispossessed, Christian missionaries were often no less culpable than those wielding rifle or plow. As historian Homer Noley (Choctaw) states, "On the one hand, church denominations geared themselves up to take the souls of Native American peoples into a brotherhood of love and peace; on the other, they were part of a white nationalist movement that geared itself up to take away the land and livelihood of Native American people by treachery and force."[9]

Though numerous non-Native historians have produced well-documented treatments of the Native/Christian encounter (most notably Henry Bowden's *American Indians and Christian Missions: Studies in Cultural Conflict* and John Webster Grant's *Moon of Wintertime: Missionaries and Canadian Indians in Encounter since 1534*), scholarly discussion of these events by Natives has been lacking. In the early 1990s two volumes attempted to begin to fill this lacuna: *Missionary Conquest: The Gospel and Native American Cultural Genocide* by George Tinker and *First White Frost: Native Americans and United Methodism* by Homer Noley.[10] Although there are many areas of basic agreement between the two authors, a comparison of the two works yields important differences and provides an illustration of the complexity involved in rehearsing Native religious history.

While Tinker is willing, at least in the case of historic missions, to give missionaries the benefit of the doubt for their good intentions, Noley is less generous in his overall interpretation. Tinker declares, "To state the case baldly and dramatically, my thesis is that the Christian missionaries—of all denominations working among American Indian nations—were partners in genocide. Unwittingly no doubt, and always with the best of intentions, nevertheless the missionaries were guilty of complicity in the destruction of Indian cultures and tribal social structures—complicity in the devastating impoverishment and death of the people to whom they preached."[11] This was so because "the kerygmatic content of the missionary's Christian faith became confused with the accoutrements of the missionary's cultural experience and behavior."[12] Putting aside the difficulty of attributing intentionality, it must still be noted that the systemic nature of racism, of which Tinker himself makes quite a lot, organizes and structures personal intent (however good) so as to mask the racist ends it may serve. Tinker himself declares, "It would have been impossible for these earlier missionaries to see and acknowledge their own sin in this regard." Yet, elsewhere, he also states with regard to missionary cooperation in Amer-European economic and political power structures, "At some level, they must have known what they were about."[13] Tinker, it appears, wants to have it both ways.

By contrast, Noley asks consistently how the missionaries, whose work, as Tinker notes, was clearly so destructive, could *not* have known what they were doing.[14] He declares, "Given the political intrigues that spanned most of the eighteenth century . . . the integrity of missionaries and their mission was in doubt. The biblical dictum 'You cannot serve God and Mammon' (Matt. 6:24) was set aside as missionaries, on the one hand, offered a religion of love and eternal life, and colonists, on the other hand, were forming militia to kill tribal people or drive them from their homes in order to take their lands and crops."[15] Intellectual and historiographic rigor force the question of how different the missiological experience would have to be before Tinker would surrender his assertion as to the "best intentions" of the missionaries, since such a belief cannot be reconcilable with *any* amount of Native suffering and *any* amount of culpability on the part of the evangelists. In the end, I suspect, Tinker's claim is empty because, given the grimness of the historical record and the role of missionaries in it, absent the improbable "smoking gun" stating baldly a divergence between stated and actual goals, it seems apparent there could be no circumstance, real or imaginary, that would dislodge Tinker from his much-repeated faith in the European and Amer-European bearers of the gospel.[16]

The second major difference between Tinker and Noley, dealing as it does with the way they approach their material, is more fundamental. Tinker limns the history of evangelical activities among Natives by focusing on the stories of four prominent missionaries from different regions and eras (John Eliot in Puritan New England; Pierre-Jean De Smet in the Northwest; Junípero Serra in old California; and Henry Benjamin Whipple, Episcopalian bishop of Minnesota during the second half of the 19th century). Other exemplars could have been chosen, but, for Tinker, the unrelenting sameness of the stories makes further renditions unnecessary.[17] Tinker hopes that his study "becomes a contribution to our understanding of why Native American peoples have generally failed to enter the American mainstream and continue to live in poverty and oppression, marginalized on the periphery of society. By and large, Indian people have not found liberation in the gospel of Jesus Christ, but, rather, continued bondage to a culture that is both alien and alienating, and even genocidal against American Indian peoples."[18]

Tinker's method, however, has an unintended and unfortunate consequence. By concentrating exclusively on the four non-Natives of his case study, Natives are erased from the picture. In the process Native agency is destroyed and Native subjectivity is damaged. The missionaries are portrayed as the only actors in the story. Indians are passive recipients, merely acted upon.[19] Noley agrees—it would be impossible for him to do otherwise—that Natives

> were not involved in the preliminary discussions and planning sessions that took place prior to the deployment of missionaries to mission assignments. Their lot was to respond to the implementation of strategies that they had nothing to do with in the planning stages. They were not party to the assessments of their needs and the consequent decision making about how to go about meeting those needs. They were not involved in interdenominational agreements about who could work among which people. It is no wonder that they often became incredulous spectators of events that drastically affected their lives and reflected on their status as intelligent human beings.
>
> From the very beginning of the major missionary movements, when the American Board of Commissioners for Foreign Missions debated heatedly on the subject of whether to "civilize" the Indian first and then "Christianize him," or vice versa, to Reconstruction Era top-to-bottom mission deployment . . . Native people have generally been unwilling spectators of the frustrating results.[20]

In contrast to Tinker, however, Noley depicts the broad sweep of missiological history. He discusses the many prominent Native missionaries and clergy (e.g., Peter Jones, George Copway, John Sunday, Harry Long) who labored, and continue to labor, effectively among their own people. Natives were, of course, actors in the drama as well. A response *was* required of them. Remarkably, despite brutality, a great many Natives did willingly embrace the alien faith, and some of them went on to carry the message to others. This difference between Noley's and Tinker's accounts is crucial. In it lies the question of whether Natives were (and are) self-determined or selves-determined.[21]

Missionaries, in their colonialist drive to assimilate Natives, told those they converted that to become Christian meant to stop being Indian. An example is the experience of Natives after the purchase of Alaska by the United States. In 1897, Dr. Sheldon Jackson, a Presbyterian missionary, was appointed the first territorial commissioner of education. With the support of his colleague Dr. S. Hall Young, Jackson set eradication of Native culture and language as a priority and established boarding schools along the Carlisle model. They encountered, however, a basic problem: these Natives did not fit their stereotypes of Indians. Instead of "rude savages," they found Alaska Natives who were already literate and multilingual, already educated in a Western sense, and already Christian and theologically astute. In fact, the Aleuts had been sending missionaries to other tribes for generations.[22] The first response of these "uncivilized" Natives was to send letters of protest to the Russian ambassador in Washington and to President McKinley. It did not work. In the place of the bilingual education system created by the Russians, Amer-Europeans taught the same self-hatred and internalized loathing that characterized American boarding schools.

Today, only between 10 and 25 percent (depending on what set of statistics one chooses to believe) of Natives consider themselves Christian. Missions still often are conducted in a manner unchanged in over a hundred years. Natives are still taught that "Christian Indian" is an oxymoron. For all too many, to become Christian still means to cease being Indian. Because of the intimate connection between culture and religious traditions for indigenous peoples, an additional irony is that converts are often told the same thing by their traditional relatives. For those who choose to practice Christianity, the result can be ostracism and isolation from community, as illustrated by the story of Samuel Checote in vignette #5 above. Referring to the brutal assimilationist methods of Christian evangelism, traditionalist and peyotist Leonard Crow Dog (Sicangu Lakota) states, "Indians became Christian by force. Often they were killed if they did not convert. Indian Christians have a very hard time these days as they are caught between two ways of seeing the world. I feel sorry for those of you who don't know who you are."[23]

IRONIC READINGS:
NATIVES AND BIBLICAL HERMENEUTICS

William Baldridge (Cherokee) confirms these ironic histories as well as their continued contemporaneity:

> Many missionaries served as federal agents and in that role negotiated treaties which left us no land. Most missionaries taught us to hate anything Native American and that of necessity meant hating our friends, our families, and ourselves. Most refused to speak to us in any language but their own. The missionaries func-

tioned as "Christ-bearing colonizers." If it were otherwise the missionaries would have come, shared the gospel, and left. We know, of course, that they stayed, and they continue to stay, and they continue to insist that we submit to them and their definitions. The vast majority of Native people have experienced the missionary system as racist and colonial."[24]

Much of that racism can be traced to the biblical hermeneutics of those who came to colonize the Americas and the theological anthropology that flowed from those interpretive systems. From the outset of the invasion of the continent, the Bible was read in a manner oppressive of indigenous peoples and employed to justify conquest.

In his paper "Native Americans and the Hermeneutical Task" Homer Noley stresses the role of "theological presuppositions and constructions which were put in place by Colonial America to describe Native Americans in the nation's theological themes."[25] Jonathan Edwards was one of many who spoke of the Western hemisphere as a "promised land" whose inhabitants were "wholly possessed of Satan until the coming of Europeans." John Rolfe proclaimed in 1616 that the British were "a peculiar people, marked and chosen by the finger of God" for the colonial enterprise "to possess [the Americas], for undoubtedly he is with us."[26]

Both Alfred A. Cave, in his article "Canaanites in a Promised Land: The American Indian and the Providential Theory of Empire," and Djelal Kadir, in his book *Columbus and the Ends of the Earth: Europe's Prophetic Rhetoric as Conquering Ideology*, have demonstrated that biblical language was used to spawn and spur the colonial enterprise. Cave quotes Sir George Peckham, a prominent Catholic nobleman who envisioned America as a refuge for Catholics, as viewing the Native population as the Canaanites inhibiting conquest of the Promised Land; these heathens would either be exterminated or, like the Gibeonites, submit "as drudges to hewe wood and carie water."[27] Kadir shows conclusively that colonizers crossed the Atlantic convinced that they were exercising their God-given right to lands held in escrow for them from the foundation of the world. Reverend Alexander Whitaker of Henrico, Virginia, exemplified this opinion when he wrote in 1613 that "this plantation, which the divill hath so often troden down, is by the miraculous blessing of God, revived. . . . God first shewed us the place, God first called us hither, and here God by his special providence hath maintained us."[28] Anders Stephanson shows in *Manifest Destiny* that such beliefs did not cease with the end of the colonial experience but persisted in the American Republic well into the nineteenth century.[29] When Natives were not conceptualized as Canaanites, they were viewed simply as part of a hostile landscape that needed to be ordered and tamed by European civilizers, little more than one more type of fauna to be either domesticated or driven toward extinction. Typical, and illustrative of such a mindset, was the declaration of Eliphalet Stark in a letter to a relative in 1797: "The Yankees have taken care of the wolves, bears, and Indians . . . and we'll build the Lord's temple yet, build it out of these great trees."[30] The roots of such racism were sunk deep in biblical exegesis.

In March 1493, the church was suddenly presented with a problem. Columbus returned home from the "New World" with captives who appeared to be human. The question immediately arose as to how to account for this when the biblical account of creation in Genesis clearly mentioned only three continents (Europe, Asia, and Africa), each populated by the progeny of a different son of Noah after the Deluge. In response, Pope Alexander VI issued his bull *Inter Caetera*. This bull sanctioned the Conquest, reading, "Among the works well pleasing to the Divine Majesty and cherished in our heart, this assuredly ranks highest, that in our times especially the Catholic faith and the Christian religion be exalted and everywhere increased and spread, that the health of souls be cared for and that the barbarous nations be overthrown and brought to the faith itself."[31]

The papal instruction did little, however, to answer the basic questions concerning the humanity and origins of the indigenes of the Americas. Some considered Natives merely human in form but devoid of a soul. Some contended that the newly discovered Natives must be "sons of Ham," the same stock as the "racially inferior" peoples of Africa.[32] Still others, observing the degree of civilization among their cultures, declared the Indians to be the lost tribes of Israel. Though all three ideas coexisted, the last gradually became dominant and persisted relatively unchallenged until well into the nineteenth century. John Wesley, for instance, echoed the prevailing opinions of the day when, addressing the urgency of Christian missions to Natives, he fretted:

> One thing has often given me concern. . . . The progeny of Shem (the Indians) seem to be quite forgotten. How few of these have seen the light of the glory of God since the English first settled among them! And now scarce one in fifty among whom we settled, perhaps scarce one in an hundred of them are left alive! Does it not seem as if God had designed all the Indian natives not for reformation but for destruction? Undoubtedly with man it is impossible to help them. But is it too hard for God? Pray ye likewise the Lord of the Harvest and he will send out more laborers into his Harvest.[33]

The argument over Native humanity itself was not finally resolved until 1512 when Pope Julius II, faced with "mounting evidence of man-like creatures inhabiting the Americas," declared that Native peoples were indeed human beings, descended from Adam and Eve through the Babylonians.[34] Thus by the grace of God and declaration of the Holy Pontiff, Indians were found to possess divine souls and were thus eligible for salvation.

Europeans' first reaction to inhabitants of the Americas was thus not alterity but sameness. Behind the debate over origins was a belief not only in the literal truth of the biblical witness but also that no people could attain any degree of civilization—even language—unless they could be shown as springing from the same roots as those of the known "Old World." They were not Other but Same. Yet, while the debate over the humanity of indigenes was settled, at least nominally, in the Natives' favor, questions as to the value of their cultures were not so resolved.

Edwards was hardly alone in proclaiming American Natives "wholly possessed of Satan" until the arrival of Europeans. Colonists and missionaries, regardless of the country from which they came, universally regarded Native cultures and religious traditions as pagan and diabolic, to be eradicated and replaced with Western values and ways of life. Even Russian missionaries, who on the whole were more sympathetic to the Native cultures they encountered, could not transcend and escape this Eurocentric bias.

An 1894 letter from Orthodox Bishop Petr discussing the traditional beliefs of the Aleuts and Kodiaks states that the morality and religious views of these people "are in essence similar to the Bible stories." The cleric considers this proof of the common origins of all humanity from a single pair of progenitors as depicted in the Hebrew scriptures. He concludes:

> The incomplete and fragmentary nature of the religious views of the Aleuts and Kadiaks [sic] can simply be explained by the fact that they have been too long . . . removed from the direct influence of God's Revelations, which alone can communicate to people in all its fullness the knowledge they need to have about God and the World, whereas originally God's Revelation was limited in all its purity to the European peoples alone. It must be noted that in accordance with God's Holy Revelations the Aleuts and the Kadiaks were not completely bereft of God's Grace, as a result of which there remained with them a sense of morality which prevented them from falling into ultimate sin.[35]

In daring to admit that there was something of the divine in Native religious traditions, albeit fractured and diminished, Bishop Petr was affirming the classical doctrine of the *logos*, which had been interpreted so that the ancient Church could cast itself as the "heir of the pagans" and claim for itself the wisdom of the Greek philosophers—a doctrine that Edwards and others implicitly denied when they saw only deviltry in indigenous traditions. The Gospel according to John begins:

> In the beginning was the Word [*logos*],
> and the Word was with God,
> and the Word was God.

It then continues that this *logos* is "the true light, which enlightens everyone" and that it became flesh and lived among humanity (Jn 1:1, 9, 14). According to historian Justo González, "Since this Logos enlightens everyone, it follows, so the ancients said, that wherever people have any light, they have it because of this eternal Word of God, who became incarnate in Jesus Christ."[36] If the church had been consistent in its treatment of the *logos*, the doctrine should have provided a means to affirm indigenous cultures. Of course, it was not consistent. González writes:

> If the Word incarnate in Christ is the true light which enlightens everyone, it follows that the Word of God can be found wherever humans have any light whatsoever. . . . Once it attained a position of power within the Roman Empire and Greco-Roman culture–partially through its use of the doctrine of the Logos–it did not even consider the possibility that the same Word may have illumined those whom the "best" of culture considered "barbarians." *They* had no Logos. The Word had to be taken from them. Ever since, Christians seem to have remembered the doctrine of the Logos only when approaching cultures and civilizations they had no possibility of overpowering. When, on the contrary, they faced cultures or civilizations they were determined to overrun, or which had not advanced the art of killing as Western civilization had, they saw in those cultures and civilizations nothing but idolatry and ignorance.[37]

Not until the Second Vatican Council did significant theologians take seriously the notion that indigenous peoples might have something to contribute to the understanding of ultimate reality. In the wake of Vatican II, Italo-German theologian Romano Guardini queried whether truths might not "require their own soil in order to develop." Articulating a doctrine of division of labor among religions, he writes:

> Here too we might discern a kind of division of labor, by which, for example, certain truths became clear in India whereas Europeans had not yet grasped them. Hence we might find in the spiritual realm of the Vedas some insights which could be useful for a deepening of the doctrine of the Trinity, or it might be that in Buddhism–the strict Buddhism of the south–experiences

emerged clearly which might be valuable for the problem of the "negative" knowledge of God.

And what of the matter of mythology; indeed the whole question of myth? Shall we simply reject it, and shall those concerned about the purity of the message confine themselves to freeing this message from its mythical elements? Or is it not possible that a way of experiencing and thinking, in which all peoples lived for a time, should contain images which could contribute to a deepening of the Christian faith?[38]

Such expressions, while falling unfortunately short of setting Native traditions on an equal footing with Jewish/Christian traditions, are nonetheless far more accepting than earlier attitudes.

The older ideas, however, persist. Views that see Native religious traditions as worthless and demonic and Natives as the progeny of Ham remain staples of fundamentalist Christianity. The myth of the ten lost tribes remains alive in the Mormon description of American Indians as the Lamanites and continues to recur in popular discourse. Successionist, fulfillment, and anonymous Christ theologies continue to claim a superior position for Christianity over Native cultures. Even conceptualizations of Natives as Canaanites impeding the *eisode* have yet to die out completely. Noley notes that in *The Light and the Glory* Peter Marshall and David Manuel claim that the divine scheme that America should be the "new Jerusalem" was "to be worked out in terms of the settlers' covenant with God and with each other." In such a plan Natives are listed along with droughts, smallpox, and wild animals as "enemies from which God delivered his people."[39] Worse yet, Amer-European missionaries, continuing the ironic history, still teach such theologies and the biblical interpretations that support them to their Native American charges. As George Tinker observes, it is not unusual for entire Indian congregations to remain faithful "to the very missionary theology that was first brought to them, even when the denomination has long ago abandoned that language for a more contemporary articulation of the gospel. One must at least suspect that the process of Christianization has involved some internalization of the larger illusion of Indian inferiority and the idealization of white culture and religion."[40] When such self-hatred has been internalized to its fullest extent, the Conquest will finally be complete.

IRONIC PHILOSOPHIES:
NATIVES AND POST-COLONIALISM

For Native Americans, perhaps the most pervasive result of colonialism is that we cannot even begin a conversation without referencing our words to definitions imposed or rooted in 1492. The arrival of Columbus marks the beginning of colonial hubris in America, a pride so severe that it must answer the charge of blasphemy.[41]

The idea of the *post-colonial,* referring to "a general process of decolonisation which, like colonisation itself, has marked the colonising societies as powerfully as it has the colonised (of course, in different ways)," has gained a great deal of currency in academic circles and exerted an important influence on the developing discipline of cultural studies.[42] It has been most fully articulated by literary critics. To a certain extent this is natural because "literature offers one of the most important ways in which these new perceptions are expressed and it is in their writing, and through other arts such as painting, sculpture, music, and dance that the day-to-day realities experienced by colonized peoples have been most powerfully encoded and so profoundly influential."[43] Yet this also has posed a limitation for post-colonial analysis because these same literary scholars "have been reluctant to make the break across disciplinary (even post-disciplinary) boundaries required to advance the argument"[44] or, indeed, truly to test its utility as a way of apprehending the lived reality of persons and peoples.

On its face, the concept has much to recommend it to Native scholars engaged in American Indian studies or religious studies, including biblical hermeneutics. As Bill Baldridge's statement above demonstrates, Native cultures were decisively different after the ruptures of invasion and colonization. It is self-evident that they were different from how they would have developed if left in isolation. New and extreme pressures, erratic and oppressive government policies, and the reduction of indigenes to less than 1 percent of the population have led to new constellations of identity.

Stuart Hall, a leading force in cultural studies, observes:

> The argument is not that, thereafter, everything has remained the same—colonisation repeating itself in perpetuity to the end of time. It is, rather, that colonisation so refigured the terrain that, ever since, the very idea of a world of separate identities, of isolated or separable and self-sufficient cultures and economies, has been obliged to yield to a variety of paradigms designed to capture these different but related forms of relationship, interconnection and discontinuity.[45]

While I do not want to be accused of the charge of "banal reductionism," which Hall hurls at critic Arif Dirlik, I do believe that there are potentially troubling aspects of post-colonial discourse that must be seriously debated before American Natives can determine whether it is useful to hop aboard the post-colonial bandwagon.

If Ella Shohat is correct about the ahistorical, universalizing, depoliticizing effects of the post-colonial, there is nothing in that analysis for Natives.[46] If Ruth Frankenberg and Lata Mani are right in their assertion that too often the sole function post-colonial analysis seems to serve is as a critique of dominant, Western philosophical discourse—"merely a detour to return to the position of the Other as a resource for rethinking the Western self"—then Natives will want little part of it.[47] Unquestionably, as Dirlik states, "post-coloniality represents a response to a genuine need, the need to overcome a crisis of understanding produced by the inability of old categories to account for the world."[48] The "old categories" of Western discourse, however, never accounted for Native worldviews, and since the time of the first contact with Europeans, American Indians' reality has been all too much monotonously the same, controlled by those who conquered them.

A basic question concerning postcoloniality is that raised by Hall in the title of his essay "When Was the 'Post-Colonial'? Thinking at the Limit." Shohat has pointed out the "problematic temporality" of the term. Bill Ashcroft, Gareth Griffiths, and Helen Tiffin contend that the post-colonial is that period which commences at the moment of colonization and continues to the present day.[49] Hall, for his part, maintains that one thing the post-colonial is not is a periodization based on epochal stages "when everything is reversed at the same moment, all the old relations disappear for ever [sic] and entirely new ones come to replace them."[50] For him the term is not merely descriptive of *there* versus *here* or *then* versus *now*. Nevertheless, in Hall's thinking, as for many post-colonial critics, the term has a temporal scope much more limited than that given to it by Ashcroft, Griffiths, and Tiffin. *Post-colonial* truly represents a time *after* colonialism and temporally means that time of post-independence of the former colonial world, even if the struggle for decolonization is not yet complete.

The problem is that for much of that two-thirds of the world colonialism is not dead. It is not living merely as "after-effects," as Hall implies. Native Americans remain a colonized people, victims of internal colonialism. *Internal colonialism* differs from classic colonialism (sometimes called blue water colonialism) in that in colonialism's classic form a small group of colonists occupy a land far from the colonial metropolis (*métropole*) and remain a minority, exercising control over a large indigenous population, whereas in internal colonialism, the native population is swamped by a large mass of colonial settlers who, after generations, no longer have a *métropole* to which to return. Today, Native American life is characterized by the same paternalistic colonialism that has marked it for over a century. The heavy hand of

federal plenary power still rests heavily upon Native American affairs.

An ironic aspect of post-colonial critique for Natives is its relationship to postmodernism. Post-structuralist discourse provides its
"philosophical and theoretical grounding," and like post-structuralism,
it is "anti-foundational."[51] To understand the irony of this predicament,
one must turn back to the previous century. In the late nineteenth century two great rationalizing sciences rose to prominence, sociology and
anthropology. The former purported to study that which was normative in the dominant culture. The latter, which Claude Levi-Strauss labels
"the handmaiden of colonialism," studied the Other and advised colonial masters in the manners and mores of native peoples that they might
be more effectively controlled.[52] In like manner, in the late twentieth
century two systems of critical thought have arisen to explain the world.
It is no coincidence that just as the peoples of the Two-Thirds World
begin to find their voices and assert their own agency and subjectivity,
postmodernism proclaims the end of subjectivity. By finding its theoretical roots in European intellectual discourse, post-colonialism
continues, by inadvertence, the philosophical hegemony of the West.

Like postmodernism, post-colonialism is obsessed with the issues of
identity and subjectivity. Hall writes that

> questions of hybridity, syncretism, of cultural undecidability and
> the complexities of diasporic identification . . . interrupt any "re-
> turn" to ethnically closed and "centred" original histories.
> Understood in its global and transcultural context, colonisation
> has made ethnic absolutism an increasingly untenable cultural
> strategy. It made the "colonies" themselves, and even more, large
> tracts of the "post-colonial" world, always-already "diasporic" in
> relation to what might be thought of as their cultures of origin.[53]

Putting aside for the moment the diasporic nature of much of modern
Native existence, one must nevertheless admit that there is something
real, concrete, and centered in Native existence and identity. Joseph
Conrad can become a major figure of English letters and Léopold Sédar
Senghor a member of the French Academy, but either one is Indian or
one is not.[54] And certain genuine consequences flow from those acci-
dents of birth and culture. It is part of the distinction drawn by Edward
Said between filiation and affiliation.[55]

The problem is that at base post-colonial discourse *is* depoliticized.
As Shohat notes, in its legitimate and sincere effort to escape essentialism, "post-colonial discourse sometimes seems to define *any* attempt to
recover or inscribe a communal past as a form of idealisation, despite
its significance as a site of resistance and collective identity."[56] Its error,
like that of postmodernism, is that it mistakes having deconstructed

something theoretically for having displaced it politically.[57] Jacqueline Rose, in her book *States of Fantasy*, observes that the postmodern in its "vision of free-wheeling identity . . . seems bereft of history and passion."[58] Said responds, "Just so, particularly at a moment when, all over the globe, identities, civilizations, religions, cultures seem more bloodily at odds than ever before. Postmodernism can do nothing to try to understand this."[59] The same case could be made against post-colonialism.

After more than five hundred years of ongoing colonialism, Native Americans wrestle with two different pulls of identity, one settled and the other diasporic.[60] The settled is that of traditional lands and a continent that was once wholly theirs. The diasporic is that of new homes to which they were exiled by their conquerors, of urban existence far removed from even those territories, and a grim realization that their colonizers are here to stay. Only the most winsome dreamer and the most prophetic visionary believe that Amer-Europeans are going anywhere—short of the success of the Ghost Dance or cataclysmic destruction brought upon themselves. Post-colonial critique provides a useful tool for analyzing Native literatures, which reflect these divergent pulls on identity, and for deconstructing the ironic and destructive biblical readings that have been imposed upon us. As long, however, as those readings and the theologies that spring from them are still taught, as long as denominational factionalism and Amer-European missionization continue to divide families and force Natives to choose between their communities and their religion, the post-colonial moment for Native Americans will not yet have arrived.

DISSOLVING IRONY:
SEARCHING FOR A COMMUNITY HERMENEUTIC

In his book *The Irony of American History* Reinhold Niebuhr delineates three distinct types of history: the pathetic, the tragic, and the ironic. Pathos is that element of history that inspires pity but deserves neither admiration nor contrition. Suffering resulting from purely natural consequences is the clearest example of pathos. Tragedy is the conscious choice of evil for the sake of good. For Niebuhr, writing at the height of the Cold War, that the United States supposedly had to have and had to threaten to use nuclear weapons in order to preserve itself and its allies was tragic. Irony "consists of apparently fortuitous incongruities of life which are discovered, upon closer examination, to be not merely fortuitous."[61] It is distinguished from the pathetic in that humans bear responsibility for it. It is distinguished from the tragic in that the responsibility rests on unconscious weakness rather than conscious choice. Irony, unlike pathos or tragedy, must dissolve when it is brought to light. It elicits laughter. American history for Niebuhr is ironic: there is a gap between the ideal of America's self-image and the reality of its history and existence.[62] Natives have been representing themselves in print for more than two hundred years and have striven to bring to light, in the hope of dissolving them, the ironic histories, readings, and philosophies that have been imposed upon them by the dominant culture. Without falling into the post-colonial/postmodernist naiveté of believing that theoretical deconstruction necessarily means ultimate efficacy, they have asserted their own subjectivity and have attempted to develop and spell out their own histories, readings, and intellectual discourse in a way that affirms their personhood.

Noley states, "If the Native American clergy are satisfied with their training, there may not be an interest in a new basis for Native American ministries. If they are not satisfied, there is a place for Native American Biblical scholarship."[63] He remains skeptical, however, because most Native clergy "reflect the fundamentalism of rural white non-Indian Christianity."[64] The remarks are consonant with Tinker's contention that Natives often adhere to the missionary theology first brought to them generations ago. In point of fact, however, at least a few Native clergy and laity always have expressed their dissatisfaction with the transmitted biblical interpretation of the dominant culture.

The work of William Apess (Pequot), writing in the 1820s and 1830s, must be viewed as resistance literature, repeatedly employing indirection and signification to affirm Indian cultural and political identity over against the dominant culture. For example, in his autobiography, *Son of the Forest,* he rejects any use of the term *Indian* as a disgrace. Looking to the Bible, he finds no reference to "indians" "and therefore deduces that it is a word imported for the special purpose of degrading us." He concludes, "But the proper term which ought to be applied to our nation, to distinguish it from the rest of the human family, is that of '*Natives*'—and I humbly conceive that the natives of this country are the only people under heaven who have a just title to the name, inasmuch as we are the only people who retain the original complexion of our father Adam."[65] Here Apess's subversion through rhetoric can be seen clearly. He invokes the language of evangelical Christianity with its appeal to the Bible. In all his writings, he constantly throws up the norms, language, and tools of Christianity into the face of Amer-Europeans in order to expose their racism and to subvert their use of the same material for racist ends.

A key example of Apess's use of signification can be found in his use of the contention that America's indigenes are the ten lost tribes of Israel. As quoted above, Apess states that Indians are the only people with Adam's original complexion, an assertion he repeats, a reference to his belief that Indians were the lost tribes. As such, they, like the Jews, whom he considers people of color, would be Semites and thus closer to Adam's coloring than the pale Anglo-Saxons. He includes a lengthy appendix to *Son of the Forest*, outlining all the various arguments in favor of this thesis. He returns to the theme in a sermon, "The Indians: The Ten Lost Tribes." Far from using this myth of dominance to slur his own people, however, Apess uses it to claim their common humanity. If Natives are the ten lost tribes, they are every bit as human as their Amer-European invaders. If they are human, they are entitled to equal treatment. Beyond this, if they share a common ancestry with Amer-Europeans, how is there any basis for racism against them? In a scathing pun, Apess looks at Amer-Europeans' complexion and their treatment of Indians and concludes that their Christianity must be only "skin-deep."[66]

Likewise, Peter Jones (Anishinaabe), writing in the decades immediately after Apess, examines the biblical text and employs it against the established order. Jones concludes that Whites have more to atone for in their treatment of Natives than they will ever be able to achieve. In language reminiscent of Apess, he looks to the ultimate judgment, writing, "Oh, what an awful account at the day of judgment, must the unprincipled white man give, who has been the agent of Satan in the extermination of the original proprietors of the American soil! Will not the blood of the red man be required at *his* hands, who, for paltry gain, has impaired the minds, corrupted the morals, and ruined the constitution of a once hardy and numerous race?" Such judgment, however, extends to crimes far more numerous than the introduction of liquor. Jones declares sarcastically, "When I think of the long catalogue of evils entailed on my poor unhappy countrymen, my heart bleeds, not only on their account, but also for their destroyers, who, coming from a land of light and knowledge, are without excuse. Poor deluded beings! Whatever their pretensions to Christianity may have been, it is evident the love of God was not in their hearts; for that love extends to all mankind, and constrains to acts of mercy, but never impels to deeds of death."[67]

One hundred and fifty years later, Marie Therese Archambault declared:

> When we read the Gospel, we must read it as *Native people*, for this is who we are. We can no longer try to be what we think the dominant society wants us to be. . . . We must learn to subtract the chauvinism and cultural superiority with which this Gospel was often presented to our people. We must, as one author says, "decolonize" the Gospel, which said we must become European in order to be Christian. We have to go beyond the *white gospel* in order to perceive its truth."[68]

For Robert Warrior, in his important and widely reprinted article "Canaanites, Cowboys, and Indians," the Native experience *is* that of the biblical Canaanites, dispossessed of their homeland and annihilated by a foreign invader. His argument takes on added force in the case of the tribal groups who were subjected to a genocidal reverse Exodus from country that was for them, literally, the Promised Land. Thus, for Warrior, to read the biblical witness as a Native, as Archambault suggests, is to read it with "Canaanite eyes."[69]

Tinker, trained as a biblical scholar, contends that a Native biblical reading "presents an interesting challenge to the predominant, Eurocentric tradition of biblical scholarship." It will differ, he avers, from "Euro-American" hermeneutics in three ways: "First, the theological function of the Old Testament in a Native American context will differ. Second, the sociopolitical context of Native American peoples will characteristically generate interpretations that are particularly Native American. Moreover, the discrete cultural particularities of cognitive structures among Native Americans will necessarily generate 'normatively divergent' readings of scripture."[70] Each of these points requires some elaboration.

According to Justo González:

> The "modern" worldview is so prevalent, and so successful in its manipulation and the exploitation of the natural world, that in many circles it currently passes for the only rational or reasonable understanding of the world. The net result in theology, and in particular in biblical interpretation, has been the need to demythologize, as Bultmann correctly pointed out—or perhaps better, to re-mythologize into the myth patterns of the twentieth-century Western technocratic myth system. Passages in the Bible dealing with miracles, demons, and divine intervention in human and natural affairs, many of which have been sources of strength for believers throughout the centuries, have become problematic for many in the dominant culture—and, precisely because of the dominant power of that culture, for many in other cultures.[71]

Needless to say, however, the "modern" worldview is not the only possible way of seeing reality, nor is its logic as inescapable as its proponents would have one believe. Michael Oleska points out, "Traditional societies, as have existed since homo sapiens first appeared, have almost universally shared certain common attitudes toward fundamental experience. They perceive time, space, and nature in ways remarkably different from those of the post-Renaissance West."[72] Native worldviews are, in fact, much closer to the worldview of the ancient Israelites than that of the modern West. After all, Yahweh was first and foremost the tutelary, local tribal deity of the Hebrew people, whose acts they recognized in their lives. Stan McKay (Cree), former moderator of the United Church of Canada, writes, "For those who come out of the Judeo-Christian background it might be helpful to view us as an 'Old Testament People.' We, like them, come out of an oral tradition which is rooted in the Creator and the creation. We, like Moses, know about the sacredness of the earth and the promise of land. Our creation stories also emphasize the power of the Creator and the goodness of creation. We can relate to the vision of Abraham and the laughter of Sarah. We have dreams like Ezekiel and have known people like the Pharaoh. We call ourselves 'the people' to reflect our sense of being chosen."[73]

These divergent worldviews will generate culturally relevant and specific interpretations of the biblical text. Native Christians give authority to scripture specifically because it resonates with their experience. Even while reading with Canaanite eyes, they locate themselves and their perceptual experience in the story. They report relating to Moses trudging up Sinai to meet the divine as one about to embark on a vision quest. They recognize Mary, the mother of Jesus, because she is *la Virgen de Guadalupe*, or White Buffalo Calf Woman, or Corn Mother, or *La llorona* refusing to be consoled at the death of her child. They can chuckle knowingly at the exploits of Jacob because he is the trickster familiar to them as Coyote, or Raven, or Iktomi. This is not the hermeneutics of professional exegetes. Rather, it is the folk theology upon which Christianity at the ground level has always thrived as a living faith. This process of appropriation of the text is no different than that which goes on in the lives of ordinary Christians anywhere in the world. Native Christians give authority to the biblical witness because, to paraphrase Coleridge, there is something that "finds them" where they live their lives.

Any post-colonial biblical hermeneutic for Natives must affirm traditional religious expressions, which previously have been denied and denigrated. As Steven Charleston (Choctaw), former Episcopal bishop of Alaska, reminds us: Natives had a covenant with the Creator lived long before missionaries came to them. According to Charleston, that original covenantal relationship forms the "Old Testament of Native America."[74] Yowa of the Cherokee, Wakan Tanka of the Lakota, the Great Energy of the Gwich'in, and countless other manifestations are as much *logoi* as any of the faces of deity in the Jewish-Christian tradition. Noley explicitly rejects the assimilationist, missionary hermeneutic that speaks of Native missions in terms of the parable of the tares (Mt 13:24-30, 36-43).[75] In such an interpretation, the tares sown by the enemy are Natives who continue to adhere to their indigenous religious traditions or those who practice religious dimorphism (a very common occurrence among Native peoples), whereby a person participates in Christianity but also still participates in his or her traditional culture and ways without mixing the two. A post-colonial hermeneutic rejects any interpretation that divides Native community.

A post-colonial hermeneutic also will take seriously the importance of land for Native peoples. This imperative has several layers. First, Natives tend to be spatially oriented rather than temporally oriented. Their cultures, spirituality, and identity are connected to the land—and not simply land in a generalized sense but *their* land. The act of creation is not so much what happened *then* as it is what happened *here*; it is the story of the formation of a specific land and a particular people. Thus, when Indian tribes were forcibly removed from their homes, they were robbed of more than territory. Taken from them was a numinous world where every mountain and lake holds meaning for their faith and identity. For example, the Cherokee word *eloh'*, sometimes translated as "religion," also means, at precisely the same time, "history," "culture," "law"—and "land."[76]

George Tinker, in particular, has written repeatedly about this spatiality. He claims that a Native reading of the Greek scriptures "begins with a primarily spatial understanding of the *basileia*." In the predominant Western biblical scholarship, since the late nineteenth century when eschatology emerged as a central aspect of interpretation of the Greek scriptures, the *basileia tou theou* (the realm of God) has been seen almost exclusively in temporal terms. According to Tinker, "That is, the only appropriate question to ask about the *basileia* has been When?" For Natives, however, thinking spatially, "it is natural to read *basileia tou theou* as a creation metaphor." It is an image of the ideal of harmony and balance. Tinker concludes, "To this extent, the ideal world is the real world of creation in an ideal relationship of harmony and balance with the Creator. It is relational, first of all, because it implies a relationship between the created order of things and its Creator, and, second, because it implies a relationship between all of the things created." It is the real world within which we hope to realize the ideal world of harmony and balance.[77]

Naturally flowing from this is the question of humanity's relationship to the earth as a creation of the Creator. Natives traditionally do not relate to the land as landscape. Landscape is related to the German *landschaft*, "a territory shaped by people, a working country carved by axe and plough."[78] It is a word rooted in a belief that the earth must be subdued by human effort before it has worth. (Though many Natives have "tooled" the land, by irrigating it or clearing it for crops or pasture, for instance, there is not the concomitant view that it is inferior or worthless without such ministrations.) In that sense, it shares a common origin with the injunction of Genesis 1:28 to have dominion over the creation. By contrast, in traditional Native cultures the relationship to the creation is quite different. There is no superiority assumed or claimed for humanity, and humanity is, in some sense, undifferentiated from the rest of the created order. The world around the Native is a point of communion with the divine because it is a visible expression of the one who created it and still undergirds it.

Finally, when one speaks of land, the issue arises as to ownership. Before the advent of Europeans and the imposition of foreign notions of land tenure, which divided up the land that it might be rendered tame, land was not "owned" in a modern sense. It was held in common by all. It was not property but community. Once again, the affinity with the worldview of the ancient Hebrews is evident. Such a belief compares readily to that expressed in Leviticus 25:23: "And the land shall not be sold in perpetuity; for the land is mine: for ye are strangers and sojourners with me." When he attempted to rally the Native nations into a grand alliance to halt White expansionism, Tecumseh (Shawnee) declared, "The only way to stop this evil is for all the red men to unite in claiming a common and equal right in the land, as it was at first, and should be now—for it never was divided, but belongs to all. No tribe has a right to sell, even to each other, much less to strangers, who demand all and will take no less."[79] This raises the ultimate question of ownership of land; namely, that of how it was wrested from its original occupants. Noley states the matter bluntly, "The fundamental question has never been addressed, even after two hundred years of white presence on this continent: namely, the validity of white presence on a continent already possessed and cultivated."[80] A post-colonial hermeneutic must take account of Native land claims.

The final fundamental, and most basic, element of a post-colonial hermeneutic is its communal character. As is often said, community is the highest value for Native peoples, and fidelity to it is a primary responsibility. Native religious traditions are not practiced for personal empowerment or fulfillment but rather to ensure the corporate good. There is generally no concept of salvation other than the continuance of the people, and the closest approximation of the Jewish-Christian doctrine of sin is a failure to live up to one's obligations to the people. A post-colonial hermeneutic for Natives rejects the individualistic interpretations brought by assimilationist missions in favor of more communal and communitarian methods and understandings.

No professional exegete or theologian can say what a text means, let alone *should* mean, for Native communities. Only the communities themselves, gathered in dialogue (though modern mass communications may permit them to be geographically distant), can perform that task. The community as the proper locus of the hermeneutical task means that what emerges resembles what Justo González, for Hispanics, labeled *Fuenteovejuna* (sheep trough) theology, "meaning . . . a theology undertaken with such a sense of community that it belongs to the community itself, and at the end no one knows who first proposed a particular idea."[81] In traditional cultures the thought that an idea or a story could belong to an individual—belong to such an extent that he or she could have enforceable proprietary rights to it—would seem as irrational and bizarre as a single person owning the land.

A post-colonial Native hermeneutic, a "we-hermeneutic," however, "goes far beyond the proposal that Scripture is best understood within the circumstances of a community, and when interpreted by a community."[82] Community is not only a tool or a framework for the hermeneutical task but also its ultimate goal.

> Thus, the community is not just a hermeneutical tool and a neces-
> sary context in which to understand a text, but also the goal of
> every interpretation and every text to be interpreted. Without such
> a perspective, we fall into I-hermeneutics, which fails, not merely
> because it misinterprets its text, but also because it misinterprets
> its task. The task of hermeneutics is not merely for an individual—
> or even for a community—to understand a text, but is even more
> for building the community.[83]

I have called such an approach *communitist* (a combination of *community* and *activist*). A truly post-colonial we-hermeneutic is communitist because it possesses an active commitment to Native community. The community itself "stands at the very center" of such an interpretive system.[84]

Though such a hermeneutic will, of necessity, be culturally specific (Natives have too long been subjected to the universalizing impulses of Western discourse), as Hall claims for the post-colonial critique in general, it moves beyond the "clear-cut politics of binary oppositions" of "us" versus "them."[85] Though it seeks to be inclusive, as much as possible, of the entire Native American community, it does not stop there. Nor does it stop at the entire human community; rather, it seeks to embrace the entire created order, plants, animals, Mother Earth herself.

In his book *Tribal Secrets* Robert Warrior speaks of the need and ability of American Natives to assert their own "intellectual sovereignty."[86] What exactly a post-colonial we-hermeneutic will mean for Natives must emerge out of the community itself as we critically reflect upon our own communitist commitments. If, however, we are ever to dismantle the colonial paradigm and move to a place "after" and "beyond" colonialism[87] and the imperialist readings it engenders, we must have hermeneutical sovereignty as well.

Notes

[1] I am indebted for this title to a paper delivered in 1988 at the Roundtable of Ethnic Minority Theologians by Stephen S. Kim of the Claremont Graduate School entitled, "From I-Hermeneutics to We-Hermeneutics: A Prolegomenon to Theology of Community from an Asian-American Perspective." That I find

it applicable as a title for this present article attests to the many commonalities people of color have shared in the colonial experience.

[2] David A. Rausch and Blair Schlepp, *Native American Voices* (Grand Rapids: Baker Books, 1994), pp. 130-31.

[3] Marilyn M. Hofstra, ed., *Voices: Native American Hymns and Worship Resources* (Nashville: Discipleship Resources, 1992), pp. 14-15.

[4] Ibid., p. 39.

[5] Homer Noley, *First White Frost* (Nashville: Abingdon Press, 1991), pp. 165-66.

[6] Vine Deloria, Jr., *Custer Died for Your Sins*, 2d ed. (Norman: University of Oklahoma, 1988), p. 112.

[7] Noley, pp. 198-200.

[8] In Jace Weaver, "Native Reformation in Indian Country?" *Christianity and Crisis* (Feb. 15, 1993), p. 40.

[9] Noley, p. 85.

[10] Although the history of Natives and Methodism is Noley's primary focus, the volume is much fuller, providing a broad history of Native/Christian interaction.

[11] George Tinker, *Missionary Conquest* (Minneapolis: Fortress Press, 1993), p. 4; George Tinker, "Reading the Bible as Native Americans," *New Interpreters Bible*, vol. 1 (Nashville: Abingdon Press, 1994), p. 174.

[12] Tinker, *Missionary Conquest*, p. 4.

[13] Ibid., pp. 10, 18.

[14] Noley, p. 191.

[15] Ibid., p. 43.

[16] See Anthony Flew, "Theology and Falsification," in *New Essays in Philosophical Theology*, ed. A. G. N. Flew and A. C. MacIntyre (London: S.C.M., 1955), pp. 96ff.

[17] Tinker, *Missionary Conquest*, pp. 125-26.

[18] Ibid., p. 5.

[19] See John Webster Grant, *Moon of Wintertime: Missionaries and the Indians of Canada in Encounter since 1534* (Toronto: University of Toronto Press, 1984), p. 239.

[20] Noley, pp. 205-6.

[21] See Holly Folk, "Indian Missionaries Among the Anishinaabe Tribes of the Great Lakes Region: Selves-Determined or Self-Determining," unpublished paper, Columbia University, Spring 1996.

[22] Michael Oleska, ed., *Alaskan Missionary Spirituality* (New York: Paulist Press, 1987), pp. 21-24. The Russian Revolution of 1917 threw Russian Orthodox missions in America into a turmoil that would not end fully until fifty-three years later when the Russian Patriarch recognized the American church as autocephalous.

[23] In James Treat, ed., *Native and Christian: Indigenous Voices on Religious Identity in the United States and Canada* (New York: Routledge, 1996), p. 18.

[24] William Baldridge, "Reclaiming Our Histories," in *New Visions for the Americas: Religious Engagement and Social Transformation*, ed. David Batstone (Minneapolis: Fortress Press, 1993), p. 25. Baldridge's original title for the article in which this statement appeared was "Christianity after Colonialism."

[25] Homer Noley, "Native Americans and the Hermeneutical Task," unpublished paper, delivered at the Roundtable of Ethnic Theologians, 1988.

[26] Perry Miller, *Errand into the Wilderness* (Cambridge: Harvard University Press, 1957), p. 119.

[27] Alfred A. Cave, "Canaanites in a Promised Land: The American Indian and the Providential Theory of Empire," *American Indian Quarterly* (Fall 1988), p. 287.

[28] In ibid., p. 288.

[29] Anders Stephanson, *Manifest Destiny: American Expansion and the Empire of Right* (New York: Hill and Wang, 1995), pp. 15-65.

[30] In Donald A. Grinde, Jr., and Bruce E. Johansen, *Ecocide in Native America* (Santa Fe: Clear Light, 1995), p. 7; Jace Weaver, *Defending Mother Earth: Native American Perspectives on Environmental Justice* (Maryknoll: Orbis Books, 1996), pp. 14-15.

[31] In Terry Tafoya and Roy De Boer, "Comments on the Involvement of Christian Churches in Native American Affairs," in Marilyn Bode, *Christians and Native Americans in the Late 20th Century* (Seattle: Church Council of Greater Seattle, 1981), p. 17.

[32] Jace Weaver, "Original Simplicities and Present Complexities: Reinhold Niebuhr, Ethnocentrism, and the Myth of American Exceptionalism," *Journal of the American Academy of Religion*, 63:2 (1995), pp. 234-35.

[33] Noley, *First White Frost*, pp. 43-44.

[34] Ibid., p. 18.

[35] In Oleska, p. 71.

[36] Justo González, *Out of Every Tribe and Nation: Christian Theology at the Ethnic Roundtable* (Nashville: Abingdon Press, 1992), p. 43.

[37] Ibid.

[38] Romano Guardini, *The Church of the Lord: On the Nature and Mission of the Church* (Chicago: Henry Regnery Company, 1966), pp. 8-9.

[39] See Noley, "Native Americans."

[40] Tinker, *Missionary Conquest*, p. 3.

[41] Baldridge, p. 24.

[42] Stuart Hall, "When Was 'the Post-Colonial'? Thinking at the Limit," in *The Post-Colonial Question: Common Skies, Divided Horizons*, ed. Iain Chambers and Lidia Curti (London: Routledge, 1996), p. 246.

[43] Bill Ashcroft, Gareth Griffiths, and Helen Tiffin, *The Empire Writes Back: Theory and Practice in Post-Colonial Literatures* (London: Routledge, 1989), p. 1.

[44] Hall, p. 258.

[45] Ibid., pp. 252-53.

[46] See Ella Shohat, "Notes on the Postcolonial," *Social Text* 31/32 (1992).

[47] Ruth Frankenberg and Lata Mani, "Crosscurrents, Crosstalk: Race, 'Postcoloniality' and the Politics of Location," *Cultural Studies* 7:2 (1992), p. 101; Hall, pp. 248-49.

[48] Arif Dirlik, "The Postcolonial Aura: Third World Criticism in the Age of Global Capitalism," *Critical Inquiry* (Winter 1992), p. 353.

[49] Ashcroft, Griffiths, and Tiffin, pp. 2, 6.

[50] Hall, p. 247.

[51] Ibid., pp. 255-56.

[52] Edward Said, *Culture and Imperialism* (New York: Alfred A. Knopf, 1993), p. 152.

[53] Hall, p. 250.

[54] See Thomas King, *All My Relations* (Toronto: McClelland & Stewart, 1990), p. x.

[55] Edward Said, *The World, the Text, and the Critic* (Cambridge: Harvard University Press, 1983), pp. 19-20.

[56] Hall, p. 251.

[57] Ibid., p. 249.

[58] Jacqueline Rose, *States of Fantasy* (New York: Oxford University Press, 1996).

[59] Edward Said, "Fantasy's Role in the Making of Nations," *Times Literary Supplement* (Aug. 9, 1996), p. 7.

[60] Ibid.

[61] Reinhold Niebuhr, *The Irony of American History* (New York: Charles Scribner's Sons, 192), pp. vii- viii.

[62] Weaver, "Original Simplicities," pp. 233-34.

[63] Noley, "Native Americans."

[64] Ibid.

[65] William Apess, *On Our Own Ground: The Complete Writings of William Apess, a Pequot*, ed. Barry O'Connell (Amherst: University of Massachusetts Press, 1992), p. 10.

[66] Ibid., pp. 34ff.

[67] Peter Jones, *History of the Ojebway Indians: With Especial Reference to Their Conversion to Christianity* (London: A. W. Bennett, 1861), pp. 29-30.

[68] In Treat, p. 135.

[69] In Jace Weaver, "A Biblical Paradigm for Native Liberation," *Christianity and Crisis* (Feb. 15, 1993), p. 40.

[70] Tinker, "Reading the Bible as Native Americans," p. 174.

[71] González, p. 48.

[72] Oleska, pp. 7-8.

[73] In Treat, p. 52.

[74] Steve Charleston, "The Old Testament of Native America," in *Lift Every Voice: Constructing Christian Theology from the Underside*, ed. Susan Brooks Thistlethwaite and Mary Potter Engel (San Francisco: Harper & Row, 1990), pp. 54-55.

[75] Noley, *First White Frost*, p. 187.

[76] Weaver, *Defending Mother Earth*, p. 12.

[77] Tinker, "Reading the Bible as Native Americans," pp. 176-80.

[78] Stephen Daniels, "This Land Was Made for Us," *Times Literary Supplement* (Aug. 9, 1996), p. 8.

[79] Noley, *First White Frost*, pp. 71-72.

[80] Ibid.

[81] González, p. 53.

[82] Ibid., p. 54; see also Kim.

[83] González, p. 54.

[84] Ibid.

[85] Hall, p. 244.

[86] Robert Allen Warrior, *Tribal Secrets: Recovering American Indian Intellectual Traditions* (Minneapolis: University of Minnesota Press, 1995), pp. 97-98.

[87] Hall, pp. 253-54.

2.

The European Concept of *Usen*

An American Aboriginal Text

VIOLA F. CORDOVA

The American aboriginal concept of *Usen* is a term of such abstraction that it has, thus far, proven too complex to the understanding of those cultures that can be termed European, that is, all of those peoples who either occupy the European continent or are descendants of those people.

It is necessary, first of all, to say something about the use of the term *European* to signify a group of people who, themselves, object to any generalization concerning the many groups subsumed under the label European. It must be pointed out that the European has invented the term *Western* to signify the shared notions that set off European, or "Western," peoples from all of the other of the planet's peoples. The term indicates, through its prevalent use, that there are some agreed-upon ideas, a matrix, if you will, that are held–in general–that would allow such a designation to carry any meaning for Westerners and non-Westerners alike.

Any further objection to the use of the term *European* and its cognate *Western* should be set aside by the following remarks of the Spanish philosopher of the early twentieth century Jose Ortega y Gasset. In his work of the 1930s, *The Revolt of the Masses*, Ortega undertakes an analysis of the European character. He points to the "homogeneity" of the group that prefers to see itself as "modern":

> In each new generation the souls of men grew more and more alike. To speak with more exactitude and caution, we might put it this way: the souls of the French and Spanish are, and will be, as different as you like, but they possess the same psychological

architecture; and, above all, they are gradually becoming similar in content. Religion, science, law, art, social and sentimental values are being shared alike. Now these are the spiritual things by which man lives. The homogeneity, then, becomes greater than if the souls themselves were all cast in identical mould. If we were to take an inventory of our mental stock today—opinions, standards, desires, assumptions—we should discover that the greater part of it does not come to the Frenchman from France, nor to the Spaniard from Spain, but from the common European stock. Today, in fact, we are more influenced by what is European in us than by what is special to us as Frenchmen, Spaniards, and so on. If we were to make in imagination the experiment of limiting ourselves to living by what is "national" in us, and if in our fancy we could deprive the average Frenchman of all that he uses, thinks, feels, by reason of other sections of the Continent, he would be terror-stricken at the result. He would see that it is not possible to live merely on his own; that four-fifths of his spiritual wealth is the common property of Europe.

As to the term *modern*, Ortega has this to say: "The very name is a disturbing one; this time calls itself 'modern,' that is to say, final, definitive, in whose presence all the rest is preterite, humble preparation and aspirations toward this present." I have found no more succinct explanation of why it is that one can generalize about the European or the West. "The homogeneity," according to Ortega, is a result of shared notions about "religion, science, law, art, social and sentimental values," as well as shared "opinions, standards, desires, and assumptions."

In making comments about the term *Usen* it is also necessary to locate it within a specific context. The term is derived from the Apache and Athabascan people of the American Southwest, specifically the state of New Mexico. The term signifies a concept that may be "pan-Indian." That is to say, it may be more widespread throughout Native North America. The Blackfoot speak of *natoji*, the Sioux of *wakan tanka*, the Navajo of *nil'ch'i*, and the peoples of the northeastern United States have the term *manitou*. In all circumstances the term signifies something "of a substance, character, nature, essence, quiddity beyond comprehension and therefore beyond explanation, a mystery; supernatural; potency, potential" (the description of Basil Johnston, an Anishinaabe writer). The concept of this mysterious force also shares the notion of its being all-pervasive. It is everywhere and in all things, perhaps is all things. Again, Basil Johnston states, "[Scholars] continue to labour under the impression that the word 'manitou' means spirit and that it has no other meaning. . . . They do not know that the word bears other meanings even more fundamental than 'spirit.'" The term *Usen*, which will be the one employed here, may or may not contain all of the features that individual tribal groups use throughout North America. It does, however, encompass the notion of something that simply *is*, that remains unidentifiable, mysterious, "supernatural" in the sense that it is beyond pointing to. Nevertheless, this mysterious *something* precedes everything else; it serves at the same time as the ground of things and the manifestation of itself.

That the notion is not unknown to Western thinkers is obvious. The idea of *Usen*, or its other manifestations, is that which early Christian missionaries chose to relate to the Western concept of God. It is most familiar to non-aboriginal peoples as the notion of the Great Spirit. The fact that Europeans, when first encountering the idea, sought to relate it to some notion that came within their range of understanding is what allowed the popularity of the term *Great Spirit.* I imagine something like the following to have taken place: The missionary tries to tell the indigenous person about his focus of worship—the extraterrestrial deity that creates but exists outside and apart from its creations. The missionary talks about the "Great Father" in the sky. The indigenous person seems to understand and points at the sun. "No! No!," insists the missionary, who tries another tack. He tells a story about God the Son. Again the indigenous person seems to relate to the story; he points to some geographic feature of his landscape and proceeds to share the story of how a legendary figure became that mountain, or rock, or ravine. Again the missionary is frustrated. "No! No!," and he tries once more. This time the missionary describes the "Holy Spirit," which seems, only seems, to the indigenous thinker to approach the concept of *Usen*. The missionary emits a sigh of relief: "At last!," and proceeds to tell the potential indigenous convert about what it is that this "Great Spirit" wants the convert to do. "Wants?," the indigenous person shakes his head at the missionary. "Wanting" is a *human* desire. To credit something on the order of sacredness as *Usen* with any anthropomorphic characteristics is a bit further than the indigenous person is willing to go for the sake of "understanding."

The imaginary missionary, in this instance, illustrates a typical response to the indigenous person's attempt to explain a concept that is crucial to understanding everything else about Native cultures and traditions. Some contemporary Western researchers have actually declared *Usen*, or "the all-pervading force," to be "too abstract" and therefore beyond the grasp of indigenous peoples. In actuality, it is the Western thinker who cannot deal with the ultimate of abstractions: the concept of *Usen*.

European thinkers pride themselves on being masters of the art of dealing with the mental act of abstraction. Abstraction, by its very definition, means to take away everything from a certain idea or object until only the essential stands out. A good example of abstraction is a simple line drawing of a vase. It may be only one continuous line, but there is no doubt in the eye of the viewer that the line depicts a vase. The viewer does not then make the mistake of seeing the line drawing as the vase of all vases. He does not, in effect, become an automatic Platonist. The abstraction remains an abstraction, a "standing for" something that is much more complex. The Western thinker suffers from a tendency to reify all his or her abstract notions, that is, to make an abstract idea concrete or "real."

Another example of the Western proclivity to reify is the concept of time. For most of the world's peoples time is an abstraction derived from the fact that there is motion and change in the world. For the ancient Greek philosophers (e.g., Aristotle and Plato) time was the number or measure of motion. Time was not a thing. For the Western thinker time becomes a thing, a dimension; it is something that is in itself measured. A reification of the idea of time allows Westerners to speak of traveling "in" time. They can postulate traveling "into the future" or "into the past" as though the future and the past were places or things that exist somewhere "out there."

Yet one more example of Western reification can be shown through the idea of God. Joseph Campbell, a philosopher of religion for whom I generally have little regard, said something very interesting in one of his last television interviews before he died. When asked about the concept of God, he pointed out that the term was a metaphor. We see all around us, he said, the vastness and mysteriousness of the universe. This experience frightens us and awes us at the same time. Out of our terror and awe we produce a metaphor. That metaphor is the term *God.* Once having created the metaphor we need never be troubled by the origin, or cause, of that terror and awe. We can control God. We refine the metaphor and give it attributes. We call it "him" and give "him" desires, needs, purposes, and, in some cases, even claim to talk to "him." The awesome universe that overwhelms us has been made endurable. The West has come to worship a metaphor. The terror has been reified.

The Native American's response to the terror and awe inspired by the universe is to call it (the universe and the terror) sacred. Its mysterious qualities are maintained. It is sacred precisely because it is beyond reification. To assign anthropomorphic qualities to such a "substance" would be to reify human characteristics. One could say that the Western idea of God is a reification of human "being." Of course, we are all familiar with the results of this reification: numerous conflicts over the descriptions of God and over what it is that God wants of human beings. There is certainly conflict over what this God has allowed to be written as "his" word, as evidenced by the development of numerous sects within the Christian fold.

Despite the inability to be comfortable with pure abstraction on the part of most Europeans, there have been instances where the notion of the mysterious sacredness has surfaced in a European context. Most prominent in this vein is the seventeenth-century philosopher Benedict de Spinoza. Spinoza, born a Jew, was expelled from his community of relations and religion because of his views about the world. There is a story told–it is without any real foundation but has survived nonetheless–that Spinoza was excommunicated from the church as well lest he try to join after being cast out by the Jewish community. Spinoza's primary philosophical idea is that of *monism*. Monism, as depicted by Spinoza, is the idea that whatever it is of which the world is composed can only be one thing. He called this one thing *God, Substance*, and *Nature*–terms that he had no problem seeing as interchangeable. To the general European thinker accustomed to the belief that God was necessarily extraterrestrial and thereby separate from his creations, Spinoza's concept was an absolute threat. His theory meant that if God/Substance/Nature was all of one piece, then, in effect, everything was God! Some called Spinoza a "God-intoxicated" man. Others called him an atheist. Most contemporary philosophers refer to him as "too complicated." His writing style is faulted for being "too geometrical." What he did was a very thorough logical analysis of the views of others (primarily Descartes). He tore away all of the extraneous factors by showing that they were untenable and thus demonstrated that there could be, logically, only one thing. The many things with which the universe seemed to be populated were "aspects" of the one thing. Furthermore, he insisted that this "one thing" was matter.

His use of the term *matter* (Spinoza claimed that he saw no problem in calling such matter sacred) was not clarified until the twentieth century. Albert Einstein, when asked whether he believed in God, replied that he "believed in the God of Spinoza." What Einstein did was similar to what Spinoza had done: they both narrowed the field of what there was in the universe. The difference between the two was that the hold of the church on the exploration of the world in which Westerners found themselves had loosened by the time of Einstein. Knowledge derived from an examination of the world did not have to have the imprimatur of the church in order to be declared valid.

What the findings of Einstein, as well as the investigations of many others in the fields of mathematics and physics, did was to offer us not a world that was composed of the dualities of matter and energy but of something more clearly akin to "matterenergy"– there was only one "substance." This is the information encoded in Einstein's famous $E=mc^2$. Energy and matter are two "aspects," interchangeable under certain circumstances, of one something. The fact that scientists have since gone on to find that that something may be capable of being many more things–tachyons, quarks, mesons, and so on–does not negate the findings of Einstein, who saw himself as exploring the world of Spinoza's God.

The claim that people usually seen by Europeans as preterite to themselves could hold a view that is only now coming to be examined by Westerners is very threatening. Benjamin Whorf, a linguist who lived in the first half of the twentieth century, actually claimed that the language of the Hopi might be a "better vehicle" for explaining the "modern" views of twentieth-century physics than the languages of the "SAE" (Standard Average European). Whorf's claim is often vehemently criticized, usually by those who have no familiarity with Native American languages. The contention concerning the Hopi language is based on his studies that showed that language to be built around the concept of motion. Hopi, as do many other Native American languages, depicts a dynamic universe. Whorf contrasts this view with the static universe of the SAE. In the static universe nothing happens without a cause or an agent of causation. In the dynamic model, something is always happening without an agent because that is what the universe, by its very nature, does.

The view of the universe as dynamic rather than static is not solely a description of the contemporary scientist. The ancient Greeks and Romans also occupied a dynamic universe, despite the presence within their ranks of thinkers who denied that there was any motion at all, or any substance. This is why I persist in excluding Greek and Roman thinkers, in general, from the ranks of Western thinkers. Chinese philosophies also portray a dynamic universe. One notable ramification of a dynamic universe model is that there need not be an anthropomorphic creator deity (which must itself be explained as uncaused), nor is a human being the goal toward which all the universe is striving (especially, as Ortega points out, a *European* human being).

Regardless of the fact that the concept of *Usen* can be shown to be present in Western thought, it remains equally a fact that the Western/European culture and tradition is not much affected by this concept. Despite the findings of physicists about the existence of "matterenergy," which does not substantiate the sharp dualities typical of Western thought (matter/energy, mind/body, material/spiritual, animate/inanimate), common notions about the world and human beings in that world persist. The new physics insists on presenting a world of interrelationships and interdependencies just as does a theory of *Usen.* Ideas that the North American indigenous peoples arrived at intuitively through their observations of the world and their circumstances in that world have finally arrived in the West. How long it will take Westerners to adapt to a more realistic description of the world is not, at present, answerable.

Deeply held notions of the constituents of "reality" are not easily given up. Such ideas serve as the "givens" of a culture that no longer questions the validity of ancient explanations. At one time the issue of whether the universe was infinite or finite was a serious one. Those who declared that it was infinite were burned at the stake. Today, those on the North American continent who persist in saying to the missionary (in our current era, they are as likely to be scholars) that he or she fails to understand our concept of *Usen/ wakan/ natoji/ nil'ch'i/ manitou* is not scheduled for burning: he or she is, however, most likely to be dismissed as showing a lack of understanding (of Western ideas) or as exhibiting a persistent type of ignorance due to his or her "undeveloped" (or perhaps "preterite") state of being.

As more Native peoples engage in the methodologies of philosophical analysis, perhaps there will be greater clarification of Native ideas and concepts that are the product of a Native context. Equally important to Native indigenous thinkers is the need to study the Western culture and tradition. It is as important for us to say *what we are not* as it is to say *what we are.*

3.

A Study of Nahua Religion
after the Conquest

LEANA HICKS

There exists in Mexico (and among Mexican Americans and Natives in the United States) a fascinating and strong devotion to Mary in the form of the Virgin of Guadalupe. Over the centuries she has become a powerful symbol and uniting force for Mexicans. Her cult is often stated to be a perfect example of syncretism of Native and Christian religion—a fusion of an Aztec earth goddess and the Spanish Catholic Virgin. It is commonly believed that the cult originated among the Nahuas (Indians of central and southern Mexico, including the Aztecs) because it gave them an opportunity to hold to their old religion and yet, at the same time, be accepted by the Christian church. As a result, the early colonial Nahuas were supposedly converted in large numbers to devoted followers of Guadalupe. I originally set out to examine Mexican Indian devotion to Guadalupe, concentrating on the Guadalupe-Aztec goddess relationship, but I found that many of the widely held beliefs about the "Indian" Virgin are simplifications of a much more complex devotion to a figure that is much more than a superimposing of the two images.

The Guadalupe cult did not spring up like a phoenix from the ashes of the conquest with a high Indian following. Rather, it developed over time, and Guadalupe's symbolism changed over time to match the changing spiritual needs of the Indians. The relation of the Virgin to the old Aztec religion goes beyond a comparison to an earth-mother-goddess, and the Nahuas' view of Mary was heavily influenced by the views of the Spaniards, as well as by circumstances of post-conquest Indian life.

LEGENDARY BELIEFS OF THE VIRGIN OF GUADALUPE

Her Apparition

The apparition story of the Virgin is based on two documents: one written in Spanish in 1648 by an Oratorian priest named Miguel Sánchez, and the other written a year later in Nahuatl (the Aztec language) by the vicar of Guadalupe, Luis Laso de la Vega. Vega's version is much more articulate and detailed, revealing more Nahuatl contributions to the story. The following summary is based on his version.[1]

On an early December morning in 1531, on the outer border of Mexico City, a poor Indian named Juan Diego was walking to a nearby town. As the sun rose, he was passing the hill of Tepeyac, and he heard the singing, as of precious birds, on the hilltop. He wondered if this was the flower land, the sunshine land that "our first old men, our grandfathers," spoke of. The song came from the east, and when he reached the top of the hill, he saw a splendid woman calling him; her garments were beaming like the sun, and the rocks on which she stood looked as though they were precious jades or bracelets. The mezquites (pear cactus) and other plants growing there looked like quetzal-green jades and turquoises.

The noblewoman spoke to Juan Diego in Nahuatl, addressing him as "my youngest child," telling him that she was the always-maiden Mary, mother of God, and she expressed her desire for a temple to be built at that spot, so that she could show her love and mercy as the mother of all who confide in her. She ordered him to tell the bishop of her desire.

Juan Diego immediately went to the bishop and told of all that had happened, but the bishop did not believe him. So Juan returned to the hilltop and told the noblewoman to find a well-known, noble person to tell the cleric, "for I am a little poor one. . . . I am a vassal." But she ordered him to go and report again.

The next morning Juan visited the bishop again, and the priest listened more closely but said he needed to see a sign as proof. Juan agreed to the condition.

On Monday, Juan Diego stayed home because his uncle was very sick. The next day, he went to get a priest for his uncle, and on his way the noblewoman appeared to him again. She told him not to worry about his uncle, for he had already been cured. Juan asked for a sign to give to the bishop. Indeed, he found roses there, despite the cold season and rocky terrain, where usually no flowers could be found. He put them in his cloak and went to show them to the bishop.

Juan told the bishop of the morning's events, and as he unfolded his cloak, the image of St. Mary miraculously appeared imprinted on it.

The image is that of a dark Virgin, standing on a crescent moon, wearing a star-studded greenish cloak, with rays of light surrounding her. Everyone marveled at the sight; then they accompanied Juan to his home, finding his uncle in good health. The uncle said he had been visited by the noblewoman, who told him that she was the always-maiden St. Mary of Guadalupe.

A church was built at Tepeyac, in which the holy image was placed. Devotees began to be miraculously cured. Eight accounts of such events, involving both Spaniards and Indians, follow in Vega's document.

Guadalupe and Tonantzin

A popular theory among anthropologists and historians is that Guadalupe, a "dark virgin," is a syncretic goddess that had a large Indian following since its beginning or was a "spiritual aspect of protest against the colonial regime."[2] Several factors lead to this conclusion.

Tepeyac was known to be the former site of a shrine to the ancient Aztec mother-goddess Tonantzin, which means "our mother" in Nahuatl. Tonantzin was one of several earth-mother goddesses worshiped by Aztecs, the most important being Coatlicue. Coatlicue herself was a product of syncretism within the multicultural fabric of Aztec religion and was often confused with Tonantzin. Tonantzin was originally a goddess of the Aztec-conquered Totonacs that was later acquired by the Aztecs as well. Coatlicue was the mother of all, as well as of the gods; this included the stars, moon, and sun, which grew to be stronger than their mother. The stars and moon were more identified with Tonantzin.

The priests of the time, considering the word *Tonantzin* an appropriate translation, used this name in reference to the Virgin and encouraged the Nahuas to do the same. Sahagún, a Spanish missionary of the time, angrily wrote:

> Now that the Church of Our Lady of Guadalupe has been built, the Indians also call her Tonantzin, on the pretext that the preachers call Our Lady, the Mother of God, "Tonantzin." . . . This is an abuse which should be stopped, for the true name of the Mother of God . . . is "God" and "nantzin" (Dios-nantzin). To me this looks very much like a satanic invention to palliate idolatry by playing on the ambiguity of this name Tonantzin. The Indians today, as in the old days, come from afar to visit this Tonantzin, and to me this cult seems very suspect, for there are everywhere numerous churches consecrated to Our Lady, but they do not go there, preferring to come from afar to this Tonantzin, as in the past.[3]

Putting on top of this the nature of the myth itself–that an Indian, ten years after the conquest, passing by Tepeyac saw a wondrous noblewoman, standing on a moon, which is said to be a symbol of Tonantzin, and asking that a shrine be built on the spot–there is considerable reason to believe that Guadalupe was a new incarnation of Tonantzin, and that she "brought comfort and motherhood to the Indians after a period of total disruption. . . . As a result the Indians spontaneously flocked to her in the aftermath of the conquest . . . and thousands were converted in the early days of devotion."[4]

The theory continues to assert that her image symbolized a rebellion against the Spaniards and was used to promote action against them; it symbolized the rights of the oppressed and poor Indians. This perspective, however, does not take into account much of the actual history of the Virgin of Guadalupe. The complexities of Indian devotion to Guadalupe can be better understood by examining more closely the development of the Guadalupe cult, as well as the religious lives of the newly Christianized Nahuas.

HISTORY AND ORIGINS OF THE BASILICA, THE IMAGE, AND THE LEGEND

It was common practice for the missionaries in Mexico to build their churches on or near the sites of pre-Columbian shrines. The constitutions of the first council of Lima, written in 1552, directly state: "We order that all the cult idols and edifices found in the villages where Christian Indians reside be burned or destroyed, and if the site is suitable, a church or at least a cross should be planted there."[5] Torquemada, a missionary of the time, wrote, "Wishing to remedy this great evil [of the worship of Tonantzin] our brethren . . . decided to build a church in the place called Tonantzin, near Mexico City, a temple to the very Holy Virgin, who is Our Lady and Our Mother."[6] It is apparent that the missionaries built the shrine as a way to replace the worship of Tonantzin with devotion to the Virgin. The actual date of the erection of the shrine is unclear; several chronicles, Spanish and Nahuatl, state that devotion to Guadalupe began in 1555-56.[7] In 1575, Viceroy Martín Enríquez wrote that the shrine became popular after a herdsman regained his health when he visited the shrine in 1555 or 1556. The apparition story, as I will later discuss, was probably developed years later to explain the existence of the shrine. Such a reversal is common in the history of Marian apparitions.

Guadalupe was named after the popular Virgin of Guadalupe of Estremuda in Spain. The province of Estremuda was the homeland of many *conquistadores*, including Cortez, and had reached its height in devotion in the sixteenth century.[8] *Conquistadores* were very loyal to this Virgin because she symbolized the struggle of Spanish Christianity against the Moslems, and therefore she was also a symbol of the struggle against Indian pagans.[9] The devotion was centered around a wooden statue of a dark Virgin, which according to legend had been hidden from the Moors during their occupation of Spain and was later found by a shepherd after Mary appeared to him and told him of the statue. His son was miraculously brought back to life after dying from an illness. The image of the Virgin at Tepeyac, chronicled to have been painted by an Indian, does not resemble the statue but does closely resemble a statue of the Immaculate Conception in the choir of the Estremuda shrine at the time. Both Virgins are standing on a crescent moon, with alternating straight and wavy lines surrounding them. This type of iconography, rather than being a symbol for Tonantzin, came from the identification of Mary as the Woman of the Apocalypse in Revelation, which describes a woman "clothed with the sun, and the moon at her feet, and upon her head a crown of twelve stars" (Rv 12:1). The painter of Tepeyac's Virgin probably based it on a reproduction of the choir Virgin brought over by the Spaniards. It is reported that, after seeing the image at Tepeyac, many Spaniards proclaimed it to be the Virgin of Guadalupe from their home.[10]

The first written documentation of the apparition did not occur until 1648, written by Miguel Sánchez. Although the appearance was said to have occurred in 1531, Sánchez openly stated that there were no previously written documents on the subject, and that he based his writings on oral sources. Several reports indicate that the apparition legend was not widely known either to the Spanish missionaries or among the Nahuas. Before 1648 the only miracles that were noted commonly related to the healing power of the image, not to its origins. The document written a year later by Luis Laso de la Vega contained many more details and Nahua characteristics and was written in such fluent and idiomatic Nahuatl that Laso de la Vega was "probably guided by an already existing model; indeed, the tale itself is so smooth that it gives the impression of having been through the polishing process of frequent telling by various narrators."[11] A survey of the time found that Sánchez's and Vega's accounts were consistent with the few already existing beliefs of the area.[12] Therefore, although the story was not well known, it was not simply invented by Sánchez or Laso de la Vega. It is reasonable to conclude that the myth developed over time, was not yet very widespread, and that both Spanish and Nahua elements made their way into the story. Perhaps the Nahuas had overheard the Estremuda myth, a theory that is not improbable considering the strong Spanish devotion, and then confused it with their own Guadalupe, changing the story through time and adding their own details.

After the publications of Sánchez and Laso de la Vega, Guadalupe become most popular among the Creoles (Mexicans of Spanish descent). William Taylor's 1987 study of naming patterns shows that at no point did Marian devotion among Indians spread spontaneously, and

Mary was most popular in the heavily Hispanicized urban areas. Other contemporary documents show that the Day of the Virgin of Guadalupe was not really celebrated in outlying Indian villages before the 1750s.[13] Although Sahagún wrote that Indians came from afar, as in former times, to worship Guadalupe, he does not elaborate on where they came from or who they were. As Taylor states, "Perhaps the Indian cult of Guadalupe in the early colonial period corresponded roughly to the territory of pilgrimage and worship of . . . Tonantzin at Tepeyac (whatever that territory may have been), but too little is known at present about the cult of Tonantzin to elaborate on this relationship."[14] Although the early history of the cult is unclear, I believe that Guadalupan devotion by the early colonial Nahuas was probably strongly tied to her relation to Tonantzin; unfortunately, the exact nature of this cult is unknown. (There is still a small group of Nahuas–those that live in a region of east central Mexico–that indeed worship a deity that is an obvious syncronization of Tonantzin and Guadalupe; I will examine their special case later.) In any case, this devotion was fairly localized, and when Guadalupe gained widespread popularity among Indians centuries later, her connection to Tonantzin, as I will show, was no longer the main factor in that popularity.

Indian devotion did not begin to spread until the 1750s, when priests realized that the dark, Nahuatl-speaking Virgin would be a perfect tool for increasing Marian devotion among Indians. Priests, few of whom were Indian, purposely began raising awareness of Guadalupe through their sermons.[15]

Having explored many of the elements of the formation of the Guadalupe cult, I will now examine the true beliefs held by the Nahuas about Guadalupe. In addition, I will discuss the development of the cult among them.

NAHUA BELIEF IN MARY AND IN GUADALUPE

Characteristics and Causes of Strong Marian Devotion

The Nahuas were part of a Marian cult long before Guadalupe gained widespread popularity. This cult was influenced by a combination of the Spaniards' beliefs, Aztec mythology, and the circumstances of early colonial Nahua life.

The Aztecs believed in cyclic time, in which a world ruled by certain gods would be created and after a time be destroyed, being replaced by a new world with different gods. Before the arrival of Cortez, several strange occurrences were seen as omens that the current world would soon come to an end. When Cortez invaded Tenochtitlan, he carried a banner of the Virgin Mary above him; the first two images that confronted the Indians were those of Mary and St. James. Tales existed among the Spaniards that Mary had appeared in battle and helped the Spanish soldiers conquer the Indians. As a result, Nahuas believed that their old gods had been defeated by the more powerful Christian deities, including Mary.

The Aztec religion before the conquest was dominated by two male gods: Quetzalcóatl, the self-sacrificing god, and Huitzilopochtli, the young warrior/sun god.[16] It is possible that their defeat "caused the faithful to return to the ancient female deities ... [and] to the maternal womb."[17] Mary, although generally addressed as "Our Lady" or "Mother of God" by the Europeans, was most often referred to as *totlacotatzin*, "our precious mother," by the Indians.[18] However, while the Nahua mother-goddesses were fertility goddesses, connected to the earth, agriculture, and cosmic patterns, Mary was more of a protector, healer, intercessor, and consoler for the weak; this reflects the changing circumstances and needs of the colonized and marginalized Indians.

The Aztec goddesses were creative as well as destructive forces who demanded sacrifices and were often monstrous in appearance. They did not love or have passion; nor were they loved by the Aztecs. Christian thought, however, separated the good from the evil, with God, the saints, and the angels on one side, and the devil and demons on the other. The mother-goddess therefore became all-good and lovable in the form of Mary.[19] Another reason for this change, according to Taylor, was that while "in Spanish popular belief, God and Jesus were more feared than loved ... Mary, on the other hand, was the beloved intercessor who worked to deflect or soften the harsh judgments of a stern God."[20] Aztec fear of pagan deities was transferred largely to the Christian God.[21] Thus Mary lost the negative features of the ancient goddesses, which were absorbed by the Father-God. Mary became a non-threatening, loved, and loving image. The Nahuas did continue, however, to perform acts of penance, to make offerings, and to say prayers to receive her help, similar to the sacrifices required by the ancient goddesses.

Another interesting aspect of the Nahua's Marian devotion is related to the Nahua perception of heaven. The Nahuas did not separate paradise from the earthly world as the Christians did; instead, they saw it as the ultimate reality of this world. It was the earthly ritual transformed so as to make visible the sacredness and beauty inherent in nature. This paradise was the "flower world," a "sunny garden filled with flowers, brightly colored tropical birds, and precious stones like jade and turquoise."[22] It was full of light, fragrance, and music; it was sometimes said to be on a mountaintop.

The Christian notion of a purely spiritual heaven was incomprehensible to the Nahuas, who simply related heaven to their flower world. This is evident in many Nahua songs and Nahua descriptions of heaven. At the same time, Christians often used the lily and the rose as symbols for Mary; in addition, they portrayed her as an inhabitant of the sacred enclosed garden of the Song of Solomon, with angels at her side. The Nahuas saw this as placing Mary in the flower world, and the angels became the precious tropical birds of this sacred realm.

The Nahuas also connected Mary with the sun and dawn. Christians often used metaphors, such as Christ being the "sun of righteousness" who took people out of darkness and shed the light of salvation upon the world. Mary, being Christ's mother, symbolized the dawn of this enlightened Christian era. In addition, the birth of Jesus was accompanied by the bright morning star. For the Nahuas, these metaphors acquired other meanings: Christ became the sun that animated the flower world, as well as the sun that brought the Nahuas out of the darkness of their pagan religion and into the light of Christianity.[23] One Nahuatl storyteller, describing the birth of Jesus, said, "It was dark, very dark. And why did it dawn? He was appearing. It was dawning. He was appearing beautifully; he was shining as he came."[24] Mary, as the mother of Jesus, was the catalyst for these transformations; she was often equated with the dawn and the sun in Nahuatl songs and myths. Further, a connection to Coatlicue may have been made, for Coatlicue was also the mother of the Sun.

Mary's virginity was easily understood by the Nahuas, perhaps for several reasons. Before the conquest "young noblewomen often spent a year in temple service prior to marriage. For the sake of ritual purity in their service to the gods, chastity was strictly required of these girls."[25] It would be fitting for Mary, being the ultimate servant of God, to be pure and virginal. Yet another parallel to Coatlicue may have been made, because Coatlicue was also a virgin. Mary's virginity may have had still another meaning to the Nahuas: degraded by the widespread rape of Indian women by Spaniards, the Nahuas may have seen Mary's virginity as a symbol of resistance as well as the retention of Indian pride and identity.

Mary's popularity increased for other reasons as well. While pre-conquest Nahua religious life mostly consisted of shared, collective experiences such as song, dance, offerings, processions, or other ceremonies, the Christian devotion to God consisted of passively listening to sermons of God's judgment and punishment. On the other hand, the Spanish-Catholic forms of Marian devotion matched very closely the religious traditions of the Nahuas. Of the twelve annual Christian festivals that Nahuas were made to participate in, four were Marian. They consisted of processions, offerings of food and flowers, singing, dancing, and reenactments of celebrated events. Religious confraternities (organizations in which volunteers performed religious and charitable activities and cared for images) became very popular, especially among women, who were excluded from most other religious activities. Many of these organizations were devoted to Mary. Also, Christian hymns and chants were very popular among the Nahuas, and many of these were directed toward Mary as well.

God was seen as a distant, not very merciful force; reaching God often required Mary's loving intercession. Mary's more direct role in Nahua life increased her importance. For example, the rosary, called a "flower necklace" by the Nahuas, became popular because they were taught that it would grant them favors. One myth of the time told how an Indian was saved from lightning because he was wearing a rosary.[26] All of the missionary sects had in their texts many stories of miracles performed by Mary, put in the context of the New World. With all these accounts circulating, in addition to several miracle-working images in the area, Nahuas came to see Mary as the deity who directly intervened in their lives to help them. They often reported such miraculous occurrences to their priests.

A main cause for the strong Marian devotion among the Indians was simply the strong devotion of the Spaniards. Many of the first conquerors, including Cortez, were from very devoted parts of Spain. The first missionaries, especially the Franciscans, and later the Jesuits, were very devoted to Mary. As previously noted, the Indians were exposed to many Spanish festivals, myths, hymns, and chants related to Mary. In addition, the Nahuatl catechism that all the Nahuas had to memorize contained prayers to Mary: the *Ave Maria* and the *Salve Regina*. It is interesting to note that the Spaniards had a special devotion to Mary of the Immaculate Conception. At the same time that the cult of the Immaculada was reaching its peak in Spain, the Third Mexican Provincial Council of 1585 declared the feast of the Immaculate Conception obligatory. This devotion could be explained by the strong belief in the Second Coming by the mendicant orders, as well as in the anguish of sin.[27] Mary the Immaculate, the only human who was free of original sin, bore the promise of redemption. She also had special importance to the Mexican situation, as anthropologist Jacques Lafaye writes: "Mestizos and Creoles, treated with the same scorn [as the Indians] by the *gachupines* (those born in Spain), felt the weight of centuries of idolatry and mortal sin. The Virgin Mary brought them grace and dignity in the form of 'prodigious' apparitions,"[28] almost all of which occurred in the late sixteenth and early seventeenth centuries. Mary the Immaculate came to symbolize the salvation of the New World, and the cult of Mary became very closely tied to the cult of the Immaculate Conception.[29] Guadalupe would later become a faction of this cult.

It is clear that early Nahua devotion to Mary was not related to the Virgin of Guadalupe, demonstrating that Guadalupe's connection to Tonantzin was not a prime factor in the strong Nahua tie to Mary. Although some parallels exist between Coatlicue/Tonantzin and Mary, the forms and factors leading to widespread Nahua Marian devotion were varied as well. The forms of Nahua devotion were highly influenced by the Spaniards' practices and folk beliefs, as well as Aztec religion, and changed according to the needs of the Christianized Nahuas. The Nahuas venerated Mary with a love unknown to the Aztec goddesses and saw her as a symbol of the rising sun rather than of the earth. Mary was the embodiment of the flower world, able to speak to God on their behalf; she was a mother, a helper, and a comforter.

The Development of Guadalupanism among the Nahuas

There are numerous Nahua contributions to Guadalupe's apparition account. Juan Diego immediately asks himself if Tepeyac is the flower land, the sunshine land, of which his grandfathers spoke. The song he hears comes from the east–the direction of the rising sun–and Mary appears at dawn, her garments shimmering and beaming like the sun. (Spanish influence may also be present here. In one version of the Estremuda myth, Mary is surrounded by sunbeams; the Woman of the Apocalypse is also "clothed with the sun.") The rocks and plants surrounding her look like precious stones (jade and turquoise are mentioned), tropical birds are heard, flowers bloom supernaturally, and light is everywhere–all characteristics of the flower world. Native plants, such as the prickly pear, are described as being transformed, matching the Aztec notion that the flower world changes the locale to a sacred place. The placing of the event in 1531 rather than 1555 may be a result of the Nahuas' desire to be seen as having willingly and immediately converted to Christianity. As Burkhart states, "This [was a] useful fiction for the Indians, who wished to be seen as legitimate Christian citizens of the colony." In addition, the Nahuas saw Christianization as the most significant result of the conquest, and placing Guadalupe's apparition closer to the date of the conquest better coincided with this belief. Here, Indian Christianity seems to rise from the ashes of the conquest, the new era dawning like Guadalupe herself.[30]

As previously mentioned, the Guadalupan cult did not begin to spread among the Indians until the 1750s, when the cult was fostered by the priests. At this time Indians were ready to venerate a non-local image. In the sixteenth and early seventeenth centuries, Indians were oriented above all toward their local communities. They centered on community patron saints, Mary included, but never on images from other communities. By the late seventeenth and early eighteenth centuries, however, Indian communities interacted more with the outside; bilingualism was common, boundaries were fragmented, and many Indians migrated through central Mexico in search of work. There was more direct contact with Hispanics in residential, commercial, and work settings. The Indians could now identify with an image that represented the larger society, centering on the capital city, one that removed the emphasis from their local units to the Indian and Mexican community as a whole.[31]

Perhaps one of Guadalupe's main appeals to the late colonial Indians was her role as intercessor. The rural Indians had a relationship with colonial authority similar to their relationship with God and Mary. Spanish rule in Mexico consisted of a system of administration and justice that depended on intermediaries, and this system was fairly successful in carrying out justice. As Taylor states, "[Rural Indians] were inclined to take their grievances over land and taxes to the courts, to work through legal intermediaries, and to appeal to a higher authority within the colonial structure if the verdict went against them. . . . Ritually, the Virgin was approached as the colonial governors were–humbly, hat in hand."[32] Just as Mary mediated between the people and God, she also interceded with the authorities, helping Indians survive in the colonial system: "In this way she sanctified the authority of the colonial system . . . and carried a message not to take matters into your own hands. . . . Turn them over to Mother Mary."[33]

Although Mary may have been used to keep Indians submissive, Guadalupe especially had the potential to symbolize rebellion against authority. She was first used in this way by Creoles, who employed her as a way to validate their rights as Mexicans–Guadalupe made Mexico a "chosen nation," sparking patriotic sentiments. Guadalupe became a symbol in the Creole-led War of Independence from Spain. This war did not have, however, high Indian involvement. In fact, the Indians were, in some ways, better off under the colonial bureaucracy than they would be under the Republic, which took away communal land holdings and special protections they previously had enjoyed.[34]

In the Mexican Revolution of 1910, led by Emiliano Zapata (who was of Nahua descent), the mostly peasant army marched under the banner of Guadalupe. It was not that Guadalupe came to stand for the rights of the oppressed Indians on a large scale. While the Creoles had seen her as a symbol of patriotism and rebellion against Spanish authority, the Indians now saw her in terms of class conflict and social revolution.[35] Another example of this can be seen in the Indian uprising in Tulancingo in 1769, in which rebels sought to replace Spanish priests with Indians, dreaming of a time when both bishops and *alcaldes* would be forced to kiss the rings of Native priests, a new theocratic utopia led by a Native whose consort was reputed to be Guadalupe herself.

Although I have argued throughout this article that Guadalupe and Tonantzin are largely unrelated, some possible connections between the two deserve examination. Just before the conquest, Tonantsi (another name for Tonantzin), who preferred only sacrifices of birds and small animals, had begun to triumph over Coatlicue, the more bloodthirsty and malevolent mother-goddess. Perhaps Guadalupe is the final, most benevolent form of a mother-goddess.[36] Another similarity between the two comes from the fact that Tonantsi had given the Nahuas the cactus plant to provide them with *pulque,* an alcoholic drink. This *pulque* made warriors more courageous in battle. Perhaps this has some relation to the way Guadalupe helped soldiers win battles.[37] Another point of interest lies in an Aztec legend that describes an encounter between Tonantsi and the Judeo-Christian God, in which she will not allow him to punish her children. She challenges God–now seen as her son– "to produce mother's milk (as she had done), to prove that his benevolence equaled his disciplinary harshness. It is God's role to punish; it is her role to intercede."[38] This story coincides with the role Nahuas gave to Mary, mentioned previously, as with the role of Guadalupe.

In addition, I have found what appears to be an isolated case in which there seems to be a strong and interesting relation between the two images. This is found among the Nahuas who inhabit the southern Huasteca region of eastern central Mexico.[39] There are about 100,000 Nahuas in this area, most of them living a traditional lifestyle in the countryside, where they grow maize, beans, squash, and chiles. Their religion contains both Nahua and Christian elements. Their most important deity is the goddess Tonantsi, whom they refer to as the Virgin of Guadalupe when they speak in Spanish; for them, the Virgin and Tonantsi are the same. Every year the Nahuas perform a ritual devoted to Tonantsi from December 20 until December 24. The ritual is called *Tlakatelilis,* meaning "causing birth," and is very different from the Christian Christmas. It is a fertility ritual in which villagers ask Tonantsi for fertility for both their fields and their families. The ceremony celebrates the fact of birth itself rather than the birth of a god.

Sandstrom examines this ritual closely, revealing many qualities of the Tonantsi cult. In the four-day ritual, an image of Tonantsi–which is actually an image of the Virgin of Guadalupe–is carried around to the households in the village. She is accompanied by statues of Joseph and Mary. Interestingly, Joseph is seen as Tonantsi's son, and Mary–a completely separate individual–is his wife. They represent the work spirit (*ekihte*) and his wife; human work is needed to convert desire into successful fertility, especially in the case of growing crops. Tonantsi's image is carried around the village by a group of young virgin women, symbolizing potential fertility. Another important characteristic of the ritual is that it is a sort of transaction: the Nahuas make offerings to Tonantsi, and in return, she will bring them fertility. This reward does not come directly from Tonantsi; it is expressed in the natural environment, in the elements and processes represented by Tonantsi.[40]

Tonantsi carries both male and female qualities; she is the interaction between the two that leads to fertility. Tonantsi's role as a mother, however, involves more than simple fertility; she is also associated with productivity, growth, birth, conception, motherhood, well-being, food, generosity, and the unity of siblings. Tonantsi is seen as an "actual mother who takes a direct interest in human affairs"[41] and can be approached through ritual. This present-day Tonantsi has undergone syncretism with Christianity in obvious ways: her image is now that of Guadalupe, and she is the mother of Joseph and Mary, although these figures also have taken on new roles. Yet in most other respects she seems to be quite independent of the Christian image of Mary: her association with Jesus is practically nonexistent; she is a completely separate character from Joseph's wife Mary; and she retains a strong image as a fertility goddess.

On the other hand, Tonantsi seems to have influenced the "mainstream" Guadalupe in several ways: Indians throughout Mexico call upon Guadalupe to help in childbirth; she is a uniting force for all Mexicans; and she can be approached relatively easily through prayer and processions. The unification of male and female also can be seen in Guadalupe's dual role as mother and as warrior and protector. Both images are related to virginity. It cannot be denied that Guadalupe shares some of Tonantsi's attributes.

There are many different ethnic groups in Mexico, and the above illustrations show that it is hard to generalize about the Nahuas' beliefs in the Virgin of Guadalupe. There are without doubt some Nahuas who still tie Guadalupe and Tonantzin closely together; it seems that in general, however, Nahua devotion to Guadalupe involves many other factors that have nothing to do with the Aztec goddess. The symbolism of and devotion to the Virgin of Guadalupe continue to change according to the spiritual and practical needs of her followers. The fact that Guadalupe is now seen as a joining of Aztec goddess and Christian Virgin may be due to Mexicans' growing pride in their Indian roots.[42] The myth of Guadalupe, even though it is of unsure origins, is full of symbolism that can apply to many aspects of the Mexican condition, and Mexicans continue to take advantage of this feature.

CONCLUSION

It is amazing that there are so many coincidental similarities between Spanish and Nahua beliefs, allowing for endless possibilities of syncretism. At times it is unclear from which culture a certain feature of Guadalupe may have originated. Even if a certain aspect is of Spanish origin—for example, the moon on which Guadalupe stands—who is to say that the colonial Nahuas did not give it their own symbolism? Most studies concerning the Virgin of Guadalupe tend to go to either side of an extreme: some do not question the syncretism with Tonantzin, while more recent studies deny it completely. Guadalupe definitely contains more facets than a simple fusion of Tonantzin and Virgin, and the eventual growth of the cult among the Indians was due mainly to different reasons. It cannot be denied, however, that there are some parallels between the two images and that the initial, although small, Nahua cult was probably heavily influenced by this relationship.

Although there has been a fair amount of research done on Nahua devotion to the Virgin of Guadalupe, little of it has had a Nahua directly involved in its conduct. It would be of great help if Nahuas were directly interviewed about their beliefs in Guadalupe; even though their present beliefs may be very different from those of the past, they definitely would provide a clue to early Nahua devotion to her.

Being a believer in the legend of Guadalupe, I was initially disappointed when I discovered that several of the beliefs and myths concerning her might not be literally true. After examining the true history of the Guadalupe cult, however, I found it to be much more interesting than my original beliefs. The development of her cult is like a mystery full of contradictions, and the deeper I went, the more pieces I had to solve the puzzle. Her history and apparition story reveal many aspects of the Mexican and Indian cultures. My faith in the Virgin of Guadalupe has taken on a different form. Whether or not she literally appeared to a humble Indian soon after the conquest, the myth itself continues to have meaning as a symbol of her relationship to the Mexican Indians as well as non-Indians, and perhaps, more generally, to all people.[43]

Notes

[1] Louise M. Burkhart, "The Cult of the Virgin of Guadalupe in Mexico," in *South and Meso-American Spirituality* (New York: Crossroad Publishing, 1993), pp. 200-3.

[2] William B. Taylor, "The Virgin of Guadalupe in New Spain: An Inquiry into the Social History of Marian Devotion," *American Ethnologist* 1:4 (1987), p. 10.

[3] Bernardino de Sahagún, *Historia general de las cosas de Nueva España* (Mexico, D.F.: Editorial Porrúa, 1981), vol. 3, p. 352.

[4] Ena Campbell, "The Virgin of Guadalupe and the Female Self-Image: A Mexican Case History," in *Mother Worship*, ed. James J. Preston (Chapel Hill: University of North Carolina Press, 1982), p. 32; Stafford Poole, *Our Lady of Guadalupe: The Origins and Sources of a Mexican National Symbol, 1531-1797* (Tucson: University of Arizona Press, 1995), p. 5.

[5] Jacques Lafaye, *Quetzalcóatl and Guadalupe, the Formation of Mexican National Consciousness 1531- 1813* (Chicago: University of Chicago Press, 1974), p. 215.

[6] Ibid.

[7] James Lockhart, *The Nahuas after the Conquest* (Stanford: Stanford University Press, 1992), pp. 246-47.

[8] Lafaye, p. 224.

[9] Ibid., p. 231.

[10] Ibid.

[11] Lockhart, p. 250.

[12] Lafaye, p. 247.

[13] Taylor, p. 15.

[14] Ibid.

[15] Ibid.

[16] Octavio Paz, *The Labyrinth of Solitude* (New York: Grove Press, 1961), p. 84.

[17] Ibid.

[18] Lockhart, p. 252.

[19] Burkhart, p. 210.

[20] Taylor, p. 11.

[21] William Marsden, *Magia de la Risa* (1960; SEP/Sententas edition, 1971), p. 223.

[22] Burkhart, p. 210.

[23] Ibid., pp. 210-12.

[24] James M. Taggart, *Nahuat Myth and Social Structure* (Austin: University of Texas Press, 1983), p. 103.

[25] Burkhart, p. 212.

[26] Ibid., p. 213.

[27] Lafaye, p. 227.

[28] Ibid.

[29] Ibid.

[30] Burkhart, p. 217.

[31] Lockhart, p. 248.

[32] Taylor, p. 20.

[33] Ibid.

[34] Taylor, p. 23; Burkhart, p. 220.

[35] Burkhart, p. 220.

[36] Campbell, p. 12.

[37] Ibid.

[38] Ibid.

[39] Alan R. Sandstrom, "The Tonantsi Cult of the Eastern Nahua," in Preston, p. 25.

[40] Ibid., p. 46.

[41] Ibid., p. 48.

[42] Burkhart, p. 221.

[43] See Virgil Elizondo, *Guadalupe: Mother of the New Creation* (Maryknoll, N.Y.: Orbis Books, 1997); see also Ana Castillo, ed., *Goddess of the Americas: Writings on the Virgin of Guadalupe* (New York: Riverhead, 1997).

4.

The Interpreters

HOMER NOLEY

In the early 1800s, when the Choctaw tribe was being forcibly removed from its homeland, it traveled in groups of families, clans, or districts instead of one single mass movement to Indian Territory. One such group was making its way following paths blazed by previous Choctaw groups. In this group was a young Choctaw named Kanchi. He became the leader of this contingent of Choctaws, which was made up of a cross section of the tribal population. There were whole families, many children, teenagers, and older persons. The terrain through which they traveled by foot was one which included treacherous and dangerous swamps, almost impenetrable underbrush, and a very hilly and uneven surface. They also faced the dangerous Mississippi River, which they would have to cross en masse before plunging into the swampy canebreaks of what is now southeast Arkansas.

Kanchi had become the leader of this group because of his courage and his sensitivity to the human and spiritual needs of the Choctaw people. He was a Christian, and that was the only negative thing about Kanchi as far as the Choctaw were concerned. Christianity was regarded as a White Man's religion, and the people responsible for the Choctaws' loss of their homeland were White Christians.

At the end of each day's ordeal, Kanchi would help people get settled in for the night, see to the distribution of available food, and help make the sick ones as comfortable as possible. He would then gather around him those who were willing, mostly teenagers, and talk to them about the gospel. He would read the Bible and explain its teachings to those who would listen. Most of the Choctaws would withdraw to their camps. A small number of youth would remain with him out of respect for him and out of curiosity for the strange things Kanchi was teaching.

Such were the days of suffering for this struggling band of Choctaws who had been driven from their homes, leaving extensive fields of crops that would be harvested by Whites who took over their properties even before the long, dangerous march began.

Sometimes they would have to pause in their journey to bury a person who had died from the ordeal. After many days of torturous travel the group reached the Mississippi River. The Choctaws knew this river well and knew when it was safe to navigate and when it was unsafe. It was clearly unsafe during this time. The river was swollen and a strong surface current was moving debris speedily downstream.

The U.S. Government had alerted Whites living close to the river about the large contingent of Choctaws who would be arriving and needing to cross the river. These White persons were prepared for the group and offered to let them cross on rafts they brought for that purpose, providing the Choctaws could pay for the privilege. Kanchi saw the swiftly moving river and observed that the rafts being offered were not in good shape. Some of the logs and timber were rotting and appeared waterlogged. After assurances that other groups had safely made it across on the rafts, the Choctaws began to board the rafts. The perilous trip across the river began. Besides the surface current, the river also was frequently visited with a swirling undercurrent that often was so powerful that it dragged whole trees beneath the surface and sent them swirling crazily underwater, dragging surface debris and anything else that got caught in the branches under the water.

It was one of these undercurrents that precipitated the severe surface turbulence that caused a raft to suddenly lift, spilling several teenagers over the side into the water. Kanchi immediately began diving into the murky waters and pulling them onto the raft one at a time. Not knowing how many had fallen off, Kanchi dove once more into the water to make sure he had gotten everyone out. The undercurrent in its turbulent journey had dragged a fallen tree underneath the surface and at that moment it passed through and dragged Kanchi into the dark and ruthless depths. Kanchi was lost, but the little band of Choctaw made its way across the river. The group gathered on the bank of the river and in a quiet moment of reverence said goodbye to a good man and a good leader. Then they turned west and moved slowly through the dangerous swamps. Finally, when evening came, they made camp.

When the people were settled in for the night, a small group of teenagers came together around a campfire. One of them had Kanchi's Bible and read from it in remembrance of Kanchi. Thereafter, at the end of each day's journey the small group of youth would gather and read from Kanchi's Bible; each evening they would be joined by a few adults and other young people for these periods of worship and scripture reading.

By the time they reached the vicinity of Skullyville in Indian Territory, a nucleus of a worshiping Christian community had been formed. It is said that one of the youths who huddled with the small group that kept the practice of Bible-reading alive after Kanchi's death was the legendary Willis Folsom, who went on to become one of the great evangelists and pastors in the Indian Territory—now Oklahoma.

Methodism and other denominations of the Christian church entered Oklahoma by way of the forced removal of Native peoples from their ancestral homelands. In most cases they came through the agency of members of the respective tribes who bore witness to a faith that came to them by way of an oppressor people.

At about the same historical period, in the Northeast, a woman of the Housatannuck tribe, which occupied an area now occupied by the state of Massachusetts, began a spiritual journey that also would terminate in Indian Territory. Electa Quinney became a Christian and with tremendous vitality expressed her witness by organizing and teaching in church schools in the area where her work began. She made her way to the Oneida tribe in New York and continued her work. When the Oneida people were forcibly removed from their homeland, Electa Quinney traveled with them. As they made their way by foot through the mountains and forests, they encountered other tribes and communities of Native peoples who helped the exiles with food and shelter. It is said that whenever they camped, Electa Quinney would organize a class and leave a nucleus of another worshiping community. Along the way she met Daniel Adams, a Mohawk evangelist who himself was an untiring worker preaching the Christian gospel. They married and became a powerful team as they made their journey from the Northeast to the center of the continent. When they reached the area now known as Green Bay, Wisconsin, they helped to found the Oneida Methodist Church. Whites in the area decided they wanted the original land on which the Natives settled, so the Oneida people moved once again.

Quinney's work apparently did not cease then, however, because the last time she is mentioned in historical accounts is when she hosted Bishop Thomas Morris and his entourage in 1844. Bishop Morris had made his way by foot and by wagon to organize the Indian Mission Conference of Oklahoma at Riley Chapel. Electa Quinney Adams, now a widow, provided food and shelter for the bishop and on the Sabbath invited her neighbors of different tribal groups, as well as Blacks and Whites, to her home to take part in a worship service led by the bishop. She and Daniel Adams had accepted an assignment to work among the Senecas of Indian Territory. Though Daniel Adams died, she continued her ministry until her death, shortly after the bishop's visit. She left a trail of new Christians from Massachusetts to New York, Wisconsin, and on to Indian Territory.

In the Central Plains, Protestant denominations are today without large-scale Christian movements among Native tribes. It was not always that way, however. Christianity was not banned by the Central Plains tribes but was received with respect. In spite of the predatory acts of so-called settlers moving into Native lands, missionary activity was taking place among the many communities of tribal people. Many Native people responded and provided leadership for the fledgling communities of converts.

Among the Native people who responded to Christianity was a Chippewa by the name of Duane Porter. Porter was challenged to the ministry by S. G. Wright, a Presbyterian missionary working among the Natives in Wisconsin. In his personal journal Porter told how he followed Indians trails and struggled through the wilderness for two hundred miles. He traveled that distance on foot with a pack on his back. He reached a White settlement known as Tower, Minnesota. From there he paddled a birchbark canoe thirty miles and arrived at a Chippewa village at the head of Lake Vermillion, at Wakimup Bay. There he began his ministry.

When Porter explained why he had come to the village, he was welcomed by the tribal headman. After preaching in the village Grand Medicine Lodge for a considerable length of time, he realized the need to be in an official relationship with a church to authenticate his ministry. He went by canoe back to Tower and then to Sudan, where a Methodist Conference was in progress. He made a public profession of faith at the conference and asked to be admitted to church membership. His reception was positive and he was licensed to preach with an "exhorter's" license. Another thirty-mile trip by canoe took him back to Wakimup Bay "with renewed courage." After a few weeks he reported, "I had finished, with the help of my people, a rough tabernacle built of trees and bark."

Duane Porter traveled hundreds of miles by canoe and on foot ministry in the upper Midwest. He built a large number of churches and tabernacles and a number of "preacher's houses." The designation *preacher's houses* indicates that other Chippewa leaders answered the call to ministry and carried on the work in Porter's absence. Some of these unsung heroes of the cross are Ah-be-dad-sung, a traditional Holy man who befriended Porter; Joe Baptiste, who built a church at Sawyer, Minnesota; and Frank Paquette, a member of the Northern Minnesota Conference in the late 1930s.

Only one of Porter's churches has survived through the years. It is the Pine Bend United Methodist Church near Fosston, Minnesota. Even this church struggles to survive today because of the unavailability of pastors in the Minnesota Conference for the tenacious congregation. The descendants of Duane Porter's family still reside in Pine Bend and provide spiritual support for the church.

The sad part of the Duane Porter story is that the Methodist church, after its friendly acceptance of Porter as a member, did not support him as it did White missionaries. It is reported that Porter never received more than $600 a year at the peak of his ministry. When a missionary of another denomination called this fact to his attention, Porter responded by saying, "I have built my house on that foundation rock, and I can't pull off my house for little things like these."

There are numerous stories of Native Christian leaders carrying the gospel among the original inhabitants of this land. These leaders, although they were the true vehicle through whom the message of Christianity took root among the Native people, have very seldom been lifted up and given due recognition for their work. Historically, the church has credited White missionaries with accomplishing the spread of Christianity among this land's Native peoples. The obvious reason is that reports from the mission field were written and filed by White missionaries. For the most part, Native American concerns were represented by non-Indians, and Native leaders were never given a forum through which they could state their own perceptions of the state of the ministry among their own people. Consequently, the respective perception and, most important, the goals of institutional missionaries serving Native communities and the Natives themselves were often not only different but in clear opposition to each other. Native American Christians were not aware that the underlying goal of White institutional missionaries was to de-culturize Native peoples through their missionary techniques. In their reports missionaries referred to this process as the "civilization" of Indians through the spread of the gospel. The churches were joined in this effort by the U.S. Government, which established a "Civilization Fund" in 1819. On the other hand, Native American people were responding to a gospel message that expressed a spiritual imperative that was appropriate to their needs both as a community and as individuals. Tribal leaders were angered to hear words of hope and salvation coming from the mouths of White missionaries who represented the very oppressor people who were systematically destroying hopefulness for hundreds of Native communities. Even so, they came to respect a message that seemed to have its origin in a source transcendent of human control. But regardless—something had happened. Today there are many different expressions of Native Christianity. There are Native American Christians who remove themselves from their cultural heritage and others who choose to maintain their cultural identity while embracing Christianity. Still others have allowed themselves to stand aloof from the necessity of seemingly having to choose between culture and religion.

How did Christianity finds its way into Native American communities? What was the initial message brought by its messengers? Why were Native peoples inclined to hear and accept these messengers along with their message? There are at least two sources to turn to for possible help in responding to such questions. Many clergy kept journals to use in reporting their mission work and these, if available, are very useful. Otherwise we are left with the reports recorded by the respective mission boards. Denominational histories of their origins in the respective states also stress their relations with the indigenous people. In addition, Native American "interpreters" or "assistants" kept journals of their work. These were not always received by the church since the White missionaries they were assisting did the reporting on behalf of the mission. Written church records, then, are one source.

Oral traditions of Native peoples are another source. Ironically, in most instances these are available to us only when committed to writing by an interviewer. One of the best known of these sources is *Black Elk Speaks.* Other such accounts claim to be the actual words of the Native holy man or headman whose name appears in the title.

We are entering an era in which eye witnesses to overt institutional moves against Native American culture will be unavailable. These overt institutional moves began to be phased out by both church and state during the civil rights era of the '60s. New generations of Native Americans are born into a society that seeks to accomplish the same ends as the policies of the historical period prior to the civil rights era in a more studied and subtle way. These new generations, not having experienced the blatant public policies of church and state in the era prior to the '60s, are more vulnerable to these maneuvers. Yet there are people who remember those years, and a way should be made for them to be heard. These people lived under the teaching and influence of the eye witnesses. They still hear the essence of oral tradition but lack the means by which it can be passed on to the present and future generations.

Many contemporary sources must be considered suspect and read employing techniques not unlike textual criticism and other forms of literary criticism that help to determine the validity of the written material. It is possible to learn from all sources if one is vigilant about the integrity of the material. Someone once said that it is possible to learn a lot about someone by reading that person's enemies. That may be true if one reads objectively and studiously attempts not to identify with the author. As in a courtroom trial, one must sometimes treat some materials (missionary reports, for example) as a hostile witness. In such a case the truth derives not in the intent of the witnesses' remarks but in analysis of the face value of the remarks.

Christianity has long been controlled by Europeans. From the time of the earliest Gentile converts first to Judaism and then to Christianity there was an attempt to tailor Christianity for acceptability among Gentiles. This included using European symbols to explain the essential beliefs of Christianity, which was born in the Jewish community. By mid-first century of the Common Era, inculturation of Christianity was well under way. In the defining years of the second, third, and fourth centuries, Christianity was transformed in its cultural format to accommodate the European peoples who became Christians in increasing numbers. Much contemporary ceremony, dogma, and philosophical underpinnings of the belief system of Christianity were put in place by the ecumenical councils of that period. Consequently, when the forbears of contemporary Native Americans referred to Christianity as a White Man's religion, there was–and is–a great deal of truth in the perception. Early missionaries did not dispute the contention. Instead, when they gained a foothold in Native American communities, they seemed to do everything they could to confirm it. Missionary planting was not a singular event but occurred in different parts of North America in different ways at different times. In the Northeast the Catholics and Anglicans were active; on the Eastern seaboard the Puritans introduced their form of Christianity. Later, the Oglethorpe colony provided a base for the introduction of still other Christian systems, notably the influential Moravians and the fledgling movement that would eventually become the Methodist Church in America. We can only speculate that along the Gulf Coast the French Catholic church and the Spanish Catholic church were active. In the great Southwest, Spanish Catholic priests, either accompanying or being accompanied by Spanish troops, forcibly did their work of planting the church. Missionaries fanned out across the land as encroachment on and theft of Native lands by White "settlers" spread West. The work of the missionaries is characterized here as "planting" the church in the Native American communities. This is to suggest that the growth and nurture of the church among Native Americans requires a somewhat different treatment and that we need to place in a more acceptable perspective the actual contribution of European missionaries.

It is tempting to concentrate on the respective European missionaries and spend a great deal of time discussing their atrocities, but in doing so we do that which they have already done–promoting their role in "Indian missions" and lessening that of Native people themselves. The missionary reports have gone to great lengths in self-promotion by the missionaries. Many of them loved to tell stories about how they bravely went among the "wild tribes" and in the woods risked their lives for the sake of the gospel. But they consistently forgot to tell of the tribal leader who granted them permission to work among the tribe and encouraged the people to attend the meetings or of the interpreters who did the actual preaching to the people in the Native languages.

Christianity found its way into Native American lives borne by missionaries and explorers fulfilling the requirements of their charters. It was not until the colonial settlements were in place that missionaries of a visionary character began to work among Native people. Ironically, it was Native American tribal communities whose existence was compromised and whose people were hit hard by European diseases and demoralized by the loss of their homes and crops to encroaching Europeans that were most susceptible to the work of European missionaries.

Tribes in the upper Eastern seaboard were almost wiped out by European diseases, mostly smallpox, and, in this setting, John Eliot began his work. Toward the South, the Moravians worked among a dispossessed and broken people. Beginning in New York and being driven out by European immigrants, the Native peoples, converts of the Moravians, began a dangerous exodus that took them from the Eastern seaboard to eastern Ohio along the Tuscarawas River; they were hounded all the way by White immigrants. The violence of the immigrants against this community continued, but they remained at that location for an extended length of time. In other parts of the East, other Native tribes, their lives disrupted by encroaching European immigrants and the colonial government that continued to remove the tribes from their homeland, were susceptible to anyone who promised relief from the atrocities they were experiencing.

Tribes whose lives had not yet been totally disrupted were more resistant to the introduction of a foreign religion, and missionaries who went among them did not find immediate success. An example is John Wesley, who approached the Creeks and went away feeling rebuffed as the Creek people indicated a preference for their own spirituality and means of observance of the Creator's activities among the People. In other instances missionaries approached leaders like Red Jacket, who declared that he was an orator rather than a prophetic leader. He was willing to listen but also wanted his opportunity to respond.

For the most part, missionaries did not find it difficult to make their way into a Native American tribal community. Native people listened politely as the missionaries told them their ways of living should be set aside and new ways adopted. In some cases missionaries would sit down with tribal officials, explain what they would like to do among the people, and solicit support from the tribal leaders. Such was the case with Jesse Walker, who was appointed by Methodist bishop William McKendree to open work among tribes in Illinois. Through his interpreter Walker arranged a meeting with tribal leaders. The Potawatomi tribal leaders joined in counsel, shared food and pipe with Walker, and then heard his request. With permission, Walker was able to establish a mission in LaSalle County, the Salem Mission. The same was true of the Wyandotte, where Reverend James Finley, John Stewart, and four of the Wyandotte headmen—Mononcue, Between-the-Logs, Hicks, and Peacock—developed the earliest mission church in the Ohio Conference of the Methodist church. In many cases, when they were consulted and their permission and support solicited, tribal leaders responded not just with permission but also made resources of the tribe available to the church for its work.

A missionary by the name of Seth Crawford was credited with helping to bring Christianity to the Great Lakes region. Crawford was unusual in that he chose to forego the usual pattern of using an interpreter to preach to the Native people. Instead he came and lived with a Chippewa family before he began his ministry so he could learn the Chippewa language. It was Crawford whom Peter Jones, one of the most prominent Native Christian missionaries of the 1840s and a Chippewa chief, credits with his own entry into the Christian church.

A great proportion of missionaries, however, went among Native people with total arrogance, and this arrogance led to failure at the least and disaster in the extreme. Jason Lee, ostensibly responding to a plea from the Flathead tribe for a missionary, chose a site for his work in the Willamette Valley of Oregon. This was located far from Native tribal settlements, but he set up a school and sent his workers out to bring Native students to board and work on the school property. Lee did not consult with Native tribal leaders and apparently never had the support of tribal groups in the area. He was able to persuade a number of youth to come attend classes and board at the school, but many of them died, apparently from diseases brought by the White mission workers to which the Native children had no immunity. At one point Lee had as many as forty enrolled in the school, but by the end of the second year only two were left. "The rest had died or fled for fear of dying." The mission failed due to this haughty aloofness but also because of the hostility of White immigrants who had preceded Jason Lee and who actively opposed the mission. Lee also had other interests. The Oregon territory was coveted by Britain, and the American immigrants who had encroached on land of the Oregon tribes desired statehood for the territory. Eventually Lee became a colonizer, promoting statehood for the Oregon Territory.

Lee's contemporary Marcus Whitman approached his work near the present-day Washington/Oregon border with an arrogance that led ultimately to disaster for him and his mission. Whitman too did not bother to consult with the tribe that controlled the area he chose for the site of his missions. Unfortunately the site Whitman chose was reserved for the headman of the Cayuse tribe. The Cayuse tribe was a small but proud people with strong territorial perceptions. They allowed him to build his mission on the site thinking that he eventually would pay the tribe for the privilege of the use of the land. He did not. He put in crops and called upon people from the Cayuse tribe and the Nez Perce to work the fields. They did, believing that it was for the benefit of their people. Matters got worse. His White mission workers used a whip on the people working in the fields if they failed to move fast enough, or, as Jason Lee commented admiringly, "Both Mr. Whitman and Mr. Spaulding use high-handed manners with their people and when they deserve it let them feel the lash." The Cayuse were still angered over the fact that Whitman had not compensated them for the use of land reserved for the headman. Further, large waves of White immigrants were arriving in the area by way of the Oregon Trail, stopping at the mission station. Finally, a young Christian man of the Cayuse tribe, a son of a Cayuse headman and a student of the mission, was shot to death by a White immigrant as the young man knelt in prayer during a church service on the Sabbath. The Whitman mission was destroyed by the Cayuse people in 1847.

By the time sectarian missionaries were purposely making their way into Native communities, these tribal communities were in desperate straits. Hounded by White immigrants and the U.S. Government, many of the tribal societies had been devastated, the leaders of the tribes compromised or killed, and the people reduced to "surviving groups" by disease and forced displacement. While many other tribes still retained their traditional strength, it is among the surviving groups that we are able to discern the character of the church's message to Native American people. William Apess, a person of the Pequot tribe of New England and a Christian minister, wrote of his experiences in several tracts and autobiographical accounts. He was born into this desperate time and as a child suffered the effects of the alcoholism that afflicted his family. Although at first he thought of himself as being rescued from the violence that attended his childhood, he eventually learned differently. At an early age he finally realized that his "rescuers," a succession of White families, were selling him among themselves as an indentured servant. He recounts for his readers his reaction to this discovery: "However, I never cried out 'Massa, Massa—Master, Master' but called them by their regular names." He never blamed the Native people themselves for their desperate condition but tried to place the blame where it belonged.

> The white will say, "What cruel creatures, to use children so!" If I could see that this blame was attached to the poor degraded Indians, I should not have one word to say. But when not a whit of it belongs to them, I have the more to say. My sufferings certainly were through the white man's measure: for they most certainly brought spirituous liquors first among My people. For surely no such sufferings were heard of, or known among our people, until the burning curse and demon of despair came among us. Surely it came through the hands of the whites.[1]

Nevertheless, Apess saw something in the gospel message that was independent of the intent and purposes of its colonial bearers. The message was evangelical, as we would describe it today, intended to convert the listener from one belief system to another. The common issue was sin, but the ultimate understanding of the nature of sin was a point of divergence. To the White missionary, even being Indian was a sin. To William Apess, disruption of harmonious life was a sin, and one who contributed to that disharmony was responsible to God. Christ died to free his followers from the bonds of sin, and to be his follower meant the freedom to rebuild one's life and to help others to be free of the destructive power of sin.

The message of the gospel in that turbulent era was as compelling as it is in our own troubled times. It was the spirituality and words of hope of the gospel soaring above the culture-bound sermons of the missionaries and the compromising acts of immigrants and soldiers that caused Native people to perceive that something greater than humankind was at work. The word transcended the actions and intent of the bearers. It was, after all, Native American Christians who were responsible for the spread of Christianity among Native Americans—not the missionaries.

All through the history of European missions to the Native peoples of the Americas, a primary role player in the spread of the church has been the interpreter. Interpreters were Native persons recruited to be the lingual spokespersons for the White missionary because he, the missionary, could not speak the Native languages. The interpreter was the preacher who was heard and understood by the Native listener, because the interpreter was himself a fellow tribesman who spoke the Native language. The missionary had to trust that the interpreter grasped the message in English and faithfully delivered it to the Natives in their own language. The interpreters became important leaders among the people, although their role was either downplayed or erased entirely in missionary reports.

Some, such as Samson Occom, rose above their role as interpreters and are known for other achievements. When he was forty years old, Occom went to England with Reverend Nathaniel Whitaker to raise funds for Eleazar Wheelock's Indian school. He preached three hundred sermons in England and Scotland and raised a considerable sum. Wheelock used the money to fund a school that eventually became Dartmouth College in New Hampshire. Samson Occom was also born into a generation that did not know the settled life of Native tribes. His tribe, the Mohegan, had been decimated; it numbered only about 350 persons. At nineteen years of age Occom sought out Wheelock to study in preparation for a goal he set for himself to teach his own people to read the word of God. He stated his own desire to read the scripture and said, "At the same time I had an uncommon pity and compassion to my poor Brethren according to the flesh. I used to wish I was capable of instructing my poor kindred." While in Montauk on New York's Long Island he was asked by the local Native people to stay among them and instruct them. He agreed to do so and worked with a Mr. Horton, the Scotch Society's missionary. Mr. Horton spent most of his time with the Shinnecock, while Occom provided the leadership at Montauk. In his report, he says that he read scripture to the people, preached in the Native language, visited the sick, and attended to their funerals. When the missionary Horton suddenly left the mission, Occom was the sole spiritual leader at Montauk and Shinnecock. He reported,

"Some time after Mr. Horton left these Indians, there was a remarkable revival of religion among these Indians and many converted to the saving knowledge of God in Jesus." In spite of his successes, he suffered the same dilemma as other Native leaders in church history. The mission boards seemed to have something against paying Native clergy equally to White clergy. Samson Occom reports that he was rebuffed and told that he wanted to live too extravagantly when he requested pay for his work. He received only £180 for twelve years of service. He compared this to the salary of a White missionary who served White "settlers." That clergyman received £180 a year!

David Fowler, a Montauk, also worked under the supervision of Eleazar Wheelock. He, like Occom, found himself solely in charge of the spiritual leadership of a community of Native people he was instructing. He apparently was in a location where visiting clergy would come, minister to the people for a while, and then leave. He described a people very receptive to the gospel and pleaded for a minister to be sent. He noted their poverty and how they tried to provide him with food from their meager provisions. He said that "most everyone of the adults have openly renounced their liquor and said that they will devote themselves to hearing the word of God."

In recent studies the names of many Native American Christians are emerging as important to the spread of Christianity among Native peoples in the formative historical years. Both men and women have literally given their lives because of the strength of their belief. In this last quarter of the twentieth century we assume that there are Native American leaders in the church, but that has not always been something that could be taken for granted. In Indian Territory most of the Native clergy of the mainline denominations started their ministry as interpreters or assistants to missionaries. These all tended to follow a similar pattern. Alexander Tally, a White missionary among the Choctaw, states in his journal that while he set up the shelter and prepared for a night's rest his interpreter was going from camp to camp gathering people together for worship services. Many outstanding Native leaders kept the church alive during the dark and dangerous days of the Civil War. Native clergy who were assistants found themselves alone in the field as most missionaries fled to states not involved in the war. In locations where ministers rarely came, Native lay persons provided the spark of leadership needed to keep the message of scripture before the people. The story of Kanchi among the Choctaw on their dangerous trek from Mississippi to Indian Territory is no doubt paralleled many times among the Creek, Cherokee, Seminole, and Chickasaw. Native American people have their heroes and martyrs in the Christian fold as do other people in the world. Their stories need to be told with as much reverence as we give to the telling of the story of the Exodus of the People of Israel from Egypt. The names of the hundreds of lives that were given in the name of the One who will restore those lives should be murmured in prayers of remembrance by contemporary generations who are building on the foundations they have laid.

Note

[1] William Apess, *The Experiences of Five Christian Indians of the Pequot Tribe* (1833), in *On Our Own Ground: The Complete Writings of William Apess, A Pequot,* ed. Barry O'Connell (Amherst: University of Massachusetts, 1992), p. 121.

5.

"If This Is Paganism . . ."

Zitkala-Sa and the Devil's Language

BETTY LOUISE BELL

Zitkala-Sa was eight when she saw the devil. Seduced by missionaries and possessing a great will even at this early age, she convinced her mother to allow her to leave the Yankton Sioux Reservation to attend White's Manual Institute in Wabash, Indiana. In her autobiographical pieces collected as *American Indian Stories*, she charts her journey from a precocious childhood to White-educated Indian teacher. Her transformation from a nonliterate, Native-speaking child to a teacher articulate and accomplished in English and the ways of the White world was testimony to the success of Indian boarding schools and literacy as a site of civilization. Zitkala-Sa was proud of her achievements and, even long after she had become alert to the cultural and spiritual costs of such a trajectory, she advocated education and the acquisition of English for Native people.

In an essay published in *American Indian Magazine* in the winter of 1919, she appeals to "the Chiefs and Headmen of the tribes" for a recognition of English as the pan-tribal language: "There is much talk among our White brothers about the importance of all Americans learning to speak English. . . . How often I have wished that you could write to me in a language we both understand perfectly. I could then profit from your advice in many things, and you would know you were not forgot." In her advocacy for a pan-tribal memory and language, Zitkala-Sa forgets that it is her tribal language and its inaccessibility to outsiders that rescues her from the devil's nightmarish pursuit at White's school. The devil cannot speak to or pursue her mother "because he did not know the Indian language."[1] The devil speaks only English. In the decades that followed, this Dakota writer dedicated much of her energies to discovering ways in which Indian experience and spiritual life could be negotiated in the devil's language.

In 1876, the year Zitkala-Sa was born, the Sioux and Cheyenne experienced a spectacular triumph in the battle of Little Bighorn, and, in severe retribution for the deaths of Custer and his soldiers, the Sioux bands of Sitting Bull were confined to the Great Sioux Reservation. The final months of the year increased despair and brought near starvation; the winter, always a time of uncertain food supplies, found hunting grounds occupied by a military still engaged in war with the Sioux. The sacred Black Hills were, after a decade of warfare, ceded to the United States. The Ghost Dance, the final hope for resurrection of all dead or lost, ended with the Wounded Knee slaughter and with the murder of Sitting Bull.

In 1891, this year of Native cultural and spiritual devastation, Gertrude Simmons (as Zitkala-Sa was then known) returned to her mother's house on the reservation and remained there for the next four years until leaving to attend the Quaker Earlham College in Richmond, Indiana. Her sense of alienation was still pronounced; after years away at school, however, it was now her mother, relatives, and the land that seemed to have a purpose and meaning separate and different from her own: "During this time I seemed to hang in the heart of chaos, beyond the touch or voice of human aid. . . . My mother had never gone inside of a school house and so she was not capable of comforting a daughter who could read and write. Even nature seemed to have no place for me. I was neither a wee girl nor a tall one; neither a wild Indian nor a tame one. This deplorable situation was the effect of my brief course in the East."[2] And it would be a quarrel over her educational ambitions and future absences from home that pushed her to self-invention. To her sister-in-law's bitter suggestion a decade later that she leave name with home, she christened herself Zitkala-Sa, translated as Red Bird, a name she wished to make known in all parts of the world. She distinguished herself as a poet and orator at Earlham and as a teacher—a teacher who refused to mimic White ways—at Carlisle Indian School. It is with her self-christening, however, that she begins to envision for herself a public identity.

At the turn of the century a group of Native intellectuals, products of Indian boarding schools, attempted to create a public and literate pan-tribal voice. They wrote about and advocated indigenous rights at a time of historical and cultural transition for Native peoples. For their work to succeed, for it to resurrect the Indian with the same tools the schools had used to suppress him, they needed to build bridges between oral and written cultures and between tradition and assimilation. These writers were mixed bloods by either blood or culture, and this middle space is evidenced in their interchangeable use of White and Indian names.

When Zitkala-Sa (Gertrude Simmons, later Bonnin), like Charles Eastman or E. Pauline Johnson, used her Indian name there was certainly a suggestion of performative authenticity–any Native writer at this point would need to demonstrate (and perhaps exploit) "real Indianness" for her mostly White audience–but there was also a genuine desire to retribalize her identity and experience, to claim what history and White education had silenced.

In this period of transition, on her return from a European engagement with the Carlisle Indian band in 1900, Zitkala-Sa takes on her Indian name and becomes a writer. Her first book, *Old Indian Legends*, was published in 1901. The previous year three of her pieces from *American Indian Stories* were published in *Atlantic Monthly*. In 1901, two short stories, "The Trial Path" and "The Soft-Hearted Sioux," were printed in *Harper's Magazine*.[3] "A Warrior's Daughter" was written in 1902. In the last month of this most creative and productive period she published "Why I Am a Pagan," which reflects a defiant swerve from her earlier celebratory embrace of America and its paternalistic ambitions for the Indian:

> We come from mountain fastnesses, from cheerless plains, from far-off low wooded streams, seeking the "White Man's ways." Seeking your skill in industry and in art, seeking labor and honest independence, seeking the treasures of knowledge and wisdom, seeking to comprehend the spirit of your laws and the genius of your noble institutions, seeking by a new birthright to unite with you our claim to a common country, seeking the Sovereign's crown that we may stand side by side with you in ascribing royal honor to our nation's flag. America, I love thee. "Thy people shall be my people and thy God my God."[4]

The essay won Gertrude Simmons second place in the Indiana State Oratorical contest in 1896. When her self-declaration of paganism appeared in 1902, Zitkala-Sa was criticized and condemned by both White and Indian readers.

Written two decades before her congressional testimony against peyote, her essay on paganism both confounds and conflates assimilation and resistance. For Zitkala-Sa, paganism is associated with open spaces, freedom, and land. Throughout her autobiographical stories the greatest crime committed against her is the attempt to domesticate and enclose her within the spaces and conventions of female gender. Her hair is cut, her blanket is exchanged for tight-fitting clothes, and her room is a close attic. White's school demanded the sacrifice of spontaneity and everyday self-determination. "It was next to impossible to leave the iron routine after the civilizing machine had begun its day's buzzing."[5] At the end of her career as a student and teacher, the prisons of Indian educational institutions produced in her a spiritual crisis, a sickness of brute and blunted feeling, and a need to return, at least emotionally, to the open spaces inhabited by the Great Spirit.

What is true for most Native writers is especially pronounced in Zitkala-Sa's work: land, mother, and tribal sovereignty are indistinguishable from one another. The most traumatic event in her early life was separation from, and loss of, her mother. And the most serious rupture in her relationship with her mother concerned the selling of land; she believed that everyone should keep land to return to. In the autobiographical stories her separation from her mother parallels her departure from a land already compromised by White encroachment. The tracks of the train taking her to "the land of red apples" are lined with telegraph poles.[6] On her final return home, she finds her mother cursing "poverty stricken White beggars" who "had rushed hither to make claims on those wild lands."[7] Their fires on the bluffs interfere with the natural beauty of the night and disrupt a daughter's visit. Her brother, educated at an eastern Indian school, tried to secure justice for his people through the Great Father in Washington only to lose his job to a White son of the Great Father.

In these stories it is the mother who seeks justice within the mercy and domain of the Great Spirit. Once she had given her daughter a Bible, the only reading material available in her home, to comfort her upon her return from boarding school. When her daughter is grown, now a teacher of students such as herself, the mother appeals to her to join in prayers to the Great Spirit for justice.

> "My child, there is only one source of justice, and I have been praying steadfastly to the Great Spirit to avenge our wrongs," she said, seeing I did not move my lips.
>
> My shattered energy was unable to hold longer any faith, and I cried out desperately: "Mother, don't pray again! The Great Spirit does not care if we live or die."[8]

It is the sickness of institutional life, the alienation from home and open spaces, that has disabled the child's faith. Zitkala-Sa's remedy is to relocate her beliefs within the vast mystery of the Great Spirit.

As many scholars have argued, the concept of the Great Spirit is a compound of early Christian influence on Native religion and a free translation of the Sioux *Wakan Tanka*, which is more literally translated as "Great Mysterious" or "Great Holy."[9] Christianity's contribution to this concept can be seen in the monolithic nature of this deity, which gives it an interchangeability—common use of this interchange is seen in the works of many turn-of-the-century Native writers—with the concept of God and, as such, makes it less objectionable to Judeo-Christian beliefs than particularized tribal religious practices. For leaders and intellectuals of the Society for American Indians (SAI), it combined and connected pan-Indian reform with a pan-tribal religion.[10] As a member of the SAI, Zitkala-Sa understood its appeal and political uses within Indian and White cultures.

In her essay celebrating the freedoms of paganism, later republished in her collection of stories as "The Great Spirit," Zitkala-Sa's primary intent is nostalgia, the regaining of childhood with its bonds and freedoms. The lyricism is reminiscent of her early autobiographical stories, capturing the swirling revel of a child circle-chasing her shadow among friends.

> When the spirit swells my breast I love to roam leisurely among the green hills; or sometimes, sitting on the brink of the murmuring Missouri, I marvel at the great blue overhead. With half-closed eyes I watch the huge cloud shadows in their noiseless play upon the high bluffs opposite me, while into my ear ripple the sweet, soft cadences of the river's song. Folded hands lie in my lap, for the time forgot. My heart and I lie small upon the earth like a grain of throbbing sand.[11]

In this passage Zitkala-Sa not only yearns for a return to her personal origins but also claims earthly origin as the domain of the Great Spirit, and, as such, the domain of indigenous peoples. This location, the habitat of the Great Spirit, is populated only by an Indian village to which she is "strongly drawn by the tie of a child to an aged mother."[12]

The effect of this romantic nostalgia is to retribalize its author, to return her to an identity uncomplicated by mother or certainly by nation and, by extension, to retribalize her readers. Zitkala-Sa's yearning for a lost time is larger than that found in human love; it must position her within the center of nature, uncorrupted by human voice or contact. Here there is no fear, and Native language is spoken and understood; here, even her black, shaggy dog understands Sioux; here, shadows become masters.

> The racial lines, which were once bitterly real, now serve nothing more than marking out a mosaic of human beings. And even here men of the same color are like the ivory keys of one instrument where each resembles all the rest, yet varies from them in pitch and quality of voice. And those creatures who are for a time mere echoes of another's note are not unlike the fable of the thin sick man whose distorted shadow, dressed like a real creature, came to the old master to make him follow as a shadow.[13]

Her only human contact is an English-speaking Indian convert, come to chastise paganism with his "bigoted creed." Zitkala-Sa identifies him as God's creature, an individual who demands as much respect as any creature within the natural world of the Great Spirit. Listening to him, she has a flash of her mother's Christian conversion—who now, like her visitor, is intent not on justice but on the avoidance of hell. It is, Zitkala-Sa again discovers, the devil that gathers faith among these converts, for God, like the Great Spirit, does not rely on fear to recruit: "There is one God who gives reward or punishment to the race of dead men. In the upper region the Christian dead are gathered in unceasing song and prayer. In the deep pit below, the sinful ones dance in torturing flames. . . . Think upon these things, my cousin, and choose now to avoid the after-doom of hell fire!"[14]

If Zitkala-Sa's celebration of nature seems something of a performance—and it is—she was too much a performer not to exploit her audience's romanticism. It is juxtaposed to her visitor's performance of hell and the visible manifestation of selection and salvation: "Knocking out the chinking of our log cabin, some evil hand thrust in a burning taper of braided dry grass, but failed of his intent, for the fire died out and the half-burned brand fell inward to the floor. Directly above it, on a shelf, lay the holy book. This is what we found after our return from several days' visit. Surely some great power is hid in the sacred book!"[15] Zitkala-Sa's response to this man of little faith is to brush away "from my eyes many like pictures."[16] Those pictures include her mother's recent conversion, but also her initial boarding school encounter with the devil.

> Out of a large book she showed me a picture of the white man's devil. I looked in horror upon the strong claws that grew out of his fur-covered fingers. His feet were like his hands. Trailing at his heels was a scaly tail tipped with a serpent's open jaws. His face was a patchwork: he had bearded cheeks, like I had seen pale-faces wear; his nose was an eagle's bill, and his sharp-pointed ears were pricked up like those of a sly fox. Above them a pair of cow's horns curved upward. I trembled with awe, and my heart throbbed in my throat, as I looked at the king of evil spirits. Then I heard the paleface woman say that this terrible creature roamed loose in the world, and that little girls who disobeyed school regulations were to be tortured by him.[17]

The devil is a distortion of shape and being, an unnatural "patchwork" of animal and human parts, informed and held together by evil, yet his appearance is undeniably and repeatedly identified as White. Historically, even Christianized Indians had difficulty imaging the devil as Native. An eighteenth-century preacher reported that Indians "accepted the existence of Satan but made him an evil brought by the whites. . . . They declare that he is not to be found among Indians but only among the white people, for if he were among the Indians they would long since have discovered and their ancestors would have told them about him."[18]

Zitkala-Sa's first punishment at boarding school resulted from her failure to understand English and to promise obedience in that indecipherable language. She and her Dakota friends had mistaken the word *no* for compliance and agreed to use it whenever addressed by a teacher. Conceived as an act of accommodation and surrender, it was quickly and viciously interpreted by a teacher as resistance and insurrection when she asked one of the pupils, "Are you going to obey my word the next time?" To which the child answered in the only word she knew and was beaten until the teacher posed a question requiring a "no" response.[19]

This image informs all of Zitkala-Sa's life and work: the hope that a voice of accommodation can enact resistance within an alien and hostile culture and its language. Many scholars have interpreted, with good reason, her embrace and advocacy of education and citizenship (and her testimony against the syncretic peyotist religion) as assimilationist. For Zitkala-Sa, tribal self-determination could be gained only through Indian accommodation with "the good intentions of a benevolent Government."[20] She failed to see that the act of assimilation, or even the appearance of it, in postcolonial cultures does not rearrange hierarchies of power but stabilizes them. Her appeal in 1919 to Americans to "revoke the tyrannical power of Government superintendents over a voiceless people and extend American opportunities to the first American–the Red Man" is a good example of how her rhetoric of accommodation undermines the strength of her political legacy.[21] She positions herself politically against Native dependence and disenfranchisement, yet the claims of indigeneity cannot be heard as "the first American." This gesture toward her White audience arrests and traps her argument within a colonial identity.

In her creative writing, however, she is able to evade the discourse that strangles much of her political writing. Perhaps this can be explained in part by the position of creative language within postcolonial cultures which do not require it to strive for "competence in the dominant tongue, but a striving towards appropriation, in which the cultural distinctiveness can be simultaneously overridden-overwritten."[22] Or perhaps it was simply that the mask of fiction allowed Zitkala-Sa to forfeit the voice of accommodation and know the demons that would silence her. The least accommodationist of her nonfiction writing, "Why I Am a Pagan," benefits from its fluid middle ground between tribal religions and Christianity. In this interstitial space that she would construct as free from personal or cultural theft, she is able to use the devil's language to return home.

By the time she died in 1938, Zitkala-Sa had lived to realize the enactment of what to her were important reforms: full citizenship for Native

Americans, the use of Roosevelt's so-called Indian New Deal to secure better health care and limited tribal self-government, and an improvement in vocational and educational opportunities for Natives. But language had become, for her, distinct from the emotion or experience it expressed. It was thus indifferent to political intention or cultural realities: "Language is only a convenience, just like a coat is a convenience, and it is not so important as your mind and heart."[23] In her latter years she did not return to Sioux country or again regain the exuberant paganism of her creative period.

Notes

[1] Zitkala-Sa, *American Indian Stories* (Lincoln: University of Nebraska Press, 1979), p. 63.

[2] Ibid., p. 69.

[3] For the exact issues and a more detailed description of Zitkala-Sa's life and career, see Dexter Fisher's foreword to *American Indian Stories.*

[4] See Dexter Fisher, "The Transformation of Tradition: A Study of Zitkala-Sa and Mourning Dove, Two Transitional American Indian Writers" (Ph.D. diss., City University of New York, 1979).

[5] Zitkala-Sa, p. 66.

[6] Ibid., p. 47.

[7] Ibid., p. 93.

[8] Ibid., p. 92.

[9] For a fuller discussion, see Raymond J. DeMallie and Douglas R. Parks, eds., *Sioux Indian Religion* (Norman: University of Oklahoma Press, 1987).

[10] For a thorough discussion of modern Indian identity and its debt to pan-Indian movements, see Hazel Hertzberg, *The Search for an American Indian Identity* (Syracuse: Syracuse University Press, 1971).

[11] Zitkala-Sa, p. 101.

[12] Ibid., p. 103.

[13] Ibid., p. 104.

[14] Ibid., p. 106.

[15] Ibid.

[16] Ibid.

[17] Ibid., pp. 62-63.

[18] Richard White, *The Middle Ground: Indian Empires and Republics in the Great Lakes Region, 1650-1815* (New York: Cambridge University Press, 1991), p. 337.

[19] Zitkala-Sa, p. 58.

[20] Ibid., p. 65.

[21] Ibid.

[22] Bill Ashcroft, Gareth Griffiths, and Helen Tiffin, *The Empire Writes Back* (London: Routledge, 1989), p. 68.

[23] Zitkala-Sa, *American Indian Magazine* (Fall 1919), p. 154.

6.

No Longer an Indian

My Story

FREDA McDONALD

I hold in my hand a card that I was given by the government of Canada at the time I married a non-Native man. It reads, "Not deemed to be an Indian within the law or any other statute." It is a record of the loss of my identity. It is my alienation, banishment, and displacement from my birthplace and country by the government and its laws. It has everything to do with history—the signing of treaties, the refusal of government to acknowledge and correct the illegal expropriation of prime lands in North America. No doubt, many will disagree with me, but the story is well documented. We are caught in this web and are still held hostage by it today. This is the brief story of one person's soul and spirit not willing to die under the onslaught of genocide practiced by the government and the industrial, avaricious ravages of our environment.

I am considered an Elder in our Native community. I did not choose to be. I grew old! Elders are individuals recognized for their work with people at the grassroots level. They hold no Ph.D.s and do not practice any "ologies" in academic careers. Elders deal with feelings, share their support and guidance in any emotional turmoil one might experience. You have to earn the trust of the people (and people do test you!) before they declare you to be an Elder. Elders are available anytime. They maintain the strictest confidentiality. They may hold different spiritual ceremonies, depending on whether they are a bundlecarrier or pipecarrier.

I am not highly educated. I only attended school to grade 10 and did not even complete that. I had the good fortune to have had one good teacher who said that the dictionary would be my greatest friend if I knew how to use it properly. She gave me that gift of knowledge. Everything else I know I learned through life experiences.

Before I share my journey as a card-toting "not deemed to be an Indian," I would like to give a brief account of my history and the background that form part of this story. I still feel my inner fear of taking the risk of exposing my thoughts and feelings, but I know that truth—no matter how scary or ugly—sets one free and allows the spirit to soar. This may be an old story, but it bears repeating in the hope that it will encourage others to let *their* truths be known. If my story reaches out and touches but one person's soul and spirit, then perhaps that person too may begin his or her walk on the path to understanding and healing. Have faith in the Creator, *manitou* in my Ojibway language. And so my story begins.

I was born on an Indian reserve called Fort Alexander in Manitoba, Canada. I was the last of my family to be born at home, coming into the world in the early morning hours of April 26, 1932. My brothers and sisters who followed me were born in the Indian hospital set up by the government through the Indian Affairs office in the mid-1930s.

Our reserve had long been exposed to the White Man as a result of the fur trade. Following this initial contact, the *mukadaykonayek*, "Black Robes," arrived to convert the *Anishnabek* "Indians" from their heathen ways. By the time of my birth, the Catholic church was long established, as was the Anglican church. The Protestants settled in Pine Falls, a small town that is legally part of our reserve but occupied by White people.

With the arrival of these religions, our community became divided. The Anglicans lived upriver and the Catholics on the lower mouth of the Winnipeg River. My parents were Catholic, and so I was baptized into that religion, which did not permit socializing with others of a different faith. This included my great-grandparents and my extended family on their side. The spiritual conflicts among the churches promoted erosive, degenerative divisions among my people and led to infighting. Yet many of my people fought to stay loyal and true to their chosen beliefs. The adage "blood is thicker than water" strongly prevailed here because, despite the stifling paternalism of the government and church authorities, we overcame with the help of our Elders.

Our Elders, our teachers, urged us to "know who we are, where we came from, and where we belong." They told us to cling to our language. Our language and tradition, they said, are God-given gifts that no human could change! Through these teachings, my family ties remained strong. We found ways to keep in touch, even though we were separated and not free to practice fully our traditional way of life.

My parents were caring, sharing, accepting, forgiving, and very community oriented. We were materially poor but very rich in values. We knew we were dependent on each other and the community in times of crisis for our own well-being and survival.

The *mukadaykonayek* built their church in the mid-1800s and added their school on our reserve around 1900, the year my father was born. The school included a seminary where young White men trained for the priesthood to help convert Indians living in the surrounding area. They did this with the help of the converted Indian souls of *Sageeng,* our Indian name for our *shkonigun* or reserve. *Shkonigun* in our language means "left-over," a clear indication that my people understood that our prime lands had been lost. The realization that this one word witnesses to this profound truth still astounds me! Our history, as our Elders said and continue to say, is indeed rooted in our language.

Like the fur traders before them, the missionaries were dependent on the Indians for their survival. They spoke to our people about this. They were sincere in their work with the people, I believe. We were fond of them. They became part of our community. But, they too, I think, became caught in the web of unresolved treaties and histories.

History is written from a grossly biased and prejudicial standpoint. When read, the records glorify atrocities of genocidal avarice visited upon invaded Native people. Perpetuated by the decreed educational system and taught to generation after generation, this leaves the Indians, including me, in a purgatory of persecution, a living hell of continual emotional and mental torment. I hated history in school, but I didn't know why. As a young child, I did not know the shame of being Indian. Education planted, fostered, and nurtured that shame within my innocent child's mind. Had our people had a written language back then, perhaps the other side of the story might have been known also. I do not say this with bitterness or malice. I personally have had to deal with my learned, corrupted, and warped thinking in order to understand from where my all consuming rage and self-destruction stemmed. For me, this is it! Now I understand, and I hear my forebears saying, "*Waybeenun!*" "Throw it away!" In so doing, one's spirit is freed.

History, jealously guarded and protected, is a self-incriminating record. Perhaps the justice lies there. If so, I can feel compassion for people who are unaware and have yet to hear, learn, and understand the other side of the story—our side of the story.

My father entered school and completed grade 12, the highest an Indian could attain at that time. Indians were not encouraged or readily accepted in higher education. But Dad tried, oh, how he tried!

My parents and our people were self-reliant. They lived off the land. They fished, hunted, and trapped. They also engaged in some small-scale farming and, at the church's urging, grew gardens. The church said farming was a better way of life. Maybe so, from its point of view.

My parents were my first teachers. Parents always are. They taught their children values and traditions in tune with our environment and way of life. We were told to observe animal life, to learn from this, and to follow the rules of the land because this is where we come from. The land is our life and the source of our survival. Everything we own comes from the land. "Look around you," my parents said, "see what we have and know where it comes from." We observed the elements, watched for disturbances to animal and plant life and took these as good signs or warnings because any disruption could threaten our lives. The church called this superstition and paganism. Today, they call it romanticizing and idolization of Mother Earth. To me it was, and still is, simply a way of life.

My mother never went to school. She was learned in tradition through her grandmother, who raised her when her mother died during her childhood. My great-grandmother was a medicine woman. It became a natural course for my *kitchi kokum* to teach her granddaughter her medicines. My mother treated us with these until the Indian hospital was established. We were informed by the Indian agent through the church that we were to use this hospital only. This was the law! Our traditional medicine practices were thus choked off and relegated to nonexistence. This affected my family directly and placed other medicine people in an awful dilemma. People were afraid of the new and alien medicine, practiced by people who did not like Indians. Many stayed away and died in the process. This is the other side of the story.

My home as a child was happy. We did not lack parental love or the nurturing all children need for healthy growth and well-being.

My generation was the first to receive family allowance— "the beginning of the welfare system." The priest announced that the government had sent application forms to be distributed to all heads of families. Parents were told to list all their children's names and ages and sign the forms. The government would pay five dollars for each child age sixteen or under. This was to benefit all children. Our people did not trust the government or the Indian agent due to past and current broken treaties, so they were reluctant to accept the forms, my father among them. I will not enter into the painful details. What struck my child's mind at the time, however, were my father's words to my mother: "*Ageenus*, when we take money for what is ours, we give up what is ours for the money. What will happen to our children?" Children hear and remember things. I did not understand the significance of my father's words then, but I fully understand what Dad meant today. It was then that I first felt fear and terror at the unknown. My father did sign under duress. My parents were caught in a stranglehold of coercive bribery.

Mandatory education became law shortly after the family allowances were received. The holocaust of the boarding school and its far-reaching, genocidal attempt at erasing a people began. Family allowances went to the schools. I became a victim, like thousands of other innocent children, who suffered the horror of literally being torn away and cut off from my life source—my parents. I did not know what was happening. They say children are resilient. I suppose this is true, because I managed to survive those long, lonely years—alone and lost! I still ache and struggle, however, to hurdle the soul-searing pain my parents must have suffered at the loss of their children, their family. We could never bridge those empty and lost years, nor did we ever speak of the occurrences afterward. An insurmountable well of mental and spiritual grief, very real and too deep, held us captive in a vise-like grip of deadly silence. It was made all the more painful because we loved each other so very much!

I have nothing against either religion or education. These have their place in serving people's needs. I have some fond memories of good teachers, priests, beautiful people I met who gave me help and encouragement to go on. I can read, write, and study words in my dictionary. It was the method used that I find most cruel and morally wrong. We are still living with the aftermath of this holocaust today.

The bottom of my world dropped out when I was handed the card reading, "Not deemed to be an Indian within the law or any other statute" because I had married a non-Native. The stigma of this life sentence entered my soul. This tore the last vestiges of my being into shreds, spiritually and mentally. By law, I could not live or be with my people anymore. I stood alone, once more, but this time naked—stripped of my identity and banished into a world of alienation and discrimination. My roots were severed. I was spiritually wounded. I entered a pit of burning, all-consuming rage! I unknowingly carried this into my marriage. I was sixteen years old. Too young to understand this devastation, I shut myself off and wrapped myself in a cocoon of deadly silence that I thought would protect me.

I walked my road of emptiness, loneliness, and complete isolation. I longed for my parents! I yearned for their love! I missed my brothers and sisters! I wanted my home back. I wanted my community back. I thought of the affection I received from my people. I remembered how beautiful my life had been on my *shkonigun.* Poor, yes! but full of love— all a person needs to survive. I wept secretly, feeling this great void of nothing. I searched for brown faces on the streets of the towns where I lived in order to assure myself that my people were still around. I longed to run up to them and tell them, "I'm Indian, too!" I was a lost soul, once again a victim of the government's one-sided history and the broken treaties.

When I agreed to set this story on paper, I thought I would sail through it. It would be a breeze, I told myself! How wrong I was! I struggle and weep revisiting my pain. It has become a giant step in my own healing. Truth purges my soul. I hear the words of my grandparents once again, "*Waybeenun!*" "Throw it away!" My spirit is free.

To my people out there, I love you! Have courage.

7.

Our Ancestors Were Charitable

MARGARET SAM-CROMARTY

Red Man

One day long ago,
White people came ashore.
Our ancestors were charitable.
The new country appealed to the White Man.

Before the White Man came,
We were humble rulers
Of the whole north continent.
It was our responsibility, our heritage.

Our country was our pride.
The White Man wanted to improve
    the red man, his country.
Should we have shared?

The red man served
His country
In world wars,
A country he found was weary of his name.

May 13, 1995

Old Age

My blood runs cold.
I saw myself old,
My hands and face
   lined with age.

I felt shame and dread.
I shrank back and cried.
I wanted the prowess
   of my youth.

I fear old age,
To be useless,
To be a burden
   to my children.

When I was born,
A little baby,
I was loved.
I dreaded not being helpless.

My parents were there.
They heard me cry
   in the night.
They comforted my fears.

Why then
Do I lack sympathy
And understanding
   for the old and helpless?

My father,
He is old and blind.
I face a responsibility
   no one is anxious to share.

"Not everyone enters,"
The Lord said,
   "into my kingdom.
Only those who are kind
To the poor, to the sick,
   to the old."

1990

Maggie's Song

My little sister Maggie,
Only thirteen,
Wanting to find a better place,
Wanting to be free.

Maggie feels chilly.
It does not matter.
She is only hungry.
She misses her mother.

Dry your tears,
    little sister.
You have a pretty smile.
I am here, so is Grandmother.

My little sister,
I don't have your gift
To see the world in the light,
To see beauty and truth.

Little sister,
Sitting still,
She hugs her old grandmother.
I hear her silent call.

Maggie laughs.
I hear the rushing of sweet waters,
Waterfalls of happy music,
Soft like Maggie's eyes.

Maggie, my little sister,
You're free,
In the sound of the big winds,
In the deep, lonely marshes.

May 13, 1995

8.

A Definition of Culture

Canada and First Nations

DENNIS McPHERSON

The primary purpose of Canada's Royal Commission on Aboriginal People (the Royal Commission), which recently concluded its work after four years, was the examination of how a "new partnership" could be brought about between Aboriginal and non-Aboriginal peoples within the constitutional framework of Canada. In reviewing the historical record between these two groups thus far, the record clearly indicates an important component of this new partnership will have to be an appreciated understanding of each other's cultures. Each group must be respectful of how, as a people, its respective *ways of behaving* may be quite different from the other's, yet acceptable to the other.

In September 1992, the Royal Commission held an Aboriginal Researchers Workshop at Nakoda Lodge in Alberta. One of the discussion groups addressed the question: "What working definition of 'culture' should the Royal Commission program be guided by?" The workshop adopted a talking-circle format and discussion began, slowly and awkwardly. Most participants prefaced their comments by qualifying them as inadequate and then hesitantly offered lists of values, concepts, traits, and activities to describe their understanding of culture. The atmosphere in the room was tense and uncomfortable. It was clear that there was a fundamental flaw in the question itself; the workshop group could not come up with a definition that satisfied *anyone* or, more important, that grasped the breadth, depth, and complexity of what Aboriginal peoples wanted to say about their "cultures."

This type of exercise demonstrates the difficulty in defining what is meant by the term *culture*. Few words possess so many different meanings for so many different people. Culture is everything. Culture is nothing specific. Culture is a way of life. Culture is history and tradition. Culture is in the here and now. Culture is found in objects. Culture is found in the soul. Culture is inherited. Culture is learned. Culture is lived by everyone in everyday life. Culture is created by specialists in the hallowed halls of learning.

If a specific definition that gives meaning to the term *culture* is beyond our grasp, then what are people talking about when they speak of culture? Aboriginal presenters to the Royal Commission public hearings talked about culture as "what makes us who we are as Aboriginal people," "the core of our identity," "the heart of our people," "the hope of our future," "the strength of our past," "the pain of our loss," "the locus of our power." They talked about culture as "spirituality," as "health," as "politics." In this vein, an Aboriginal view of culture begins to unfold with the lived experiences of real people as a seat of power as well as the power culture has to create and sustain identities, both individual and communal. This view emerged as a constant theme throughout the process of public hearings conducted by the Royal Commission.

From the Aboriginal presenters to the Royal Commission, the meaning of culture also comes to life through the telling of it. When Aboriginal people talk about *culture*, they speak of specific topics and analyses, but more important, they speak with a passion, with a pain, with an anger, with a compassion, with a hope, with a resolve, and with a commitment to themselves, to their community, to past generations, and to future generations yet unborn.

The definitional and communicative task in understanding what is meant by culture is further complicated by the fact that there is no single, agreed-upon meaning of *culture* in the English or French languages either. Anthropologists, whose work it is to study culture, themselves employ the term in a variety of ways. As Michael Asch has pointed out, however, based on a review of anthropological texts: "Certain aspects of its definition . . . are held by all," and these meanings are reflected in dictionary definitions. Among these are:

- Culture is an attribute of all human societies.
- Culture includes rules and/or behavior regarding virtually all aspects of human social life.
- Culture is passed on from one generation to another by learning rather than by instinct.
- Virtually all human social behavior is based on patterns that are cultural and learned rather than inherited genetically through biological processes.[1]

The general public and various institutions have their own working and popular definitions and usages of *culture*. Likewise, governments at various levels define *culture* for the purpose of cultural policy. But if in English and French the word *culture* is understood as an abstract category, an object of study, a policy field, a bounded topic distinguishable from other topics that are *not culture*, and, in other words, a historically, politically, and geographically specific phenomenon, then constructing separations between *culture* and *not culture* is one of the most difficult areas of cross-cultural communication between Aboriginal and non-Aboriginal peoples.

If, for the purposes of discussion, we can accept and use the notion that cultures are "the webs of significance that humankind has spun and that give meaning to its relationship to the world" and are also "the webs of mystification and legitimation spun by the few to capture the many," then we have a starting point.[2]

In the variety of Aboriginal cultural traditions in Canada today, commonalities can be found one to the other even though they are most often expressed in different words or are manifest in different environmental or behavioral contexts. This does not mean there is only one Aboriginal culture that is generally applicable to all of Canada's Aboriginal peoples or that Aboriginal culture can be understood merely as some form of "pan-Indianism," making all Aboriginal peoples in Canada behave in the same fashion. It is actually quite the opposite. The cultural traditions of the various First Nations are very different one from the other. In order to understand and appreciate the various cultural traditions displayed by Aboriginal peoples today, a brief look must be taken at the path these cultures have had to follow since coming into contact with the many influences presented to them by Europeans as European migration progressed across their lands. Aboriginal people are often told by their Elders that we cannot know where we are today unless we know where we have come from.

Earlier cultural traditions of Aboriginal peoples can be seen by looking at what the first meetings between Aboriginal people and Europeans were really like. This can be done by reading the descriptions left to us by the Europeans who first experienced such situations. For example, in his Letter to the Sovereigns in 1492, which was promptly published in Barcelona and widely distributed throughout Europe in a Latin translation, Christopher Columbus stresses the gentleness and generosity of the natives:

> They are so ingenuous and free with all they have, that no one would believe it who has not seen it; of anything that they possess, if it be asked of them, they never say no; on the contrary, they invite you to share it and show as much love as if their hearts

went with it, and they are content with whatever trifle be given them, whether it be a thing of value or of petty worth. I forbade that they be given things so worthless of broken crockery and of green glass and lacepoints, although when they could get them, they thought they had the best jewel in the world.[3]

Almost 150 years after Columbus first encountered the native people of America, and about 3000 miles distance to the north from that contact, Father Paul Le Jeune of the Society of Jesus writes in his reports back to the provincial of the Jesuits in France of his experience on June 18, 1632, at Tadoussac (now Quebec):

It was here that I saw Savages for the first time. As soon as they saw our vessel they lighted fires, and two of them came on board in a little canoe very neatly made of bark. The next day a Sagamore, with ten or twelve Savages, came to see us. When I saw them enter our Captain's room, where I happened to be, it seemed to me that I was looking at those maskers who run about in France in Carnival time. There were some whose noses were painted blue, the eyes, the eyebrows, and cheeks painted black, and the rest of the face red; and these colors are bright and shining like those of our masks; others had black, red and blue stripes drawn from the ears to the mouth.

Later, when reporting further to the Society concerning the Hurons he encountered, Father Le Jeune writes:

We see shining among them some rather noble moral virtues. You note, in the first place, a great love and union, which they are careful to cultivate by means of their marriages, of their presents, of their feasts, and of their frequent visits. On returning from their fishing, their hunting, and their trading, they exchange many gifts; even if they thus obtained something unusually good, even if they have bought it, or if it has been given to them, they make a feast to the whole village with it. Their hospitality towards all sorts of strangers is remarkable; they present to them, in their feasts, the best of what they have prepared, and, as I have already said, I do not know if anything similar, in this regard, is to be found anywhere. They never close the door upon a Stranger, and, once having received him into their houses, they share with him the best they have; they never send him away, and when he goes away of his own accord, he repays them by a simple "thank you."[4]

In their respective reports of their first encounters with the native people of America, both Columbus and Father Le Jeune speak about the different values displayed in the cultural behaviors of the native people with whom they came in contact. In their reports they describe natives who are caring, loving, and sharing among themselves and with others. Over two hundred years later, and about three thousand miles west of where Father Le Jeune had his experiences, these same values are displayed again on the far-distant prairies of what is now Canada.

> An early Ukrainian settler on the Canadian prairies told the story of working in the field clearing land by hand when an elderly Indian came by. "He got off his horse and walked over to a clump of bush. He was talking in some kind of language but I couldn't understand anything. He waved to me to come over. I was kind of scared and didn't go at first. Finally I went and as I got nearer I saw that he was eating these berries. Slowly, he picked off a berry and dropped it into his mouth. He was showing me I should do the same. I finally did and tasted the juiciest berry I ever had. I smiled and tried to thank the man. Food was not exactly plentiful and I was more than happy to learn about some edible berries. I will always remember that incident and wonder why today [1957] we always think of the Indian in such a bad way."[5]

The "early Ukrainian settler" presents an interesting question for the time—Why do we always think of the Indian in such a bad way? Perhaps it is because "we" do not understand the Indian's *culture*. But then again, do "we" understand the *culture* of the European?

Earlier policies of European governments—and in particular the British style of government, which still operates in Canada today—governing the relations between Europeans and Aboriginal peoples have seriously affected the cultures of Aboriginal peoples. These policies are well described by the Rev. George M. Grant of Halifax, Nova Scotia, who, as secretary to Sir Sanford Fleming, engineer-in-chief of the Dominion Government, traveled with Fleming's expedition across Canada in 1872 to survey a route to unite British Columbia with Eastern Canada by the Canadian Pacific Railway. According to Grant, who advanced the myth of the "Vanishing Indian," regardless of any policies, "It may be said that, do what we like, the Indians as a race, must eventually die out."[6]

But "Indians as a race" in Canada (as throughout the Americas) have managed to resist "dying out"—just as they have resisted over time the policies of extermination, paternalism, and assimilation of the "Indians as a race" instituted by other European, British colonial, and post-Confederation governments. Instead, in contemporary debates Aboriginal people demand recognition of their right to self-determination and self-government. In essence, Aboriginal people are boldly making the statement, "We are who we are, and we refuse to change."

It has been a longstanding concern of Aboriginal people why they have to change their culture and traditions (including, most important, their religious traditions) in order to receive the same benefits of the Canadian state as other citizens of the country. In order to understand the perceived need for Aboriginal people to change their cultural traditions, we again have to look backward, this time into the not-too-distant past.

Cultures, whether they are manifestations of Aboriginal ways of behaving or otherwise, do not evolve in a vacuum. In fact, it is quite the opposite. Cultures, as ways of behaving, can derive from the experiences of people within the particular environmental setting in which they find themselves; or cultures, as ways of behaving, can be influenced and changed as the result of the particular thoughts of certain individuals sanctioned by the larger group or community. These sanctions in turn become the customary practices of the community. The thoughts, produced and recorded by the individual, once sanctioned by the community, eventually become the values which that community sees as important elements used to define the structure of their society. It is this process, being forced to uphold certain values different from their own, which has drastically affected Aboriginal cultures in Canada today.

In the Canadian context this process of cultural evolution widening the gap between the culture of Aboriginal peoples and Europeans (Euro-Canadians) can be traced back in British history to the seventeenth century and the era of a particular philosopher named John Locke.

> Locke had extensive knowledge of and interest in European contact with aboriginal peoples. A large number of books in his library are accounts of European exploration, colonization and of aboriginal peoples, especially Amerindians and their ways. As secretary to Lord Shaftesbury, secretary to the Lord Proprietors of Carolina (1668-71), secretary to the Council of Trade and Plantations (1673-4), and member of the Board of Trade (1696-1700), Locke was one of the six or eight men who closely invigilated and helped to shape the old colonial system during the Restoration. He invested in the slavetrading Royal Africa Company (1671) and the Company of Merchant Adventurers to trade with the Bahamas (1672), and he was a Landgrave of the proprietary government of Carolina.[7]

Locke's theory of political society and property was widely disseminated in the eighteenth century and woven into theories of progress, development, and statehood. Debates—between jurists and humanists, free traders and mercantilists, and capitalists and socialists—over the great questions of political and economic justice have thus tended to work within Locke's basic conceptual framework.[8] It is debates carried on within this conceptual framework that have had an impact on the Aboriginal world of North America. For instance, Locke's idea "to assert the basic human rights 'of life, liberty and the pursuit of happiness'" was not only adopted by Thomas Jefferson in the American Declaration of Independence but also helped define Canada's governmental policies toward Aboriginal people.[9]

Locke himself would be the first to admit that his philosophy was not intended to provide a guiding light for the Aboriginal peoples of America, as the following discourse reveals: "Locke argued that when Indian nations entered into treaties (what he called "treaty federalism" or "treaty commonwealth") with the American nations, those treaties and the bonds they established were limited to specific purposes rather than being comprehensive subordination of Indian's will to the will of non-Indians."[10] His starting position for his argument is vastly different from that taken by Aboriginal people. For Locke, the right to rule and have dominion over others began with

> God, who hath given the world to men in common, hath also given them reason to make use of it to the best advantage of life and convenience. The earth, and all that is therein, is given to men for the support and comfort of their being. And though all the fruits it naturally produces, and beasts it feeds, belong to mankind in common, as they are produced by the spontaneous hand of nature; and nobody has originally a private dominion, exclusive of the rest of mankind, in any of them, as they are thus in their natural state: yet being given for the use of men, there must of necessity be a means to appropriate them some way or other before they can be of any use, or at all beneficial to any particular man.[11]

By contrast, Aboriginal people do not recognize a separation between themselves and the spirits and instead speak of their oneness with creation and their spiritual ties to Mother Earth.

Locke, however, is not talking about spirituality or religion. He is presenting an argument to substantiate his belief in progress, development, and the need for civil society. In his view, God has given everything in existence to all men[12] equally. God has also given all men the means to better themselves and their individual predicament. Therefore, there must be a way for each man to use all things in the world, including other men, in order to better his own position.

Locke extends his argument, which is founded in the belief that the world was made by God, to include his reasons why men should labor and improve upon the world in which they find themselves. In doing so, he sets out man's reasons for being in the world, what is required of man's presence, and what it is that man is to gain for his efforts. Locke says the world was created by God.

> God, when he gave the world in common to all mankind, commanded man also to labour, and the penury of his condition required it of him. God and his reason commanded him to subdue the earth, i.e. improve it for the benefit of life, and there-in lay out something upon it that was his own, his labour. . . . And thus, . . . supposing the world given, as it was, to the children of men in common, we see how labour could make men distinct titles to several parcels of it, for their private uses; wherein there could be no doubt of right, no room for quarrel.[13]

According to Locke, this world, created by God, exists initially as the "state of nature" where all things given to man by God are held in common. But this "state of nature," where no man has more privilege or right above the other, is a useless world unless man can find some means "to appropriate" the things found in the state of nature and, in so doing, remove parts of those things held in common in the state of nature for his own particular purpose. It is when man removes a part of those things held in common from the state of nature that the part becomes his property. Thus man makes a significant contribution to the part removed by contributing his labor. In separating the part, man makes the part more than it once was by contributing his labor, and it is this contribution that justifies the part as his private property.

At first glance this argument for the right to own private property certainly seems plausible, and none would argue with Locke's statement: "He that is nourished by the acorns he picked up under an oak, or the apples he gathered from the trees in the wood, has certainly appropriated them to himself. Nobody can deny but the nourishment is his."[14] The question, however, that also must be asked is where does man get the right to remove a part from the state of nature that he determines to be his private property? Again, John Locke must turn to the workings of God, who has constructed man in his likeness and, in so doing, has conferred on man the duties of "self-preservation" and the "preservation of mankind." Thus, following the words of Locke, we can see that in the makeup of man, man is forced to behave in the manner in which he does. Man's culture is determined by God.

A brief analysis of Locke's reasoning shows the fallacy of his argument. First, if "man" were to behave in a manner which respects the "state of nature" in which all things are held in common by "compact" or "common consent," man's respect would lead to his own demise and not only his existence, but the existence of the entire world, would be useless. In the dilemma presented to man by the dichotomy of "self-preservation" and the "preservation of mankind," man has little choice to do otherwise. If man were to respect the state of nature and its inherent law that all things are held in common by compact, as described by Locke, then man has no alternative in providing for his own self-preservation but to consider on an equal level his self-preservation and the preservation of mankind. In so doing, in order to take a single part from the state of nature for his own nourishment, man must secure the consent of all mankind. It is easily seen that to secure such consent is an impossible task and one which, even if carried out in a land of plenty, would cause man to starve long before he attained such a consensus.

Second, the concept of man holding a respect for the state of nature in which all things are held in common by agreement is also an illogical consideration in light of the fact that man has an inherent duty, conferred on him by God, for his own self-preservation. To use Locke's own words against him, it is not only the inherent duty of self-preservation that needs to be considered here but also man's reason to use the state of nature, given to man by God. Locke states, "The earth, and all that is therein, is given to men for the support and comfort of their being."[15]

Therefore, in following Locke's reasoning, it must be concluded that man has no option but to behave in the manner he does, for it is only in securing property that man (a) prevents the world from being useless, (b) provides for his own self preservation, and (c) follows the will of God. It is these values that are apparent as the value base upon which Canadian society (or, for that matter, American society) has been constructed.

The argument, however, does not end here. Instead, it perpetuates itself. Accepting the premise that (1) man does have an obligatory duty of self-preservation, stipulated by God, and (2) it is this obligatory duty that in turn drives man to separate parts of the state of nature, then (3) it follows that in separation of the part of the state of nature, it is man's labor that gives him the right to determine the part as his private property. If this argument is true and is the law of nature, then the question of how much man can separate from that state of nature to call his own property must be asked. Locke would answer this question simply by saying, "The same law of nature, that does by this means give us property, does also bound that property too. 'God has given us all things richly,' 1 Tim. vi.17, is the voice of reason confirmed by inspiration. But how far has he given it us? To enjoy."[16]

Therefore, through the law of nature, man has a right to separate parts from the state of nature to the extent that man can "enjoy," and what man separates through his labor, and improves upon by his labor from that which existed in the state of nature and that which he calls his private property, is not allowed to be wasted. For it is in the making of waste that man begins to infringe upon the right of others to fulfill their inherent duty of self-preservation.

Locke's argument establishing man's right to property stems from the will of God, and included in man's right to property is the right, by the application of his labor, to improve upon the state of nature. Fundamental to this argument is the belief that God does indeed exist.

Contrary to such a belief held by Europeans—that improvements can be made on the natural world (as it exists in the state of nature) by means of human labor, in the process giving it to man to "subdue the earth"—Aboriginals tend to view the natural world as perfect. To an Aboriginal person, the natural world as it exists in the state of nature does not need improvement; man is not meant to "subdue the earth" but to live in harmony with it. Therefore, Aboriginal people do not see themselves as entities separate from the state of nature. Instead, they see themselves as part and parcel of the same package. In the final analysis:

> The reason why Locke's concepts of political society and property are inadequate to represent these two problems [the problems of Aboriginal self-government and ecology] clearly is that Locke constructed them in contrast to Amerindian forms of nationhood and property in such a way that they obscure and downgrade the distinctive features of Amerindian polity and property. . . . First, Locke defines political society in such a way that Amerindian government does not qualify as a legitimate form of political society. Rather, it is construed as a historically less developed form of European political organization located in the later stages of the "state of nature" and thus not on par with modern European political formations. Second, Locke defines property in such a way that Amerindian customary land use is not a legitimate type of property. Rather, it is construed as individual labour-based possession and assimilated to an earlier stage of European development in the state of nature, and thus not on an equal footing with European property. Amerindian political formations and property are thereby subjected to the sovereignty of European concepts of politics and property. Furthermore, these concepts serve to justify the dispossession of Amerindians of their political organizations, and territories, and to vindicate the superiority of European, and specifically English, forms of political society and property established in the new world.[17]

As was stated at the outset, the task of exploring the apparent cultural differences between European and Aboriginal peoples has the appearance of being impossible. For example, it was recognized early in the nineteenth century by the Aboriginal interpreter and Ojibway historian William Warren that to gain an understanding of the Aboriginal requires a most intimate acquaintance with them as a people, and individually with their old story tellers, also with their language, beliefs, and customs, to procure their real beliefs and to analyze the tales they seldom refuse to tell, and separate the Indian or original from those portions which they have borrowed or imbibed from the whites. Their innate courtesy and politeness often carry them so far that they seldom, if ever, refuse to tell a story when asked by a white man, respecting their ideas of the creation and the origin of mankind. These tales, though made up for the occasion by the Indian saga, are taken by his white hearers as their bona fide belief, and, as such, may have been made public, and accepted by the civilized world.[18]

But whether Warren was correct or not in saying that an "intimate acquaintance" with the Aboriginal is necessary to find out what he really believes, and even with such an acquaintance it is difficult to separate "the Indian or original" from what is "borrowed or imbibed from the whites" may be to miss the point. Instead of relying on "Indian saga" or "Indian custom" to gain an understanding of Aboriginal culture, perhaps other means can be employed. For example, when viewing the cultural practices of the Aboriginal world of Warren's time, as compared to the well-documented histories of Europeans of the same period, a more satisfactory means by which to gain insight into Aboriginal culture becomes clear. A difference in cultural practices between these two worlds is well illustrated by Warren's description of the Aboriginal world that he knew existed in prior times. He states:

> There was . . . less theft and lying, more devotion to the Great Spirit, more obedience to their parents, and more chastity in man and woman, than exist at the present day since their baneful intercourse with the white race. Even in the twenty years' experience of the writer, he has vividly noticed these changes, spoken of by the old men, as rapidly taking place. In former times there was certainly more good-will, charity, and hospitality practiced toward one another; and the widow and orphan never were allowed to live in want and poverty. The old traditionalists of the Ojibways tell of many customs which have become nearly or altogether extinct.[19]

Following from the experiences of Warren—that it is difficult to separate the "Indian" or original from those portions borrowed from Europeans, and that many customs have become nearly or entirely extinct—one could expect the task of exploring and understanding Aboriginal culture to be even more futile in the modern era. Perhaps, however, as appears to be the case for Warren, "legitimate" Aboriginal culture is not to be found in "Indian saga," whatever the origin, or even in Aboriginal customs, extinct or otherwise. Instead, perhaps Aboriginal cultural practices have withstood the test of time, and despite the changes taking place as suggested by Warren's depiction, the values inherent in Aboriginal culture are still here today and these values can be extrapolated from the cultural interaction within Aboriginal society.

To begin a process of extrapolation by which to gain insight into the profound statement by Aboriginals that the natural world is perfect, let us borrow from the writings of the French sociologist Marcel Mauss, who states:

> In the systems of the past we do not find simple exchange of goods, wealth and produce through markets established among individuals. For it is groups, and not individuals, which carry on exchange, make contracts, and are bound by obligation; the persons represented in the contracts are moral persons—clans, tribes, and families; the groups, or the chiefs as intermediaries for the groups, confront and oppose each other. Further, what they exchange is not exclusively goods and wealth, real and personal property, and things of economic value. They exchange rather courtesies, entertainments, ritual, military assistance, women, children, dances, and feasts; and fairs in which the market is but one element and the circulation of wealth but one part of a wide and enduring contract.[20]

Combining Mauss's description of "systems of the past," a description by which, it is safe to say, he is referring to the Aboriginal world, with the Aboriginal perception of the natural world as perfect, the perfect Aboriginal world begins to look much different from the individualistic setting underlying man's relationship with the "state of nature" embedded in a modern value system based on Lockian philosophy.

Comparatively speaking, these two worldviews do differ greatly and result in divergent cultural practices. For the moment, like Good Samaritans, let us concede the point that man, of either European or Aboriginal extraction, does have property, and he has it for whatever reason it may come into his possession, whether as a condition of self-preservation, by application of his labor, or for any other reason. To do otherwise and argue that Aboriginals do not relate to property is both naive and foolish. Although Aboriginals do not see things as outside of themselves, they do project their view that things apart from themselves take on their own personalities, and ultimately, in this projection, all things become as one. In other words, as is expressed in the following quotation, Aboriginals view property in an entirely different sense than do Europeans driven by a Lockian philosophy.

> The capitalistic principle is, simply stated, private property and all that accrues to private property. We native people did not have the concept of private property in our lexicon, and the principle of private property was pretty much in conflict with our value system. For example, you wouldn't see "No Hunting," "No Fishing," or "No Trespassing" signs in our territories. If you said to the people, "The Ontario government owns all the air in Ontario, and if you want some, you are going to have to go see the Bureau of Air," we would all laugh. Well, it made Indians laugh too when Europeans said, "We are going to own the land." How could anyone own the land.[21]

If, for the sake of argument, we can accept the notion that property as it is held by both worldviews is similar–that is to say, that property is something that exists outside of ourselves–then we can get away from the question of a right to property and instead look at the purpose of property. This change in venue, addressing the purpose of property rather than the right to it, allows an escape from two unresolvable problems that are central to the two worldviews and cultural practices under discussion. These twin problems are, on the one hand, whether God in fact does exist and whether all power derives from God, while on the other, whether the natural world *is* perfect or needs to be improved upon. It can be seen that these problems, founded in two fundamentally different systems of belief, give rise to cultures that respect entirely different values.

Again we will look first at the Lockian view, wherein the purpose of property is very clear. Locke says, "We see in commons, which remain so by compact, that it is the taking any part of which is common, and removing it out of the state nature leaves it in, which begins the property; without which the common is of no use."[22] Following the logical reasoning of this argument, it becomes clear that the paramount motivating force behind Locke's approach to property is the principle of accumulation. Rights to property are gained by the labor of one man, applying that labor to (a) improve upon those things he found in the state of nature, and (b) "subdue" the earth to benefit his life. It is in this way that he makes his wealth. This "accumulated" wealth can be passed on to his sons as their property rights. To do otherwise, such as to leave things as they are found in the state of nature and held in common by all mankind, according to Locke, makes all things in the state of nature useless to anybody.

By contrast, as Mauss points out, "property for the Aboriginal is a gift to be given and as such it is at the same time property and a possession, a pledge and a loan, an object sold and an object bought, a deposit, a mandate, a trust; for it is given only on condition that it will be used on behalf of, or transmitted to, a third person, the remote partner."[23] Here again, when looking at the purpose of property, we come across a discrepancy between the values central to two disparate cultures. If a European's motivation for having property is accumulation for purposes of enjoyment, and the motivation of the Aboriginal is based on the principle of distribution, the giving away of property, then, with certainty, cultural practices regarding property will not be the same.

The Aboriginal view of property is again substantiated by Mauss, who, in his studies, focused on the social function of the *potlatch* practiced by Aboriginal cultures.[24] As a ceremony, Mauss found the potlatch to be a time when the clan, group, or tribe gathered together to distribute property. In this forum, value was placed on the act of giving the gift, not on the gift given. He found that in this transaction respect accrued to the person performing the act of giving.

At first, a system based on gift giving seems simplistic and incomprehensible. Analysis of such a system, however, finds it to be driven by sound principles and mechanisms binding upon the participants. Mauss says, "Many ideas and principles are to be noted in systems of this type. The most important of these spiritual mechanisms is clearly the one which obliges us to make a return gift for a gift received."[25]

The implications stemming from the perception of property in each of these two cultural settings undoubtedly has a strong impact upon the organizational structure of their respective societies. As Locke says, "The great and chief end, therefore, of men's uniting into commonwealths, and putting themselves under government, is the preservation of their property."[26] In Locke's view, man enters into civil society to protect his property against the wrongful actions of "degenerates" who hide among his fellows. "Degenerates," for Locke, are those persons who are not willing to apply their labor to improve upon the things found in the state of nature and instead prefer to take the rightful property of others. By comparison, social interaction or society for Aboriginal people provides them with the opportunity to exercise their privilege to give property away to others rather than giving them protection against the loss of property to "degenerates."

If one is to accept Locke's argument that the "great and chief end" of man entering into civil society follows from the need for man to protect his property, one needs to question what it is that man must give up in order to enter society and receive that protection. It seems suspicious that man would be allowed to receive a benefit from civil society without first surrendering something in exchange for the benefit to be received.

Looking to the words of John Locke, it appears that man is quite capable of protecting his property while in the state of nature, for he says:

> Man being born . . . with a title to perfect freedom, and uncontrolled enjoyment of all the rights and privileges of the law of nature, equally with any other man, or number of men in the world, hath by nature a power, not only to preserve his property, that is, his life, liberty, and estate, against the injuries and attempts of other men; but to judge of and punish the breaches of that law in others, as he is persuaded the offence deserves, even with death itself, in crimes where the heinousness of the fact, in his opinion requires it.[27]

It appears that, in Locke's view, instilled in every man's "title" to "perfect freedom and uncontrolled enjoyment" is an innate "power" to protect his "title." He states that "in the state of nature every one has the executive power of the law of nature."[28] Accordingly, in this view, executive power is the power of man to judge the wrongful actions of others. Even as Locke states, however, "it is unreasonable for men to be judges in their own cases, that self-love will make men partial to themselves and their friends: and, on the other side, that ill-nature, passion, and revenge will carry them too far in punishing others; and that therefore nothing but confusion and disorder will follow: and that therefore God hath certainly appointed government to restrain the partiality and violence of men."[29] And so Locke concludes from this that even

> though men, when they enter into society, give up the equality, liberty, and executive power they had in the state of nature, into the hands of the society, to be so far disposed of by the legislative as the good of the society shall require; yet it being only with an intention in every one the better to preserve himself, his liberty and property (for no rational creature can be supposed to change his condition with an intention to be worse); the power of the society, or legislative constituted by them, can never be supposed to extend farther than the common good; but is obliged to secure every one's property, by providing against those three defects above-mentioned, that made the state of nature so unsafe and uneasy.[30]

Locke's own words confirm the suspicion: man must first give up something in order to receive the benefit derived from joining "civil society." Man must give up his "equality, liberty, and executive power" in order to receive protection for his property. If this is the trade-off, then one must ask, what does this mean for man?

In further examining Locke's argument, we find that "God hath certainly appointed government to restrain the partiality and violence of men." If this view is correct, then it follows that God never at any time meant for man to enjoy the power or right of self-government, which Locke admits man was born with and held in the state of nature. It would then be fair to say that, according to Locke's view, God meant only for man to join civil society and receive protection for accumulated property. In the process, God intended for man to give up his individual rights to "equality, liberty, and executive power." In other words, God meant for man to give up his autonomy.

This point represents the fundamental difference in the perspectives and cultural practices of Europeans and Aboriginals. In ordinary parlance the word *autonomy* means "the power or right of an individual to be self-governing." In a legal context it means the political independence of a nation, the right (and condition) of the power of self-government. Self-governance, in turn, means the power or right of man to direct and control his own destiny.

Within Aboriginal society, each member exercises his or her individual right to give to the group, each exercises "equality, liberty, and executive power," each exercises autonomy. Each has a right to self-governance. One must be careful, however, not to confuse the concept of the individual with that of autonomy or vice-versa. Nor should one even consider the two terms to be in any way synonymous. The concept of individual rights, along with concomitant strict, legalistic regulation of individual behavior, are foreign to most Aboriginal traditions.

In a comparison of European culture with Aboriginal culture we do see significant differences. In the case of the Europeans, individuals exercise their individuality by giving up elements of their condition, their "equality, liberty, and executive power," to a government appointed by God in order to receive the benefit of civil society, and in so doing, give up their autonomy. In the case of Aboriginals, individuals exercise their "equality, liberty, and executive power" and in so doing maintain their autonomy.

When investigating cultural practices as ways of behaving as demonstrated by Europeans, we find that man must remove himself from the state of nature. With the contribution of his labor man improves on the things found in nature and subdues the earth within the context of a rightful duty conferred upon him by God. His actions directed toward the accumulation of property are sanctioned by government, which is also ordained by God.

When examining cultural practices as ways of behaving as evinced by Aboriginal people, we find that they view themselves as a part of nature and see as their duty their manner of working in harmony within their environment. In their view of the world they see themselves as having an integral part to play, and that part is dependent only upon their interactions. Actions are achieved as a result of their own self-determination.

The European sees the world as a hierarchical structure to be controlled—the prime authority for which rests in the hands of God. For the Aboriginal person, the world is a dynamic, ever-changing process within a natural framework. For the Aboriginal, inclusion in the world is for a purpose, not for right, and the struggles are with use, not with ownership or control. The wisdom of the Aboriginal acceptance of the world as it is given is found in what John Locke labels the "state of nature."

As noted previously, the primary work of the Royal Commission was devoted to an examination of how a "new partnership" can be brought about between Aboriginal and non-Aboriginal peoples within the constitutional framework of Canada. No one who addresses this problem can expect it to be an easy task, but at least one particular method to achieve this goal was presented to the Royal Commission by a Native Elder. He stated:

> I've a tremendous sense of honour to be among the Elders today. Part of your process for me has been very real. To learn of sisters and brothers among the Inuit and the genocidal process that goes on in their lives and ours. Of imperialism about politics, about economics, about religion. Imperialism that has never been dealt with. So my expectations of the Commission, of the possibilities that are before you, although they are not tremendously high in terms of what can happen politically on this land, I think the potential for education and growing awareness among three and four year olds in the wider society, new Canadians and old Canadians, Aboriginal and other Canadians who are here, who have been given wrong stories about who we are and what it is we might share together, *I think is an educational process that is primarily in this land.* Otherwise we'll hold to old myths, and we'll fight old battles that were never completed in Europe and other parts of the world. (Stan McKay–Cree)

The rationale used by this Elder is unquestionable—there is no great expectation placed on the Royal Commission to solve all the problems facing Aboriginal people. From the Elder's perspective, an educational process needs to take place that provides all Canadians with accurate information on the identity of Aboriginal people. The importance of education within aboriginal culture resonated in the presentations of other Elders as well. Another Elder said:

> When I was brought up, education was very important to my family. Education was, in their way, the way . . . they understood

the world. They were very responsible people. They taught us at a very early age to respect, to accept and share, to be strong and determined people. They were preparing us for that in the future. They were also very strong people in their way of believing. Their spiritual values were very much a part of their lives. And they were very hard working people. They did everything for themselves. There was no such thing as welfare in those days when my parents brought me up. They had to do everything within their own power. (Mary Lou Iahtail–Attawapiskat)

Central to the Aboriginal educational system described by the Elders are the core values of Aboriginal culture—"to respect, to accept and share, to be responsible, to be strong and determined people." These values were expressed again by another Elder, who stated:

My parents used to talk about this. They used to say that the only way you can survive is to hunt out on the land and this is where you could get your clothing from the animals you catch. During the winter they would hit out into the sea where they would do their hunting. They were using bow and arrows and harpoons back then. The people used to get together and stay in one little settlement area. That is where they do their seal hunting during the long winter periods and where they would do their spring and summer hunting. They used to use grassroots for different diets besides the fish and caribou. This is what my parents used to tell me when I was a child. They would walk inland and that is where they would do their hunting to get their winter clothing. In them days, the Inuit didn't know was a God. They thought they were living by themselves until the missionaries started coming up. That is when they started learning about religions. They thought they were living by themselves in all those years. This is what my parents used to teach me, these things my parents used to tell me all about. (Moses Koihok–Inuit)

It is apparent that the core of Aboriginal culture can be found in the words of the Elders, if we accept the notion that culture is learned behavior. As learned behavior, the cultural expressions used by the Elders then become the "rules and/or social behavior regarding virtually all aspects" of Aboriginal social life and are "passed from one generation to another by learning rather than by instinct."[31] It is in this respect that implicit in Aboriginal teachings are the rules that guide the culture.

What do these teachings have to do with why we sit here? Because this is the way of life of our Indian people. They say we have to bring it up to the surface and start teaching our young ones, because they are the future. I am talking about creation. At the beginning the Creator gave them Indian law to follow in four directions. The Creator gave them four directions and put four eagles in those directions for Indian people. The east is the bald eagle, the one that brings tobacco for our people. The south brings cedar, and that is the golden eagle. The west is the spotted eagle, and it brings the buffalo sage. The north . . . is the white eagle, and it brings . . . food. The traditional drum has four gates which represent those four directions and the eagles.

Then the Creator made this woman with the power to bring life to Mother Earth. The way we see this lady, she is pregnant. When she brings life, that is the way she looks. . . . [We were taught] always to be kind. This band represents that circle of life, what the Creator put [here] for us.

When our white brothers came across in our land, our people got mixed up. (George Courchene)

Like all cultures, Aboriginal cultures have their distinctive features, and, as a result, they are not all the same. The culture of one group varies to some degree in its stories, myths, legends, narratives, or ceremonies from that of another. In all of these cultures, however, similar aspects, irrespective of their geographic location, become clear. The oneness, the integration and spiritual ties to Mother Earth, within these cultures is apparent. It is these spiritual ties Aboriginal people have with the land and with all of creation that binds them to their culture. For Aboriginal people there is no distinctive "other"; therefore, there is no reality in a concept of "a separation from others." Aboriginal people hold a strong belief and understanding that the "I" as a being in both physical and spiritual realms means having a presence in everything and everything having a presence in me.

Retention–that I am in everything and everything is in me–is of primary importance in Aboriginal cultures, for it is this strong belief that opens the cultural door to all creation. This belief allows Aboriginal people to communicate with all creation, whether physical or spiritual. In this sense, for Aboriginal people, their culture is their religion and the world is their church.

In order for Aboriginal people to retain this gift, this ability to communicate within their cultures, rules must be followed that are deeply imbedded within their languages, as are the cultural rules of any group. The major difference, however, is that Aboriginal languages are not object-oriented, as are European languages. As mentioned previously, for an Aboriginal person there is no "other" out there somewhere; therefore, there is no "thing" out there somewhere either. Instead, Aboriginal languages are process-oriented, and, as such, these languages speak to what we do rather than what we are. The impact on Aboriginal culture of this inability to define a distinctive "other" or a "thing" out there somewhere prevents people from using language to pass judgment on others. As a result, Aboriginal culture is nonjudgmental–there is no capability in Aboriginal languages to discriminate on purely moral grounds. There is no ability in the languages to see "other" or "thing" as either good or bad. In a similar fashion, Aboriginal languages prevent the use of gender differentiation. In using an Aboriginal language to refer to persons as either man or woman they are described by what they do rather than by what they are. It is not uncommon to hear gender clash in conversations with Aboriginal people unfamiliar with the usages of English. For example, an Aboriginal person may say, "That man she . . . "

In following the teachings of the culture, Aboriginal people operationalize fundamental cultural values. First of all, the Aboriginal person must be open to all available new information. The taking in and processing of information by an Aboriginal person is sometimes interpreted as slowness, an inability to think, or a measurement of lower intellectual ability, when in fact what is really happening is a complex analytical process. The Aboriginal person is intently studying the situation while making a determination of exactly what should be the appropriate behavioral action under the present circumstances.

A second value demonstrated by Aboriginal people within their respective cultures is honesty. They must react only to what is real to them, whether that is in the physical world or the spiritual world. In this respect Aboriginal people are never alone. The consequences of inappropriate behavior are seen as fatal.

The codependence and integration of the cultural teachings also reinforce the need to share. In sharing, benefit is brought to all members of the group or community.

Paramount of all cultural values is the value of respect. Respect must be given and shown to all that is in creation. Without respect for self and all that is in creation, the Aboriginal person is unable to live his or her life to the fullest and will be unable to fulfill his or her purpose for being.

It has been said that "it's the Indian who is going to understand the white man before the white man understands the Indian. This is so because the Indian can think with his whole heart, whereas the white man thinks with his head, and thinking only with the head really doesn't help to understand the other person."[32] If this new venture, this "new partnership" between Aboriginal and non-Aboriginal people, is ever to be, then all people will have to do the same within their respective cultures: all people must think with their whole hearts, not just with their heads.

Notes

[1] Michael Asch, "Errors in Delgamuuk: An Anthropological Perspective," in *Aboriginal Title in British Columbia: Delgamuuk v. The Queen,* ed. F. Cassidy (Vancouver: Oolichan Books, 1991), pp. 224-25.

[2] These quotations are paraphrases of a debate between anthropologists Clifford Geertz and Roger Keesing.

[3] Samuel Eliot Morison, *Admiral of the Ocean Sea: A Life of Christopher Columbus* (Boston: Little, Brown and Company, 1942), p. 231.

[4] S. R. Mealing, ed., *The Jesuit Relations and Allied Documents, A Selection* (Ottawa: Carleton University Press, 1990), pp. 17, 45.

[5] Donald Purich, *Our Land* (Toronto: James Lorimer & Company, 1986), p. 31.

[6] George M. Grant, *Ocean to Ocean, Sanford Fleming's Expedition Through Canada in 1872* (Toronto: Radisson Society of Canada Limited, 1925), pp. 108-10.

[7] James Tully, *An Approach to Political Philosophy: Locke in Contexts* (Cambridge: Cambridge University Press, 1993), p. 141.

[8] Ibid., p. 139.

[9] Paul Dukes, *A History of Europe 1648-1948: The Arrival, the Rise, the Fall* (London: Macmillan Publishers Ltd., 1985), p. 122.

[10] Leroy Little Bear, "Aboriginal Rights and the Canadian 'Grundnorm,'" in *Arduous Journey: Canadian Indians and Decolonization* (Toronto: McClelland and Stewart, 1986), p. 250.

[11] John W. Yolton, *The Locke Reader* (New York: Cambridge University Press, 1977), p. 289.

[12] Because Locke, writing in the seventeenth century, speaks of "man" and "men," I will continue what we now recognize as gender-exclusive language throughout my discussion.

[13] Yolton, p. 291.

[14] Ibid., p. 290.

[15] Ibid., p. 289.

[16] Ibid., p. 291.

[17] Tully, p. 138.

[18] William W. Warren, *History of the Ojibway People* (St. Paul: Minnesota Historical Society Press, 1984), p. 58.

[19] Ibid., p. 101.

[20] Marcel Mauss, *The Gift* (London: Cohen and West, 1966), p. 3.

[21] Oren Lyons, "Spirituality, Equality, and Natural Law," in *Pathways to Self-Determination: Canadian Indians and the Canadian State* (Toronto: University of Toronto Press, 1984), p. 9.

[22] Yolton, p. 285.

[23] Mauss, p. 23.

[24] Ibid., p. 4. The term *potlatch* translates as "to nourish" or "to consume." As a term for the giveaway practiced by a variety of tribes, *potlatch* is often intensely disliked among Natives.

[25] Ibid., p. 5.

[26] Yolton, p. 285.

[27] Ibid., p. 243.

[28] Ibid., p. 282.

[29] Ibid.

[30] Ibid., p. 287.

[31] Taken from the definitions of *culture* listed at the beginning of the chapter.

[32] S. M. Morey and O. L. Gilliam, *Respect for Life* (New York: Waldorf Press, 1972), p. 11.

9.

Indian Presence with No Indians Present

NAGPRA and Its Discontents

JACE WEAVER

Although wrongs have been done me, I live in hopes. I have not got two hearts. These young men, when I call them into the lodge and talk with them, they listen to me and mind what I say. Now we are again together to make peace. My shame is as big as the earth, although I will do what my friends advise me to do. I once thought that I was the only man that persevered to be the friend of the white man, but since they have come and cleaned out our lodges, horses, and everything else, it is hard for me to believe white men any more.

Black Kettle, 1865[1]

I never met Black Kettle, the great Cheyenne peace chief. He died almost ninety years before I was born, but I saw him once—or rather I saw part of him once.

When I was about six years old, my mother and grandmother took me to the site of the Washita Massacre, where, on November 27, 1868, George Armstrong Custer and his 7th Cavalry launched an unprovoked attack on Black Kettle's camp. One hundred and three Cheyenne, including Motavato (as his own people knew Black Kettle) and his wife, were slain. Of that number, only eleven were warriors. As a child, roaming the killing field, I was too interested in looking for relics to feel the overwhelming sense of grief I have felt there on subsequent visits.

After visiting the massacre site, they took me to a small museum in nearby Cheyenne. I raced amid army uniforms, rifles, and other artifacts. Then I came upon a glass museum case containing human remains,

99

a skull and a few other bones. There, surrounded by other exhibits, were the bones of Motavato. Horrified by the gruesome display, I quickly called the visit to an end. Upon arriving home I told my elder brother what I had seen. He replied, "I think it's a great step forward. When I was your age [nine years earlier], they were in the window of the local newspaper office."

White men not only "cleaned out" (stole) the lodges, lands, and possessions of Indians but robbed Indians of their persons as well–selling them into slavery, forcing assimilation and cultural genocide upon them, and, in the most bizarre turn, looting their graves as well. For decades, thousands of skeletons were gathered systematically and shipped away to be displayed and warehoused in museums. By the early twentieth century, it was grimly joked that the Smithsonian Institution in Washington had more dead Indians than there were live Indians. Amateur archaeologists and "pothunters," seeking artifacts for sale, completed the process. In the late 1980s, it was estimated that "museums, federal agencies, other institutions, and private collectors retain[ed] between 300,000 and 2.5 million dead bodies taken from Indian graves, battlefields, and POW camps by soldiers, museum collectors, scientists, and pothunters."[2] The Smithsonian alone was estimated to contain approximately 19,000 sets of remains. According to Walter R. and Roger C. Echo-Hawk (Pawnee), "Motives for Indian body snatching range from interests in race biology, to museum competition for anthropological 'collections,' to commercial exploitation, to just 'carrying out orders.'"[3] In addition to the human remains themselves, millions of funerary, ceremonial, and cultural objects were taken.

This massive theft was spawned in part by a belief that Native nations were rapidly dying out. Spurred by the myth of the Vanishing Indian, anthropologists fanned out across Indian Country to document Native cultures.[4] As Joan Mark of Harvard's Peabody Museum writes, "It was urgent to record as many of the old ways as possible before the last instance or even last memory of them disappeared completely. The reason it was considered urgent was that cultures represent alternative social arrangements from which we might learn something as well as clusters of irreplaceable historical data. For a culture to die out unrecorded, to become extinct, was analogous to a biological species becoming extinct. In each case it meant an irreparable loss of diversity and of scientific information."[5] Mark's comments reflect not only the myth of the Vanishing Indian and Amer-Europeans' stasis assumptions about Native cultures, but betray anthropology as, to use Claude Levi-Strauss's phrase, "the handmaiden of colonialism," as it likens changes in those societies to *biological extinction.*[6] The impulse is no different from that of geneticists today who, in the Human Genome Diversity Project, rush to record indigenous DNA patterns and coding with scant regard for native peoples themselves.

At the same time anthropologists rushed to record Native culture, archaeologists collected Indian remains for what they might tell scientists and future generations. As the Echo-Hawks report, however, "All tribes throughout Indian country . . . have been victimized by what has become the most grisly and frightening problem confronting Native Americans today. The impact upon Native people, regardless of the motive, is always the same: emotional trauma and spiritual distress."[7] A Department of the Interior report acknowledged this in 1979, stating, "The prevalent view in the society of applicable disciplines is that Native American human remains are public property and artifacts for study, display, and cultural investment. It is understandable that this view is in conflict with and repugnant to those Native people whose ancestors and near relatives are considered the property at issue."[8] Granted, human remains, from any period, can tell us much about lifeways, diet, diseases, and many other things. Yet we do not see archaeologists hurrying to excavate colonial cemeteries in New England churchyards for what they can say about early colonists. As the Echo-Hawks conclude:

> Systematic disturbances of non-Indian graves, on the one hand, are abhorred and avoided at all costs, while Indian people are actively searched out, dug up, and placed in museum storage. Criminal statutes in all fifty states very strictly prohibit grave desecration, grave robbing, and mutilation of the dead—yet they are not applied to protect Indian dead. Instead, the laws and social policy, to the extent that they affect Native dead, do not treat this class of decedents as human, but rather define them as "non-renewable archaeological resources" to be treated like dinosaurs or snails, "federal property" to be used as chattels in the academic marketplace, "pathological specimens" to be studied by those interested in racial biology, or simple "trophies or booty" to enrich private collectors. The huge collections of dead Indians are compelling testimony that Indians have been singled out for markedly disparate treatment.[9]

Recognizing the problem and answering the protests of Elders and other Natives, the United States Congress passed a series of laws designed to protect Natives from further theft and desecration. The first of these enactments was the Archaeological Resources Protection Act of 1979 (ARPA). Designed to provide preserve sites on federal lands, it provided for fines and incarceration for removing "archaeological resources" from federal property without a prior permit pursuant to the Antiquities Act of 1906. The law was amended in 1988, strengthening provisions concerning looting of "federal property."[10] Designed to halt commercial vandalism on federal lands, the act did nothing to protect remains on private property.

In 1990, Congress enacted the National Museum of the American Indian Act, creating a museum for Native culture and history within the Smithsonian. As part of the legislation, the Smithsonian was required to catalogue and identify the origin of Native human remains in its holdings "in consultation and cooperation with traditional Indian religious leaders and government officials of Indian tribes." If the inventoried remains could be identified as a specific individual or associated with a particular tribe, the museum was required, upon request of the descendants or the tribe, to return the remains and any funerary objects associated with them.[11] The act was the first law to require repatriation and reburial of human remains. The same year, Congress also passed the Native American Graves Protection and Repatriation Act (NAGPRA).[12] The act

> prohibits trade, transport, or sale of Native American human remains and directs federal agencies and museums to take inventory of any Native American . . . remains and, if identifiable, the agency or museum is to return them to the tribal descendants. The Act mandates the Secretary of Interior to establish a committee to monitor the return of remains and objects and authorizes the Secretary to make grants for assisting museums with compliance. The Act prohibits remains and objects from being considered archaeological resources, prohibits disturbing sites without tribal consent, and imposes penalties for unauthorized excavation, removal, damage or destruction.[13]

In addition to human remains and funerary objects, it also mandated the return of sacred objects and other cultural patrimony. NAGPRA, drafted in consultation with archaeologists, "represents a broad national reburial [and] repatriation policy."[14] Any institution receiving federal funds is covered by its requirements.

From the beginning NAGPRA has presented challenges to archaeologists, museums, and tribes alike. Museums and universities often have dragged their heels at compliance, and some have sought to impose conditions upon tribes before repatriating objects. Archaeologists have decried requests for return of remains and objects as unfairly inhibiting scientific inquiry. Walter and Roger Echo-Hawk respond:

> When non-Indian institutions possess Indian sacred objects and living gods and when they control disposition of the dead, they become little more than quasi-church facilities imposed upon Indian communities, regulating the "free" exercise of religion for dispossessed Indian worshipers. First Amendment religious freedoms are clearly controlled from the pulpit of science when museums elevate scientific curiosity over Indian religious belief

in the treatment of the dead. Should Indians protest, some scientists are quick to raise the specter of research censorship, comparing such protesters to "book-burners" and referring to Indian plans for the disposition of their deceased ancestors as the "destruction of data."[15]

One of the more interesting disputes involved hair recovered by archaeologist Robson Bonnichsen at a 10,000-year-old site in Montana. Realizing that human hair does not decay like other genetic material, Dr. Bonnichsen developed a sophisticated system of filters and recovered a bundle of hairs that he planned to subject to DNA testing. Before any tests could take place, however, the Confederated Salish-Kootenai and the Shoshone-Bannock demanded the return of the hair pursuant to NAGPRA; the Bureau of Land Management, which controlled the site, acting on behalf of the tribes, barred the Bonnichsen team from the site and prohibited the proposed tests. Bonnichsen protested that the hairs he had recovered were not "remains" within the definition of the act, since they were not associated with any burial site but were rather of the type that humans normally lose daily. He has declared, "Two years of work were totally disrupted. Repatriation has taken on a life of its own and is about to put us out of business as a profession."[16] After two years of dispute, regulations under NAGPRA have been amended to exclude naturally shed hair from the workings of the act.

Controversy over NAGPRA came to a head with the discovery of a largely intact skeleton on the banks of the Columbia River at Kennewick, Washington, in July 1996. James Chatters, a private consultant in archaeology and paleoecology, examined the skeleton at the request of the local sheriff. Upon initial review, based upon its physical characteristics, Dr. Chatters concluded that it was the remains of a Caucasian male about fifty-years-old. Sent to the University of California at Riverside for radiocarbon dating, bone samples were determined to be between 9,100 and 9,400 years old. Two other anthropologists who also examined the skeleton, Catherine J. MacMillan of Central Washington University and Grover S. Krantz of Washington State University, agreed that it had Caucasian features.

As with the Bonnichsen hair samples, the scientists proposed DNA tests. Once the find was made public, however, and before any such testing could be performed, the Umatilla Confederated Tribe, whose reservation is across the Columbia in Oregon, laid claim to it under NAGPRA, demanding that study of the skeleton cease. They were quickly joined by four other tribes with common ancestral ties to the region, the Colville Confederated Tribes, the Nez Perce, the Wanapun Band of Walla Walla Tribes, and the Yakama Nation. Because NAGPRA requires that tribal affiliation be determined as prerequisite to repatriation, and because the extreme age of the paleo-Indian remains makes specificity difficult if not impossible, the cooperation of the five claimants became crucial. Responding to the requirement of specific tribal affiliation, Bill Yallup of the Yakama tribal council stated, "We are no different one from another, we are all Indian."[17]

When the U.S. Army Corps of Engineers—who assumed jurisdiction over what was now called the Richland Man or the Kennewick Man by scientists and simply the Ancient One by Natives (out of respect for their ancestor, they refuse to use either nickname)—announced that they would turn the remains over to the tribes, scientists protested. Douglas Owsley, a forensic anthropologist at the Smithsonian, stated, "They need to reconsider this decision. Skeletons from this period are extremely rare. We know very little about them. If there is no further opportunity to examine these remains, we will be losing information that is important to every American." James Chatters, who first viewed the Ancient One, declared, "It's been like a gold mine where normal people all of a sudden go goofy. My thinking was, here was an opportunity to look at us as less separate."[18]

Two lawsuits were brought in the United States District Court in Portland, seeking to prevent repatriation and reburial. One was filed by a group of eight scientists, desiring to make further tests. A second was pursued by the Asatru Folk Assembly, a new religious movement of approximately 500 persons who claim to follow pre-Christian Norse traditions. Both complaints relied on Chatters's initial description that the Ancient One was Caucasian, contending that therefore ARPA rather than NAGPRA applied. Asatru president Stephen McNallen stated, "We don't want to offend Native Americans, because, really, we have a lot in common with them."[19] Most scientists, however, remained skeptical, claiming that based on a single skeleton it was impossible to conclude that Caucasians resided in North America more than 450 generations ago. Even Chatters himself admitted that his initial characterization was based on modern forensic standards, "When it [the Ancient One] turns out to be old, the whole equation changes. We're not sure what people looked like back then."[20]

Nevertheless, the "brief viewings" of Chatters and others and their "initial impression" were seized upon by proponents (including the Asatru Folk Assembly) of a variant of the Bering Strait theory known as the Euro-Bering migration. As described by the *New York Times,* "It [the discovery of the Ancient One] adds credence to theories that some early inhabitants of North America came from European stock, perhaps migrating across northern Asia and into the Western Hemisphere over a land bridge exposed in the Bering Sea about 12,000 years ago, or earlier, near the end of the last Ice Age."[21] Robson Bonnichsen once again lambasted the operation of NAGPRA, saying, "This is a battle over who controls America's past. We have always used the term paleo-

Indian to describe remains of this era. But this may be the wrong term. Maybe some of these guys were really just paleo-American."[22] Having used the Bering Strait theory to make Indians immigrants not fundamentally different from those who disembarked at Ellis Island, it is now used to make them European as well, the populating of the hemisphere no different than Columbus's (or Vikings') "discovery" centuries later.

At least one of the scientists party to the suit disputed the contention. Gentry Steele, a physical anthropologist at Texas A&M University, pointed out that paleo-Indians "appear Caucasoid or Asian to the untrained eye," but that traits actually fall somewhere between the two groups. He stated, "That's not to say that southern Asians populated the area. It could mean that North American Indians looked more like south Asians than they do today." He concluded, "What we're trying to say is that the individual could be the model to the ancestors of all North American and South American Indians." Dr. Steele expressed his belief that NAGPRA did apply to the discovery and that the Ancient One should be repatriated, *but* only after further study.[23]

As the controversy continued, and while litigants awaited a hearing on a preliminary injunction against the Corps of Engineers on October 23, the *New York Times*, which previously had reported the debate, decided to enter the dispute more actively. On October 22, it ran a front-page story (continued in its "Science Times" section) entitled "Indian Tribes' Creationists Thwart Archeologists." The article, heavily slanted in favor of the scientists, likened Natives seeking return of ancestral remains pursuant to the provisions of NAGPRA to Christian fundamentalists. It declared, "Since the repatriation act was passed in 1990, American Indian creationism, which rejects the theory of evolution and other scientific explanations of human origins in favor of the Indians' own religious beliefs, has been steadily gaining in political momentum. Adhering to their own creation accounts as adamantly as biblical creationists adhere to the book of Genesis, Indian tribes have stopped important archeological research on hundreds of prehistoric remains."[24]

The article rehearsed the disputes over both the Bonnichsen hair find and the Ancient One. It stated that similar cases throughout the West had "given some archeologists the feeling that their field is in a state of siege" and cited four other instances in which studies of Indian or paleo-Indian remains were halted because of NAGPRA demands. The clear message of the piece was that important, legitimate inquiry was being stymied by dogmatic Native "creationists." It quoted Vine Deloria, Jr. (Standing Rock Sioux), "a history professor at the University of Colorado and a prominent Indian advocate and legal scholar," concerning material in his recent book, *Red Earth, White Lies: Native Americans and the Myth of Scientific Fact.* According to the *Times*, "In his book, Mr. Deloria dismisses as 'scientific folklore' the theory, embraced by virtually all archeologists, that America's native peoples came from Asia across the Bering Strait 10,000 or more years ago. . . . Using some of the same arguments embraced by fundamentalist Christians, Mr. Deloria also dismisses the theory of evolution as more unsubstantiated dogma."[25]

Minimizing the comments of archaeologists sympathetic to Natives, the article focused on those who saw NAGPRA demands as anti-intellectualism. Quoting Steve Lekson, an archaeological research associate at Deloria's own institution, it read, "Some people who are not sympathetic to fundamentalist Christian beliefs are extraordinarily sympathetic to Native American beliefs. I'm not sure I see the difference."[26]

Three days later the *Times* printed two letters to the editor critical of the newspaper's reporting.[27] On November 2, however, it ran an op-ed piece by Pulitzer Prize–winning writer N. Scott Momaday (Kiowa/Cherokee). Momaday, long a believer in the Bering Strait theory and in the benefits of Western science, repeated the fundamentalist characterization. Referring to the long history of poor relations between scientists and Natives he labeled Native actions in situations like that involving the Ancient One as "vengeance" for past depredations.[28] In the context of the ongoing imbroglio concerning the Ancient One, the *New York Times* reporting and the enlistment of Momaday are troubling for many reasons.

The newspaper clearly contended that Native "religious fundamentalists" are the primary force demanding the return of human remains and opposing scientific testing. Their fear, it is claimed, is that analysis of remains will "disprove" traditional tribal protologies, which often state that the tribe in question has been on its ancestral lands since creation. Although traditional creation myths are an important part of tribal identity and are often deeply held, they are not the prime factor in NAGPRA repatriation requests.

Native traditions prescribe respect for the remains of ancestors. The fear among many Natives about scientific testing is not that it will contradict or disprove sacred accounts concerning tribal origins but that it will further desecrate the remains. Native leaders have stated as much in the tug-of-war over the Ancient One. Armand Minthorn, a spokesman for the Umatilla, ruled out DNA testing, saying, "That goes against all our beliefs [on how to treat the dead]."[29] Walla Walla chief Carl Sampson, at a conference with the Corps of Engineers, echoed Minthorn: "We're tired of the desecration of our ancestors. You don't understand us, you that aren't Indian here today. We're going to put that body back into the ground no matter what your supreme law says."[30]

Many Natives feel that any study of human remains is disrespectful. For others, however, testing is permissible provided it is nondestructive. Among the Colvilles (one of the NAGPRA claimants of the Ancient One), for instance, nondestructive study of remains, including measurement and bone scraping, is a common practice.[31] DNA testing is opposed because such analysis consumes the sample it tests. Though naturally shed human hair may not be human remains within the intended scope of NAGPRA, the objection is simply that the testing will destroy the hairs. If the real fear were that human origins in the Americas would prove to be the product of relatively recent migrations from Asia and thus cast doubt on the literal truth of tribal protologies, why would tribes, as noted by the *Times*, allow radiocarbon dating of human remains, which also could tend to lend credence to the same theory?

Reporting in the *Times*, as in most of the mainstream media, assumes the scientific fact of the Bering Strait theory. The October 22 article states that it is "embraced by virtually all archeologists, that America's native peoples came from Asia across the Bering Strait 10,000 or more years ago."[32] Beringia, the presumed land bridge between Asia and North America, is thought to have existed three or four times, beginning 70,000 years ago. If ancestors of present-day Natives migrated across such a bridge (and in his work Deloria raises serious objections to such a proposition), they certainly did so much earlier than 10,000 to 12,000 years ago and were active in the Americas at a much earlier date.

The question of the origin of humans in this hemisphere has troubled Europeans and Amer-Europeans at least since Columbus returned to Spain in March 1493. Accompanying him were captive indigenes, beings who appeared to be human. Their existence posed a threat to the prevailing biblical exegesis of the day, which assumed the literal historical truth of the story of Noah and his ark. Such a "fundamentalist" or "creationist" reading of Hebrew scripture led to a belief that there were only three continents, each peopled by the offsprings of a different son of the ark builder after the biblical flood. Many concluded that the people erroneously labeled Indians were the ten lost tribes of Israel.[33]

When early Russian explorers discovered that Alaska and the Aleutian Islands stretched out to almost touch Asia, it was imagined that the indigenous peoples of the Western Hemisphere must have originated on that continent. The Bering Strait theory in its modern form stems only from 1739. In that year, a portrait painter named Smibert arrived in Boston to paint the colonial aristocracy. Seeing Indians, he noticed the similarity to Siberians he had seen in the Russian court and pronounced them Mongolians. According to anthropologist Clark Wissler, "From that day to this, notwithstanding the intensive research of specialists, everything points to a Mongoloid ancestry for the Indian."[34] More precisely, one might say that everything has been made to point to such an origin.

For many years, Vine Deloria points out, it was contended that Indians were relative newcomers to the hemisphere, "latecomers who had barely unpacked before Columbus came knocking on the door."[35] The political/ideological value of such an assumption is clear. According to Deloria, "If Indians had arrived only a few centuries earlier, they had no *real* claim to land that could not be swept away by European discovery. Aleš Hrdlicka of the Smithsonian devoted his life to discrediting of any early occupancy of North America and a whole generation of scholars, fearfully following the master, rejected the claims of their peers rather than offend this powerful scholar."[36] Coincidentally, Hrdlicka was responsible for the largest collection of skeletal remains repatriated pursuant to NAGPRA–756 specimens excavated by him on Kodiak Island between 1932 and 1936.[37]

In 1926 a site was uncovered near Folsom, New Mexico, that revealed much earlier signs of human habitation than any previously known. Radiocarbon dating of a Folsom culture dig outside Lubbock, Texas, disclosed an age of 9883 ± 350 years. In the 1930s, a few years after the Folsom discovery, road builders near Clovis, New Mexico, found a deposit of fossilized bones of mammoths and an extinct type of bison. Associated with the find was a previously unknown type of projectile point. These "Clovis points" were about four inches long and distinguished by their concave appearance and their fluted edges. Subsequently, such points have been found in all of the forty-eight contiguous United States and into Mexico. According to Peter Farb, "So uniform was the culture across the continent, particularly east of the Rockies, that a site in Massachusetts is scarcely distinguishable from another Llano [Clovis] site in, say, Colorado." The Clovis site was dated to 11,000-12,000 years ago. Testing of any other archaeological site could yield a date no earlier than 12,000 years. Initially an unwelcomed and embarrassing discovery, Clovis ultimately was embraced, and the "Clovis barrier" of 12,000 years for human habitation in the Americas became the new scientific orthodoxy. Such a date fit neatly with the Bering Strait theory.[38]

In *Red Earth, White Lies* Deloria details the cases of a number of scientists, many of them eminent, whose careers and reputations suffered as a result of challenging this established orthodoxy. Several archaeologists, including Louis Leakey, found or evaluated sites that they believed broke the Clovis barrier. All of these, however, were discredited. Then, in 1976, local lumbermen accidentally discovered a site near Puerto Montt in south-central Chile. When an interdisciplinary team headed by anthropologist Thomas Dillehay began excavating the site, known as Monte Verde, they realized that it was extraordinary. Radiocarbon dating led to a conclusion that the most impressive remains dated to 12,500 years ago–and at the deepest level nearly 32,000 years. Proponents of the Clovis barrier, including the acknowledged dean of paleo-Indian archaeology Junius Bird of the American Museum of Natural History, joined in dismissing the discovery and attacking Dillehay. According to Dillehay:

> Much of the debate about the existence of pre-Clovis people in the Americas hinges on standards of archaeological evidence. Clovis advocates maintain, with some justification, that most pre-Clovis sites are nothing more than jumbled deposits of old soil and much younger artifacts and plant remains. Pre-Clovis advocates counter that their opponents are isolationists and chauvinists, that they too often reject sites without proper evidence of disproof. If the same standards were applied to Clovis sites, they go on to say, many of those sites would not be accepted either.[39]

Dillehay concludes:

> Although I was braced for some criticism when we first began excavating Monte Verde, I was taken aback by how quickly our work was cast into the middle of the pre-Clovis controversy. Every few months, it seems, a new instant analysis of Monte Verde and other pre-Clovis sites appeared, all without a site visit or a review of all the evidence. . . . Instant-opinion-hurling has become something of a sport in the study of the first Americans—a sport that reveals our arbitrary understanding of . . . the peopling of the Americas.[40]

In January 1997, a multidisciplinary team including some of Dillehay's staunchest critics gathered at the University of Kentucky to review evidence, followed by a three-day site visit. All agreed that the Clovis barrier had been broken, dating one stratum at Monte Verde to 12,500 years. Unspoken in reporting of the event was any discussion of the much older layers claimed by Dillehay.

The verification of a site of such antiquity, populated by a sophisticated and sedentary people, 10,000 miles from the Bering Strait raises important questions. According to a report of the January visit in the *New York Times:*

> In the depths of the most recent ice age, two vast ice sheets converged about 20,000 years ago over what is now Canada and the United States and apparently closed off human traffic there until sometime after 13,000 years ago. Either people migrated through a corridor between the ice sheets and spread remarkably fast to the southern end of America or they came by a different route,

perhaps along the western coast, by foot and sometimes on small vessels. Otherwise they must have entered the Americas before 20,000 years ago.[41]

Hearing such speculation and the words of Dillehay above, one can sympathize with Deloria's plea, "In all honesty, therefore, 'science' should drop the pretense of absolute authority with regard to human origins and begin looking for some other kind of explanation that would include the traditions and memories of non-Western peoples."[42] Larry Zimmerman, anthropologist at the University of Iowa, echoes Deloria when he states the need for "a different kind of science, between the boundaries of Western ways of knowing and Indian ways of knowing."[43]

New discoveries are made regularly, in diverse areas and branches of science, that cast doubt on the received story of the peopling of the Americas. In July 1996, the same month the Ancient One was found in Washington, paleo-Indian skeletal remains, dated at 9,700 years, were discovered on Prince of Wales Island in southern Alaska, leading to consideration that the area was occupied 30,000 or more years ago.[44] The linguistic analysis of Johanna Nichols of the University of California at Berkeley suggests humans in the New World 35,000-40,000 years ago.[45] Spears have been found in a mine in Germany, suggesting Stone Age people systematically hunted big game 400,000 years ago–as opposed to the 40,000 years previously assumed. Evidence has been found that humans lived in the harsh cold of Siberia as early as 300,000 years ago; before the find it had been assumed that human habitation before the advent of fully modern *Homo sapiens,* perhaps 40,000 years ago, was impossible.[46] Most intriguing of all is the discovery of a Clovis point in Siberia by Russian archaeologist Sergei B. Slobodin and American doctoral candidate Maureen L. King. Radiocarbon dating of material associated with the point indicates that it is 8,300 years old–more than 2,000 years younger than those at Clovis itself.[47] The find, if confirmed, would indicate that if there was travel between Asia and the Americas it was hardly the one-way street usually put forth. All of this research, though not necessarily either "proving" tribal protologies or "disproving" the Bering Strait theory, should demonstrate that knowledge of human origins and the populating of the Americas is neither as definitive nor as absolute as scientists sometimes suggest. It is a common joke in Indian Country that the only physical evidence for a Bering Strait migration is a single fossil footprint, and scientists cannot tell in which direction it is heading.

The Bering Strait theory is simply that–a theory. Alternative theories, ranging from continental drift, to polygenesis, to human genesis in the Americas, have been put forth. Such theories, while seeming outlandish to some, are vitally important in freeing the imagination and opening up the seams of what has been largely a closed discussion, conducted without the participation of traditional Natives. According to historian Homer Noley (Choctaw), "Unfortunately, today's public schools teach one of the theories as if it were fact, namely the Bering Strait land bridge theory. It is a theory not supported by adequate evidence, but it is held by those who need convenient answers to their questions. The truth is nobody knows the origins of the Native tribes on this continent."[48] Philosopher Paul Feyerabend states that science as a way of knowing the world is "inherently superior only for those who have already decided in favor of a certain ideology. . . . Science took over by force, not by argument."[49] Noley notes, "Neither anthropology nor history rests on principles or methods that are absolute, as mathematics does. The choice of a point of reference too often becomes merely the judgment of the scientist or historian. [Determinations of fact often depend] on the judgment call of the person or group making the first diagnosis. Events that follow that judgment are justified by the diagnosis."[50]

Certain evidence, in fact, militates against the Bering Strait theory. For example, Native tribes record the purest type-A and type-O blood groups in the world, plus the only groups entirely lacking type-A. Moreover, aside from those in the Arctic and sub-Arctic, there is among most groups an absence of type-B blood, the overwhelmingly predominant blood group in East Asia. How are these facts to be reconciled with an Asian migration at a relatively recent date? If such a migration did occur, how did the immigrants so quickly populate the entirety of the Americas and so rapidly adapt to widely diverse environments from frozen tundra to South American rainforest? If it occurred, how did an obviously highly mobile people manage to change so quickly into sedentary inhabitants like those of Monte Verde? Once again, one can understand Deloria's conclusion:

> Not only does the more recent interpretation of human evolution militate against American Indians being latecomers to the Western Hemisphere, an examination of the Bering Strait doctrine suggests that such a journey would have been impossible even if there had been hordes of Paleo-Indians trying to get across the hypothetical land bridge. It appears that not even animals or plants *really* crossed this mythical connection between Asia and North America. The Bering Strait [crossing] exists and existed only in the minds of scientists.[51]

It is sometimes argued that the absence of any credible scientific evidence for any alternative theory leaves only the Bering Strait theory. But it is always dangerous to draw conclusions on the basis of the absence of evidence.

It is a reasonable and well documented principle that the frequency of archaeological finds falls sharply with their age; Karl Butzer has estimated that 11,000 year old sites [for the sake of argument, roughly the date of the Clovis barrier] will be found 10-15 times more often than 30,000 year old sites, and over 100 times more often than a 75,000 year old site. Even given all the clever techniques which archaeologists have developed to locate artifacts, it is no surprise that few finds have been made in Siberia and Alaska, where sparse resources and a bitter climate probably limited the human population to small, widely separated communities, further reducing man's already vanishing fingerprint.[52]

Who knows what finds yet await discovery in the Orinoco or the Amazon? Might certain previously discredited pre-Clovis sites need to be reevaluated in light of the confirmation of Monte Verde? As Thomas Dillehay states, "Archaeologists will probably never find the remains of the very first Americans. Even if they do, they may not recognize those remains for what they are."[53]

In the October 22 article in the *New York Times* concerning the supposed travesties wrought by NAGPRA, the author writes that "according to many Indian creation accounts, natives have always lived in the Americas after emerging onto the surface of the earth from a subterranean world of spirits." This is true. Native nations, however, are possessed of a tremendous variety of creation accounts and religious traditions that often differ one from another as much as Christianity differs from Hinduism. To homogenize them and then to juxtapose them with Western science is only to conflate them and ultimately to do a disservice to all concerned. In fact, some tribes—notably the Cherokee and the Delaware—preserve myths about a migration from lands across the water.[54] Still others, such as the Hopi and the Colville, as noted by Deloria, speak of transoceanic moves by boat.[55]

Reading accounts of the controversy over the Ancient One, a reader might get the impression that NAGPRA has been an unmitigated disaster—"that the relationship between archaeologists and Native Americans is a negative one, with little in common on either side."[56] In reality, a number of tribes have cultural heritage programs or historic preservation offices that include archaeological work. William Tall Bull (Northern Cheyenne) and Ted Rising Sun (Northern Cheyenne), among others, have shown that history and archaeology, though they have been too often employed for domination, can be tools of resistance as well, "capable of allowing [dominated] groups to free themselves from participation in the dominant ideology."[57] Though presenting challenges, NAGPRA has functioned reasonably well and has led to the repatriation of thousands of remains and important ritual objects. Rather than fighting tribes in the name of science and denouncing their legitimate demands as "religious fundamentalism," the lesson for archaeologists to draw from NAGPRA is the need to cultivate good relations with the Natives whom they study and on whose ancestral lands they work. This is the sensible suggestion of William D. Lipe, president of the Society for American Archeology, in a letter he wrote in response to the dispute over the Ancient One.[58] Such an approach could benefit not only scientists but the tribes as well.

A few years ago I returned to that museum in Cheyenne, Oklahoma. I was no longer able to see Motavato. He had been buried. As I recall, an American flag flew above his grave. It was like the one that he had been given on a trip to Washington where he met with President Lincoln. The army colonel who presented it promised him that, as long as that flag flew above him, no soldier would fire upon him. That flag fluttered above his lodge at Sand Creek that day in November 1864 when soldiers did attack. This flag was the same. Only now sixteen stars, representing further theft of Native lands, had been added. I never knew Motavato, but somehow I don't think he would approve.

Author's Note: The problem with writing timely, topical essays is that time does not cooperate by standing still. The lag time between finished manuscript and publication, in either journals or books, is generally ten to twelve months. Events continue to unfold during that hiatus, with the result that a piece, while still relevant, may not be quite as to-the-moment when it sees the light of day as it was when illuminated only by the flicker of a computer screen.

With the suits by the eight scientists and the Asatru Folk Assembly pending, the Army Corps of Engineers rescinded its original decision to turn the Ancient One over to the tribes. On June 2, 1997, John Jelderks, the federal magistrate hearing motions in the case, denied the scientists' request for immediate access to the skeleton. He did, however, order the Corps to reconsider its decision.

In a written opinion in July, the judge elaborated on the June 2 decision. While making it clear that he was not deciding the ultimate disposition of the remains, he did term the decision-making process followed by the Corps flawed, finding that it had chosen "to suppress [its doubts about the applicability of NAGPRA] in the interests of fostering a climate of cooperation with the tribes." He concluded by ordering all parties to report back to the court on a quarterly basis, beginning October 1, 1997.

Notes

[1] Black Kettle, quoted in W. C. Vanderwerth, *Indian Oratory* (Norman: University of Oklahoma Press, 1971), p. 134.

[2] Walter R. Echo-Hawk and Roger C. Echo-Hawk, "Repatriation, Reburial, and Religious Rights," in *Handbook of American Indian Religious Freedom*, ed. Christopher Vecsey (New York: Crossroad, 1991), p. 67.

[3] Ibid.

[4] Edward Said states, "Of all the modern sciences, anthropology is the one historically most closely tied to colonialism, since it was often the case that anthropologists and ethnologists advised colonial rulers on the manners and mores of native people" (*Culture and Imperialism* [New York: Alfred A. Knopf, 1993], p. 152).

[5] Joan Mark, quoted in Elsie Clews Parson, ed., *American Indian Life*, 2d Bison Book ed. (Lincoln: University of Nebraska Press, 1991), pp. ix-x.

[6] Said, p. 152.

[7] Echo-Hawk and Echo-Hawk, p. 67.

[8] U.S. Department of Interior, *Federal Agencies Task Force Report, American Indian Religious Freedom Act Report* (Washington: 1979), p. 64.

[9] Echo-Hawk and Echo-Hawk, p. 68.

[10] See 16 U.S.C. § 432 (1906); 16 U.S.C. § 470aa-470*ll* (1988).

[11] 20 U.S.C. §§ 80q-9, 80q-9 (c) (1990).

[12] 25 U.S.C. §§ 3001-3013 (1991).

[13] David H. Getches, Charles F. Wilkinson, and Robert A. Williams, Jr., *Cases and Materials on Federal Indian Law*, 3d ed. (St. Paul: West Publishing, 1993), pp. 772-73.

[14] Lynne Goldstein, "Archaeology," in *Native America in the Twentieth Century, An Encyclopedia*, ed. Mary B. Davis (New York: Garland Publishing, 1994), p. 53.

[15] Echo-Hawk and Echo-Hawk, p. 64.

[16] George Johnson, "Indian Tribes' Creationists Thwart Archeologists," *New York Times* (October 22, 1996), p. C13. For Bonnichsen's account of the find and the resulting controversy, see Robson Bonnichsen and Alan L. Schneider, "Roots," *The Sciences* (May/June 1995), pp. 26-31.

[17] Valerie Henderson, "Five Tribes Seek Remains of 'The Ancient One,'" *Indian Country Today* (November 25–December 2, 1996), p. B1.

[18] Timothy Egan, "Tribe Stops Study of Bones That Challenge History," *New York Times* (September 30, 1996), p. A12.

[19] "Mistaken Man," *New York Times Magazine* (December 1, 1996), p. 31.

[20] Egan, p. A12; Danyelle Robinson, "Ancient Remains Relative to Many," *Indian Country Today* (January 20-27, 1997), p. A7; Danyelle Robinson, "Tribes, Scientists Base Claims on Separate Acts," *Indian Country Today* (January 20-27, 1997), p. A8.

[21] Robinson, "Tribes," p. A8; Egan, p. A12.

[22] Ibid.

[23] Danyelle Robinson, "Ancient Remains Linked to American Indian Tribes," *Indian Country Today* (February 17-24, 1997), p. A1.

[24] George Johnson, "Indian Tribes' Creationists Thwart Archeologists," *New York Times* (October 22, 1996), p. A1.

[25] Ibid., p. C13.

[26] Ibid.

[27] "Science and the Native American Cosmos," *New York Times* (October 25, 1996), p. A38. One of the two letters under this collective caption was from me.

[28] N. Scott Momaday, "Disturbing the Spirits," *New York Times* (November 2, 1996), p. A15.

[29] Egan, p. A12.

[30] Henderson, p. B1.

[31] Robinson, "Ancient Remains Relative to Many," p. A7.

[32] Johnson, p. C13.

[33] See Jace Weaver, "From I-Hermeneutics to We-Hermeneutics: Native Americans and the Post-Colonial," chapter 1, above.

[34] Clark Wissler, *Indians of the United States*, rev. ed. with revisions by Lucy Wales Kluckhorn (Garden City, N.Y.: Doubleday, 1966), p. 4.

[35] Vine Deloria, Jr., *Red Earth, White Lies: Native Americans and the Myth of Scientific Fact* (New York: Scribner, 1995), p. 82.

[36] Ibid.

[37] Russell Thornton, "Repatriation of Human Remains and Artifacts," in Davis, p. 543.

[38] Wissler, pp. 8-9; Olivia Vlahos, *New World Beginnings: Indian Cultures in the Americas* (New York: Viking Press, 1970), p. 16; Peter Farb, *Man's Rise to Civilization as Shown by the Indians of North America from Primeval Times to the Coming of the Industrial State* (New York: E. P. Dutton, 1968), p. 199.

[39] Thomas D. Dillehay, "The Battle of Monte Verde," *The Sciences* (January/February 1997), p. 32.

[40] Ibid., p. 33.

[41] John Noble Wilford, "Human Presence in Americas Is Pushed Back a Millennium," *New York Times* (February 11, 1997), p. C4.

[42] Deloria, pp. 68-69.

[43] Johnson, p. C13.

[44] Karen Freeman, "9,700-Year-Old Bones Back Theory of Coastal Migration," *New York Times* (October 6, 1996), p. 32.

[45] "Prehistory of Languages," *Archaeology* (July/August 1994), p. 17.

[46] John Noble Wilford, "Ancient Spears Tell of Mighty Hunters of Stone Age," *New York Times* (March 4, 1997), p. C6.

[47] John Noble Wilford, "'American' Arrowhead Found in Siberia," *New York Times* (August 2, 1996), p. A6.

[48] Homer Noley, *First White Frost* (Nashville: Abingdon Press, 1991), pp. 17-18.

[49] Bruce Schiamberg, "American-Indians Choose Spirit Over Science," *New York Times* (November 11, 1996), p. A14.

[50] Noley, pp. 16-17.

[51] Deloria, p. 107.

[52] Daniel Riegel, "On the Origins of Native Americans: A Synthesis of Ideas," unpublished paper (Yale University, December 23, 1996), p. 5; Tom D. Dillehay and David J. Meltzer, eds., *The First Americans: Search and Research* (Boston: CRC Press, 1991), p. 144.

[53] Dillehay, p. 33.

[54] Billy M. Jones and Odie B. Faulk, *Cherokees: An Illustrated History* (Muskogee, Ok.: The Five Civilized Tribes Museum, 1984), p. 10; see, generally, David McCutchen, *The Red Record: The Wallam Olum of the Lenni Lenape, the Delaware Indians, a Translation and Study* (Garden City Park, N.Y.: Avery Publishing Group, 1993).

[55] Deloria, p. 97.

[56] Goldstein, p. 50.

[57] J. Douglas McDonald, Larry J. Zimmerman, A. L. McDonald, William Tall Bull, and Ted Rising Sun, "The Northern Cheyenne Outbreak of 1879: Using Oral History and Archaeology as Tools of Resistance," in *The Archaeology of Inequality*, ed. Randall H. McGuire and Robert Paynter (Oxford: Blackwell, 1991), pp. 64, 77.

[58] William D. Lipe, "For the Good of All, Study Those Ancient Bones," *New York Times* (October 4, 1996), p. A14.

10.

Sun Dance

DIANE GLANCY

> She practiced both religions at the same time and at random. Her soul was healthy and at peace, she said, because what she did not find in one faith was there in another.
>
> Gabriel Garcia Marquez, *Of Love and Other Demons*

It is raining when I leave St. Paul on Interstate 35S for the Sun Dance on the Rosebud Reservation just west of Mission, South Dakota. It's 523 miles to the particular dance I'm going to. There are others. But this one I know through the Mazakute Native American Mission in St. Paul. I went to the Sun Dance last summer, and wanted to go again to find some words to put it in perspective. To understand more than my own way. To understand why I want to return to a ceremony that is not in my culture.

Two hours later, at Interstate 90 in southern Minnesota, I turn west. Another four hours and I stop at the lookout above the Missouri River nearly half way across South Dakota. There isn't much between the low sky and the prairie except the Missouri River which cuts into the land. The river is green in its valley. Like one of those nineteenth-century landscapes. If you don't look at the bridge. And the traffic.

I read a plaque:

Lewis & Clark / 1804 / ate plums & acorns from the burr oaks / killed a buffalo & magpie / dried equipment / repacked boats / camped again 1806 on the return trip.

I feel the raised letters on the plaque with my hand as if they are the low hills. I run my finger between them as if it is the river. I think of the site of the Mandan village farther north on the Missouri, where another plaque erroneously says the whole tribe was wiped out by smallpox.

A few hours later I exit I-90 at Murdo. I take Highway 83 south for the last sixty-three miles of the trip. At the junction of Highway 18 I turn west a short distance, then south again at a sign that says *Mission*. Later I turn onto Highway 1. The sign is a 1 on an arrowhead. Somewhere, after one turn or another, the road to Mission goes east and the open land of the Rosebud Reservation is west. The highway descends into a sharp valley, curves around a gas station and convenience store, and a few buildings of Sinte Gleska College, then climbs the hill. No name of the town. No names on streets. Nothing to let you know where you are. At the top of the hill I turn south again at a sign marked *St. Francis*. Somehow the roads shift and turn and boundaries are not remembered once passed.

My ears pop and the land seems high under the sky. I see a butte to the west and the gray trail of the highway up and down across the land to the south. And it rains. Through the nodding wipers I watch the cattle grazing. I pass the Rosebud Timber Reserve, a few clumps of pastel reservation houses, some with satellite dishes, and a trail of smoke from the garbage burn.

In St. Francis I stop and talk with a priest. I ask about the mixing of Christianity and Indian traditions. "What are you looking for?" he asks me, and I don't know the answer. I drive back to the water tower road and turn west on BIA 501. It's about seven miles to the ridge where the Sun Dance is held. Soon I see the large camp of tents and teepees. I turn left and drive through the rutted field toward the north section where I will find people I know from St. Paul.

The field is on a ridge high above a valley filled with pines. It's pasture, except the third week in July when it's used for the Sun Dance. I pass the vans and trucks and cars. I pass the teepees and tents and Coleman stoves and campfires. Children run everywhere and groups of people sit by their tents. It has stopped raining, and the smell of cedar and sage and cooking fires fills the air.

In the center of the camp is the Sun Dance arena, which looks like an old brush-arbor church-camp meeting in Oklahoma. But this is the Sun Dance, and I'm going to see it on its own terms.

In the middle of the Sun Dance arena is the cottonwood tree, which has been cut and carried into the circle and placed upright again. The cottonwood because it holds water. Its branches are tied up with ropes, and prayer-ties or tobacco-ties hang from the tree. Black for West. Red for North. Yellow for East. White for South. Green for Earth. Blue for Sky.

It is evening and everyone is resting. After the nine-hour trip from St. Paul by myself, I pull a borrowed tent from my car and unfold it. Others help me set it up.

In the dark I move my sleeping bag several places on the hard, uneven ground inside the tent.

I sleep, and at 4:30 I hear the wake-up song on the loud speaker. There's no reason to get up. I'm an observer. I know the sun dancers are on their way to the sweat lodges for purification. When I hear the drums, I picture the sun dancers. I know they begin in the first light, in their long skirts and bare chests, moving inside the circle of the arena around the cottonwood, singing the Sun Dance songs and blowing their eagle-bone whistles. The women dance in a larger circle around the men. The people sit or stand in the brush arbor that surrounds both circles of dancers and the tree.

Then the piercing begins. A man who has danced and prayed, and is in the right frame of mind, lies on the buffalo robe by the tree in the center of the circle. Two elk bone skewers are pushed under the skin on his chest. He stands connected to the tree with two small ropes and joins his group of supporters in the circle that surrounds the tree, for however many rounds he chooses. Then he pulls back on the ropes until the skewers break free and he is released.

Men are not suspended from a pole, nor do they stare at the sun until they're blind. The Sun Dance is a commitment, a way of life more than a religion. It's keeping a promise. Doing what you say you're going to do. It's a prayer service to the Great Spirit. An intercession for relatives in need. It's humility and respect and supplication. It's a strengthening ceremony. A thanksgiving. There are testimonies between rounds. And the humor of the announcer mixed with the endurance. The suffering. The seriousness. Over and over the announcer says to pray for the dancers who are having a difficult time in their fight against heat, thirst, hunger, and fatigue.

There's an assortment of people from several states at the Sun Dance. The Indians are mainly Lakota and Dakota. They open their ceremony to others. There are many white people. Some come from Europe. One family is from Australia. I don't know numbers. Maybe there were four hundred. Probably more. Cars come and go each day.

It's an old ceremony of death and resurrection. A connection to the tree. A release.

The Sun Dance continues all day until about 6:00 P.M. Then the dancers sit once more in the sweat lodge and return to their tents or teepees. They cannot eat or drink water.

There are those who are pierced. There are those who just dance. There are those who watch. I stand in the brush arbor that circles the dance arena. For the second year I forgot a lawn chair. I watch. Pray. Think of my own needs and those of others. Dance in place. Raise my hands to the tree like the dancers and the other watchers. Sometimes I walk back to the tent. I make tobacco prayer-ties, which someone will hang on the tree. I am not part of the Sun Dance and cannot enter the arena.

There are many rules.

For lunch I eat peanut butter on crackers, remembering somehow the burr acorns and magpies from the Missouri River plaque. I drink warm water out of a plastic bottle. You carry your water and food in with you. Whatever you need. I am reminded of church camp in Oklahoma where I had to put on my socks over dirty feet and felt the dust between my toes. There's an outhouse but no bath or shower. You camp in an open field under the sun on a ridge above the valleys of dark pines maybe 150 or 200 miles southeast of the Black Hills. By mid-afternoon the heat is unbearable inside the tent. The only shade is in the arbor, where sometimes a warm breeze moves the prayer-ties on the tree.

That night I drive into Mission to hear an Indian leader who I knew was speaking at the Charles Hare Center. He begins with a story about a minister who led his congregation from the church into the open air, singing a hymn as they went. Only the pastor was walking backward as he led them, and at the edge of the churchyard he fell into a newly dug grave and couldn't get out, his head appearing and disappearing as he jumped. Finally they pulled him out, and he had that white soil even in his eyebrows. As the Indian leader went on talking, the seriousness surfaced. The meanness of reservation border towns. When you pray for them, he said, pray about alcoholism, AIDS, drugs, diabetes, joblessness, poverty.

I start back to the Sun Dance ground around 9:30. The sun has gone down and the sky is like a piece of blue tissue paper. Some thought or memory is wrapped in it. The land is dark and wavy beneath the sky. There's one star up there, and the telephone poles are crosses on the hills.

I think it's about thirty miles back from Mission. I know it's a long way and I feel unsure. It's hard to see the road in the dark. There's just the prairie and the sky and the center line on the road and watching the shoulders for deer.

Sometimes, far off in the distance, I see a few lights on the horizon. I think it must be St. Francis, but the lights don't seem in the right direction. The road isn't headed toward them. I pass a lone building with a yard light. A schoolbus parked in a yard. And where are the stars? The sky in the west still has not turned out its light. Maybe it's too early for them.

Yes, the few lights I saw are St. Francis. The highway finally curves toward them. On the water tower road, right after the post office, I turn west. I wonder if I can see the camp off BIA 501 in the dark. I wonder if I will know when seven miles have gone by. There is a car behind me and I don't want to go too slow. But soon I see car lights coming through a field. I know the turn off is just ahead. I signal, and the car behind me also turns, its headlights on bright.

As I look from my tent that night, I see the stars. A sky full of them. I go to sleep on the lumpy ground.

I get up at 4:30 this time. I'm not comfortable. I want to leave. I'm into something I don't belong in. A Sun Dance in the Lakota/Dakota tradition. I'm in a magnetic field, and I feel repelled. But I have felt outside of every tradition I've been in. The Methodist church as a child because I couldn't figure out all the trouble of going to church. What did they preach other than the brotherhood of man and a sense of community? I need more than that.

I need salvation to help me out of the hurt and isolation and darkness I feel in my heart.

Through the years I also have attended the Presbyterian church, which seemed to me like the Methodist. And later, when I was saved, the fundamentalist church that was opposed to the arts and a life of the imagination. Sometimes I attend the Episcopal church.

There is no belonging here. I am not from the north, but a shadow of a place I used to live, but I'm not from there either. I was born long ago, to parents of different heritages. I've lived several places, and none of them is where I'm from.

I feel marginalized from both my white and Indian heritages. I'm neither of both. Both of neither. My great-grandfather was a full-blood Cherokee born near Sallisaw in Indian Territory in 1843. His parents got there somehow. The only way was the Trail of Tears from the southeast. My mother's people of European descent farmed in Kansas.

Because I don't have a road, because I'm in the process of the journey, I still don't know why I'm between two different cultures. I still have to jump-start an image of my broken self.

The Bible is full of journeys. It's why I think it is home.

That second morning at the Sun Dance I watch the men on the buffalo robe. I watch as the holy men push the skewers under their skin. That's where it suddenly connects for me.

My son, when he was seventeen, had open lung surgery. He had holes in his lungs and they had to be stapled. When his lung first collapsed, the doctor pushed a tube into his chest. I was sitting outside the curtain. The opening for the tube was the size of a yellow jacket stinging and stinging, and he couldn't push it away.

I am not an outsider to this. I am the mother who listened to him suffer. I smoked and drank when he was conceived, and those habits interfered with his chances for development. I think so anyway. I've had a dream of snow in the yard. He was looking from the window. I tossed the snow at the window calling him, and he disappeared. The great black hole of the mailbox. No answers coming. And into the cold outside of the house I tossed him.

He was born blue and mottled. Wrapped in the tissue paper of the evening sky. There was also a second surgery. His kidney this time. He was pierced in the side like Christ, and all the pages of the Bible cannot change it.

I wish I could go back and conceive him again. I wish I could put on his overalls and pull a shirt over his chest again. He survived. He teaches school.

That morning in the open field on the Rosebud Reservation in South Dakota, during one of the rest periods between the rounds of dancing, an Elder speaks over the loud speaker. He says the Sun Dance is a form of Christ going to the cross. For me, it finished on the cross. But the ceremony of linkage to suffering and release is still here.

A time to unload and repack the boats and start back on the river.

In the afternoon, I drive with two friends to the White River, nearly to Murdo. I hear the birds and insects in the grasses from the window of the car as I pass, like Oklahoma and the open places I've traveled. We pick some sage in a field along the road, leaving an offering of tobacco.

We have lunch at the Cook Shack in Mission and return to the Sun Dance grounds for another hot afternoon. That evening, as the dance is finished, the announcer says there is a severe storm warning. We can see the clouds to the west because you can see far across the prairie from the ridge where we camp. Less than an hour later, we're in our tents trying to hold them down in the wind.

That evening I ride out the storm in the borrowed tent, the sides puffing as if it is a large bird trying to take flight. I hear the snap and hum of the lightning. I can even smell it.

Afterward, while it is still light, I hear someone say, "Look at the rainbows." When I look from the tent, I see the two rainbows over the camp grounds. I stand in the slight rain that is still falling and the wind still whipping the tents and feel the oneness with the sky and earth. I feel survival. I feel promise. I feel what I hadn't known I'd been looking for. Significance.

Later in the night I hear the eerie noise of coyotes, the hecklers, laughing at what I have found. But I stick with it.

I want a journey of meaning in ordinary life. I've always liked the plain land under the sky. The routine of housework and grading papers and writing and teaching and traveling, transformed by the act of its own ordinariness. Just like Jesus walking through the wheat field. These moments become more than themselves.

My mother used to talk about the Maypole dance she experienced as a girl. The ceremony of the tree goes back in history. The cross of Christ. The cottonwood tree of the Sun Dance. It's a connection to the past.

> . . . I hung
> on the windy tree . . .
> gashed with a blade
> bloodied for Odin
>   myself an offering to myself
> knotted to that tree
> no man knows
>   whither the roots of it run.
>   —Brian Branston, *The Last Gods of England*

The Sun Dance is also a connection to the Plains Indian culture I had read about in school, which is different from the woodland Cherokee heritage my father had left, and which had confused me as to what an "Indian" is.

I am looking for meaning in the heat and community and sometimes the boredom as a Sun Dance observer.

I know I already have it. When my son's chest was opened during surgery. When I have been deconstructed. When I need the construction of strength and meaning and hope. It is Christ. I've always gone to church through the years. I am saved and filled with the Holy Spirit. I speak in tongues.

I believe in ceremony. There are many at the Sun Dance, which is itself a ceremony.

The next morning the clouds are low when I dismantle my tent and leave. It feels as if the day will be cool, but I know how soon the heat comes.

I watch the road ahead of me as I drive back toward Interstate 90 to the north. I watch the road reflecting in the hood of my car. I have made an expedition to a place I am not from. The low, rolling hills of South Dakota under the sky that lids them. I feel the air in the window. My hand on the wheel.

I turn east onto I-90 toward Minnesota. The cars and trucks moving along the highway are unaware of the Sun Dance just a few miles over the hills. And the sun dancers, when they come in their vans with their teepee lodge-poles tied on top and turn onto the Interstate, will pass along the road with the other traffic. They will carry with them their *significance*, which is a blanket over the pitfalls of the earth. Well, we do fall into them sometimes but get lifted out.

It's why I want to write—to touch words—because the touch of words is alive.

11.

Learning to Navigate in a Christian World

DONALD A. GRINDE, JR.

When the Christians took the Indian children off to boarding schools, the minister used to lead the children into the chapel and point up to the picture of Jesus, with long flowing hair, and tell the Indian children that they were going to learn how to be just like that man, Jesus. After this statement, the minister would send all the Indian boys off to get their hair cut short.

Rupert Costo (Cahuilla)

When I was a small child in a federal housing project in Savannah, Georgia, my mother taught me that the earth was our mother and that one of the reasons it was so hot during the summers in Savannah was that much of the earth in the city was paved and thus our earth mother found it difficult to breathe. This view conflicted with the Christian fundamentalist thought that surrounded me, which explained the meaning of life only through human behavior and the resulting harsh judgments of a patriarchal God. Since I was grounded in and knowledgeable about the place of the Yamasee people (the lower Savannah River Valley), I preferred my mother's explanation of the world. It was kinder, more loving, and related directly to the place I lived. She taught me respect for all forms of creation, not just God, and was focused on this earth, not hopes of "heaven." Later, I would read and agree with Black Elk that one must be humble before all of the myriad forms of creation to enable spiritual awareness. Native cultures do not polarize a masculine and feminine since we understand that there is a masculine spirit in the sky that impregnates mother earth with the rain (the larger processes of creation reflect the smaller processes of creation). My world was very much alive, while the spiritual world of fundamentalist Christianity that enveloped me in the post–World War II American South seemed death-dealing.

My memories vacillate between cool swims in the Savannah River and the hot fires of damnation that were generated by Christians in the revivals and camp meetings that were commonplace in my childhood. The local environment was a comforting haven from the scary psychological constructs of fundamentalist Christians. I remember being surrounded by massive projects to alter the earth and produce more wealth, but what has meaning in my memories are the gardens that my mother cultivated of corn, beans, squash, and other vegetables–planted in "hills" because they were meant to cooperate not compete. A harmonious relationship with the environment was desired over one that sought ruthlessly to exploit our surroundings for profit.

At an early age I was acutely aware of the violence in American society. My elementary school was a rough place with gangs, stabbings, and thefts on a regular basis; I was stabbed in the stomach on the school playground at the age of six. The way I navigated through that maze of anger was to enter the world of written words early and yet stay in the spoken words of my relatives. I was counseled that everyone is a human being in creation and that we should try to understand creation through interaction with the environment and other created beings. I remember being fascinated with ants as a child, with their minutest activities. I lived in a Christian society (as only the American South can be), but that religion was distant from my life–imported from the world across the big water (Europe). For me, Christianity never seemed rooted in North America, since it clung tenaciously to Old-World messages and Old-World environments.

I remember going to the funeral of a man who befriended my grandfather, when I was about seven years old. It was in a small Baptist church, and because the man had so many friends, the church was overflowing. My grandfather and I sat in one of the back pews. It was hot, so I got drowsy and put my head in his lap. As I was going to sleep, the spirit of the service changed. The preacher apparently decided that since there were so many strangers in his church he would attempt to convert them all. After a brief discussion of the deceased's life, the preacher began pacing in front of the mourning people and accusing them of being sinners. His accusatory style jolted me. It was my first experience in the house of an angry and vengeful God. The minister detailed the ways that the devil entered the lives of human beings and led them to hellfire and damnation. He ranted for about an hour and a half. Many people became uncomfortable, and a few left. Noticing my discomfort, my grandfather patted my head and told me to go to sleep. He said that these were not our ways, and the minister should have been more respectful to his friend by confining his remarks to the subject of the service, namely, the burial of his friend.

At last the imagery of the devil and eternal damnation ceased, and my grandfather and I lined up in the aisle to exit the church. The preacher had positioned himself at the door to shake hands with people as they filed out. As we drew closer to the door, my grandfather put his arm around me, and I clung to his leg. My grandfather was a relatively short man, about five foot eight inches, but as he stepped up to the six foot tall minister, he extended his hand and looked the minister straight in the eye. In a clear voice, so that everyone around us could hear, my grandfather declared, "You are the one that's going to hell because you are needlessly scaring little children with your terrible words and have neglected the funeral service for my friend." The minister looked away from my grandfather as we stepped out the door of the church into the bright summer sun. It was wonderful to be back in the warm natural environment that was so alive.

Sensing my discomfort with the house-based and anthropocentric religion of Christianity, my grandfather made it a point to discuss the rhythms of creation and the cycles of life with me. As a farmer, he was close to the workings of the earth. He preferred the world of nature to the world of religious discourse. Some of my fondest memories as a young boy are those of quietly walking behind him sowing corn as he plowed the fields with his two mules. In the hot Georgia sun, with his overalls on and no shirt, he guided the plow by looping the reins to the mules around his shoulders. Each time he leaned forward or backward or sideways, the mules would subtly change direction.

Once, during the heat of the day, one of the mules collapsed and died in harness while we were plowing a field. My grandfather unhitched the dead mule, and we walked to the shed to get shovels so that we could bury the mule in the field. When we came back, the vultures were already circling in the sky overhead. We dug for over an hour in the hot sun until we had made a deep hole. The other mule stood silently by its dead companion, seeming to understand that their relationship had been severed by death. Once the digging was completed, we put the dead mule into the hole by slowly pulling it over the edge and then we dug further underneath its carcass. Eventually gravity did its work and the mule's body slid into its grave. It took another twenty or thirty minutes to cover the grave; then we grabbed the reins to the remaining mule and led it back to the mule pen. My grandfather said that the other mule would probably die pretty soon since the two of them were old and inseparable. We tried to feed that mule and cheer it up all summer but it pined away for its lifelong companion and died by the end of the summer. At the age of seven, I had learned that, like human beings, animals were capable of strong bonds of friendship and love.

Throughout my formative years my mother and grandfather taught me about the workings of the environment. This ecological knowledge contrasted with the human behavior codes advocated by Christian sects. It was difficult to fathom the idea that if human beings behaved according to a God-given code they would be redeemed as individuals in a land far from here called heaven. Furthermore, it seemed that the Christian God was quite fickle, wanted appeasement, and was more concerned with vengeance, retribution, and pain than with love and understanding. The Christian God seemed more like a wrathful adolescent than a Creator who wanted its creation to grow nicely. What was the purpose of such a belief system? Was it to foster fear and obedience without contemplation? Christian ideology seemed to make human beings into demigods and distorted their capabilities and responsibilities on earth. As a young Indian child, I was taught that once people separated themselves from their environment and from their community, they were capable of bad things because they could no longer see the results of their actions in this world. It seemed as though Christians were busy becoming "good" individuals and then getting off the planet, while we were focused on staying here and learning the ways of the earth.

With this background, I entered a public high school. It seemed that adolescence was accompanied by an accelerated drive by school officials to repress our exuberance and curiosity. I was enrolled in the gifted classes in the sciences and humanities, and the things we learned in the early 1960s were often in conflict with the fundamental values of Christianity. For some of my classmates this was a difficult path to tread, but I had always been on the outside of Christianity looking in anyway. As adolescents, we decided to resolve some of these contradictions through guerrilla theater and politics. Some of my friends became "Anti-Christians" dedicated to the notion that overthrowing Christian hegemony would pave the way toward freedom of mind and spirit. They would publicly challenge God to strike them dead if he were real. At one point a group of atheists ran a slate of class officers (including class chaplain) that sought to blunt the effect of fundamentalist Christianity at our school. For my part, I contented myself with more intellectual pursuits in my dealings with Christianity. I supported the elimination of school prayer and Bible readings at the start of the school day. Basically, I have always had the idea that any religion that needs state support to continue its existence and further its power over nonbelievers is really not a religion but a political ideology that serves the interests of the ruling class.

It was not until I got into college that I found more liberal Christians. It was something of a shock to learn that some Christians were not into hellfire and damnation but talked about love, forgiveness, and acceptance of difference. During my undergraduate years the Civil Rights Movement was swirling about me and many African-American ministers seemed dedicated to good ideals.

In graduate school at the University of Delaware I encountered people who opposed the Vietnam War and racism in America. Some of these people were liberal Christians, so I began to get a broader picture of

Christian ideology. Throughout my years in graduate school I remained interested in Native American traditions. I disdained Christian fundamentalism. As students faced the betrayal of American institutions and ideologies in the late 1960s and early 1970s, I seemed more capable of navigating those tortuous waters than my peers. I had always known that much of what was "true" was more earthly than divinely inspired. People construct their own specific realities within the broad outlines of creation. Thus, people must find ways to alter the situations in which they find themselves.

When I became an assistant professor teaching Native American history at SUNY (State University of New York) in Buffalo in the 1970s, I learned some of the problems with liberal Christianity. Upon my arrival in Buffalo in the fall of 1973, the Buffalo North American Indian Center invited me to serve on its board of directors. I accepted the invitation, although I had some hesitancy about being in a leadership role at the young age of twenty-seven. The Buffalo Indian Center was an urban self-help center that provided health-care, job-training, educational, and recreational services to the Buffalo Native American community. Over three-quarters of its members were Iroquois people, since Buffalo was surrounded by over a half dozen Iroquois reservations. Very soon I learned that the Buffalo North American Indian Center was structured along traditional Iroquois ways. Typically, older women chose as leaders those men and women in whom they felt confidence. Before the meetings of the board, the older women would advise us of their wishes on important matters. Often there was spirited discussion and disagreement, and if there was no consensus then the discussion of differences would spill over into the general meetings that happened once a month.

Throughout my years on the board (1974-77), Ron LaFrance (Mohawk) was president. He worked for the Buffalo City Schools in their Native American Education programs and constantly prodded me to write more useful Native American history for the schools. He was a member of the Longhouse religion at the Akwesasne Mohawk Reservation in northern New York State. He instructed me about the Iroquois politics that I was experiencing. Christian Indians versus traditionalists clashed over job programs, educational policies, and other issues. The Christians wanted to abandon old ways and embrace the ways of the whites, while the traditionalists argued that the survival of Native ways was crucial in the resolution of all issues.

Buffalo in the mid-1970s was a paradox. I had only heard of the Mafia in the movies until I moved there, but organized crime was a part of daily life at that time in Buffalo. I remember learning how the law worked. One evening, a Mafia don was eating in an Italian restaurant with his family when he decided to walk a few blocks down to the cathedral and pay his last respects to a colleague. As he walked to the cathedral, a car pulled alongside him, gunfire blazed, and he was killed. There were several people on the street at the time it happened. But no one saw anything, no one could remember the license plate number of the car or its make. One woman claimed to have her back turned to the whole incident; another man stated that he was cleaning his glasses when it happened; still another person claimed to be blinded by a streetlight at the time of the crime. It was plain that no one wanted to be involved in building a case for the prosecution. The newspaper ran the usual headline: "Mafia Don Slain by Gangsters." Within a week the case was forgotten, and it remains an unsolved murder. The police were no more anxious to prosecute the case than the eyewitnesses. More-over, the larger community saw no reason to find the murderers of a Mafia leader. It was a lesson to me in urban justice, American style.

I was soon to find out, however, that American justice works differently for different people. The urban Native American community in Buffalo was plagued at the time by drug pushers. Heroin was the major drug that the Mafia brought into the neighborhood. It corrupted many people. Young men became criminals and women turned to prostitution to feed their habits. The Vietnam War was winding down and the country was sliding into an economic malaise. Most of the drug dealers would get arrested and then be out on the streets again on bail within three or four hours. They seemed to have the best lawyers, no matter how disreputable they were. Many of the leaders in the Native American community were frustrated by the inability of the police to curb the drug dealers' activities. These problems were brought home to me by events that transpired soon after I became a part of the board.

A member of the board was frustrated with drug dealing in his neighborhood. His sister had become addicted to heroin and turned to prostitution, while other people had seen their brothers' lives ruined by the effects of heroin. For over a year people called the police on a regular basis to arrest the drug dealer in the Native American neighborhood of Buffalo, but he was always freed and back on the streets in just a few hours. Frustrated by the ineffectiveness of the legal system, the board member and a group of about four friends resolved to teach the drug dealer a lesson themselves. Late one evening they cornered him in an alley and beat him up. In the scuffle the drug dealer's nose was broken. Dazed and semi-conscious, he fell to the ground with his face up as the group of angry American Indian men left him. Since his broken nose was bleeding profusely, the drug dealer drowned in his own blood.

The headlines the next day read: "Drug Dealer Found Beaten to Death, Indians Suspected." The police were determined to find the people who did it. The newspapers pointed out that the victim had been arrested over fifty times in the last few years for drug dealing, but they insisted that he was a human being and that his killers should be brought to justice. The police called on leaders in the Native American community to cooperate with the investigation. Needless to say, the members of the American Indian community were not anxious to co-operate with a police force that had failed to take a terrible drug dealer off their streets. But it seems that this drug dealer was the son of a powerful crime lord, so the police were getting pressure from the father to do something. In addition, other white people did not like the idea of Native Americans taking the law into their own hands.

What followed was as nightmare for our community. People quickly figured out who had relatives that had been corrupted by this drug dealer. I found out that the member of the board did not actually beat up the drug dealer but merely watched. Several of the men involved in the slaying fled to Canada, where they had relatives, but the board member stayed in town. For several months the local newspaper kept insisting that someone be brought to justice for the murder. Eventually the board member was arrested for murder. In the interrogation the police made it known that they knew that he did not do it, but they said they were charging him with murder so that they could force him to tell them who had really done it. For almost a year my friend was imprisoned merely to make him talk about the real murderers of the drug dealer. Fearing for his own life if he testified against the people who did it, he chose to remain silent and in jail until the police found other sources of information. Even now, over twenty years later, I look back on these events with sorrow and sadness. The justice system failed miserably to keep drugs off our streets, but it was highly effective in prosecuting the murderer of a drug dealer who had spoiled many lives in our community. Paradoxically, the police and the news media still seemed uninterested in finding the murderers of the local crime lord. This is justice American style. It's about who has power, race, and money. Regrettably, Christian values too often reinforce such power structures.

In my years in Buffalo I tended to side most often with the Iroquois traditionalists because of my personal inclinations and my ingrained distrust for a Christian ideology that seeks to dismantle old identities and replace them with being "born again." One of the crucial lessons that I learned was humility. In 1974, the Native American Comprehensive Employment Training Act (CETA) Program and the City of Buffalo approached the board with a plan to infuse more money into job-training programs to expand health-care, recreational, and educational programs in our community. I became convinced that this project would aid in moving the Buffalo Indian Center into self-sufficiency. Many of the older people, however, were resistant, saying that we, as American Indian people, did not have enough control over the funds and that we could become dependent on them and then be manipulated as a result. I argued that over 33 percent of the Native American families in Buffalo were out of work or underemployed and that we did not have the luxury of being choosy about the source of the employment money to help people who were in desperate need. Many of the Christians at the Indian Center sided with me. The issue was hotly debated, and finally those of us who opposed what the older women wanted (rejecting the money to expand employment-training programs) were told that if we resisted them further we would be removed. This was in accord with the old Iroquois tradition that if chiefs did something that the clan mothers did not like they could be removed from their leadership posts immediately.

I thought long and hard about this political turn of events. Should I stick to what I believed was right, or should I give in to the wishes of the older women? After much reflection I decided to vote against the wishes of the older women and be removed from office. I wanted to send a message that I would not bend or compromise on certain things about which I felt strongly. Within a month of my vote I was removed from office. It was not a bitter fight; I knew that my removal was coming. But I did not resign. When I was voted out of office, I quietly stepped down and became a member of the Buffalo Indian Center without a leadership role. I continued to attend meetings and voice my views on issues. There was no shame, no guilt, no uneasiness about my past status, my removal, or my continuation in the life of the Center.

However, the deindustrialization of Buffalo was continuing apace and the ranks of the unemployed continued to grow larger. Inflation also made it difficult for poor families to make ends meet. Many people with years of seniority at local Buffalo industries began to be laid off by the mid-1970s. Jobs became scarcer, and a bad situation became worse. The unemployment, food-stamp, and WIC programs were the only lifelines for many families. Slowly our community came to the realization that jobs of any kind were better than none. With such bad times, the older women came to me again and asked me to serve once again on the board. They did not apologize for removing me from office, nor did I seek to rationalize my reasons for being steadfast in my opinions with regard to the need for Native American CETA programs.

Shortly after my reinstallation on the board, the CETA grant officers came again, and this time people at the Indian Center reluctantly embraced the program. We were told that we would receive grants to facilitate the employment of Indian people in job-training programs. I remember thinking that training people for semi-skilled jobs in a deindustrializing city like Buffalo seemed futile, but I also understood that people needed some hope and some way to secure the resources that they needed to support their families.

When we wrote the grant, the government advisors told us that it really was not a job training grant. At that time in New York State people on unemployment could receive fifty-two weeks of benefits. After that time they were on relief if they could not find work. However, if they could find employment for another thirteen weeks at the end of their unemployment benefits, they were eligible for another fifty-two weeks of unemployment benefits if they were laid off at the end of their thirteenth week of working.

With this in mind, the CETA people advised us to hire people going off unemployment benefits for only thirteen weeks and then lay them off again. This would extend their benefits for another year and maximize benefits for the poor in our community. Very soon it became apparent to all that this program, as it was being implemented, was a band-aid on a deeply wounded industrial society. As a member of the board, my role was to keep families barely afloat through a system that cycled people from unemployment benefits to temporary jobs to unemployment benefits again. It had little to do with real job training, upward mobility, or self-sufficiency.

Unfortunately, we all faced a grim deindustrializing process that offered little hope for the poor and those who had lost their jobs. I cannot say that I was right or wrong in the debates in our community about this program. We did keep some families going through the distribution of its monies, but we did not help them improve their job skills. I think that both the old people and I saw a grim future, and, at first, we reacted to it differently. The fact that we all came to the realization that the CETA program was the only option available was not comforting to any of us. Only the Christians among us continued to think that they were doing good and helping the poor.

Just as I had seen as a young man, the world seemed structured not by any intrinsic values but by power. Regrettably, Christianity seemed to support the powerful and hold out very little to really aid the poor. Reform of the system seemed unattainable, so people remained trapped in a Leviathan that devoured them. This reality reinforced the lessons of my youth—that my values anchored in the environment and place served me better than a Christian ideology that changes with the reconfigurations of power in a decaying industrial society.

Traditional Native American identity is anchored in the environment and, as such, is much more difficult to alter than Christian ideology, which is constructed through the redefinition of time-specific human behavioral codes. Our environment doesn't change unless we move to a new one. This is the constant for Native peoples; it is what makes us difficult to change or "assimilate" completely into modern society. I guess this is why I am always on the outside looking in toward Christianity. It changes and reconfigures itself to adapt to the needs of a human community that has divorced itself from the environment. This process produces conflicts, inconsistencies, and ironies in my life and the lives of the communities in which I have lived. Back in the 1960s, Andy Warhol said, "Art is anything you can get away with." From my vantage point, I think that institutional religion can be characterized in the same way. A friend once told me that "being Indian is the hardest thing to do." I think that is true, because it requires us to look at our environment and balance our behavior with that contextual awareness. Many of us do not live fully within the ideological and human behavioral constructs of our Euroamerican neighbors. We are not disembodied from our surroundings. We believe that we will continue here when we are dead. That is why Iroquois chiefs are charged with taking care of seven generations buried, those now in the bellies of women, those here on this earth, and those who will come seven generations hence. For my own part, this is the only place we have, and we have to take care of it because we believe that we stay here in another reality when we die. The Creator is with us always; we only need to learn how to see it better. I hope that we will someday have a society that allows all of us to nurture our spirituality in a respectful way.

12.

Jesus, Corn Mother, and Conquest

Christology and Colonialism

GEORGE TINKER

This chapter will move in two disparate directions. On the one hand, it will press the issue of the inappropriateness in American Indian communities of the use of the customary Christian language for calling on Jesus and to propose other, more applicable metaphors, both scriptural and indigenous, for referencing Jesus and the Christ in a Christian Indian context. Then, however, it will reevaluate the suitability or appropriateness of even this project in the healing process of a colonized community damaged socially, emotionally, and spiritually by the past five hundred years of conquest and destruction. Many Indian people have been missionized and continue to find personal solace in their connection with the church, and the initial project may help them to rediscover a more culturally appropriate christology for an Indian church. A great many others, however, have found any affirmation of the Christ of Christianity to be merely another imposition of colonial control. In any event, this essay is a small exercise in neo-colonial resistance in search of genuine American Indian liberation, part of a much broader quest engaging Indian peoples today. It intends to speak somehow to both colonizer and colonized.

INTRODUCTION

"What can the death of a man two thousand years ago possibly have to do with people who live today?" Covered in black grease, my Indian-adopted brother looked up from the engine of my old truck long enough to ask a serious theological question. He had been raised a Christian Indian, but had begun incorporating traditional spiritual practices, including the Sun Dance, back into his life for several years. An insightful genius, he was always the visionary at Four Winds Survival Project in Denver, always pushing the community further than we imagined we would go, at times even further or faster than we wanted. On this occasion, he was initiating a process that would call us to reconsider the nature of the relationship between Four Winds' vision of Indian community healing and a public Christian commitment. For the moment, however, I had an answer for him that slowed him down, even if only temporarily. "Why do you dance?" was my response. Sometimes the deepest theological discussions are very short and to the point. His only reply as he dove back into the engine compartment was, "Oh! . . . Yeah." No more words were needed between us, since we both knew full well the vicarious suffering aspect of our spiritual commitments at Sun Dance, the Rite of Vigil, and the Purification Ceremony (often called the sweat lodge in English).

Virtually every tribal nation in North America had a variety of ceremonies whereby the individual might take on a discipline of ceremonial vicarious suffering for the sake of the people as a whole. In every case, the first European and Amer-European invaders of their lands, including especially the missionaries, mistook these ceremonies for something they never were intended to be. Predicated on misunderstanding, sometimes intentional, the missionaries and the Amer-European government proceeded to condemn our ancient rites as devil worship or idolatry. Yet, these ceremonies have much in common with the suffering of Jesus in the Christian gospels because the individual undertaking the ceremony willingly undergoes a discipline of suffering on behalf of the people. This is even true in the case of the Rite of Vigil, often referred to as the "vision quest" in the literature. While there are particularly individual benefits that can accrue from engaging in this ceremony of fasting and prayer, even the eventual benefits are enjoyed by the individual for the sake of the community as a whole.[1]

Our understanding of vicarious suffering in such ceremonial contexts gives Indian people an inherent understanding of the Christian concept of grace that precedes the arrival of the missionaries. We could even go so far as to insist that we already knew the gospel! We were taught differently by the missionaries, of course. They had a vested interest in separating Indian people from their ancient ceremonial structures and consistently taught that those ceremonies fell far short of the Christian ideal. They were, the missionaries insisted, merely vain human attempts to placate an angry god—an impossibility in the first place, went the message, and unnecessary in the light of God's grace revealed in the gospel of Jesus Christ.

More and more, contemporary Indians are realizing that the missionary interpretation was a self-serving lie, a colonial act of domination. There is no sense in any of our traditions as far as I can tell that reflects any attempt to make God, a god, or the spirits happy with us or to placate the judgment of God over against a sinful humanity. There is no sense of God's anger. In fact, the whole notion of *Wakonda* (the Osage concept of ultimate reality) becoming angry is far too anthropomorphic a notion of deity for Indian people. Rather, our traditions are much more complex than that. Our notion of *Wakonda* cannot conceive of ascribing human emotions to *Wakonda*. Yet we do conceive of *Wakonda* as functioning in the best interests of the created world. We know *Wakonda*, however, much more as a sacred but impersonal force that only becomes personified in order to facilitate human understanding. We were given ceremonies in order that we might do our share as two-leggeds in maintaining the world, just as all other species contribute their part. Thus we participate with *Wakonda*, the Sacred Energy or Mystery or Power. And we likewise participate with the more personified spirits that are part of *Wakonda's* self-manifestation.

There were and are ceremonies to make right an imbalance that we ourselves as pitiful two-leggeds may have instigated—through our laziness, inattention, oversight, anger, or some unknown mistake. Even here, however, the anger of the spirits is never at stake in most of our traditions when those traditions are understood at their most complex level. The spirits are, rather, neutral and follow a natural, pre-determinable course. We are mere players in this drama and have been given ceremonies and ways of being that can help to determine the outcome. Thus, our ceremonies are gifts to us, signs of what Euro-Christian theology would call God's grace, or the intrinsic goodness of *Wakonda* and all of its various manifestations and personifications as Grandmothers and Grandfathers.

If our native ways already had some notion of God's Good News, then it becomes important for us to hang on to the good news *Wakonda* originally gave us rather than blindly consume the Good News that the missionaries would impose on us at the cost of losing our own sets of cultural values and losing our inculturated sense of community and individual self-esteem.

AMERICAN INDIANS AND JESUS

My brother's question that day was much more persistent than I initially gave him credit for. Indeed, the question would not go away. Given the implicit and explicit participation of the churches' missionaries in the oppression and cultural genocide of American Indians, what relevance can Jesus have for Indian peoples? That, ultimately, was the question he was asking, and this question became a constantly recurring problem for us at Living Waters Indian Lutheran Ministry, a project with which I have been affiliated for a dozen years and which now calls itself Four Winds Survival Project. How could we proclaim Jesus to a community that has been constantly hurt by the proclamation of the gospel and those who have proclaimed it? There are three points to be made here: (1) the initial problem is not with Jesus but with Christianity and the church; (2) if Jesus is not necessarily a problem, language about Jesus can be quite problematic, and the churches might reasonably make some linguistic/theological shift that might be more inclusive of Indian peoples and their cultures and values; (3) in the final analysis, however, the historical experience of colonization and conquest may continue to make any use of Jesus problematic for American Indian people. It is difficult for many Indian people to concede efficacy to a system of religious belief that they have experienced consistently over several generations as an intimate and symbiotic part of the conquest and the ongoing colonial presence.

Jesus and the Church

Traditional spiritual elders and medicine women and men rather consistently expressed their respect for Jesus as a spiritual person and even as a manifestation of the Creator (namely, God, or something like what is meant by God). While these spiritual elders and medicine people may have significant resistance to church and to Christianity, they found that they were quite able to participate at Living Waters, since Living Waters represented, in its day, an Indian community more than it represented church. Moreover, these elders were more likely than many other traditional people to participate fully in Living Waters' liturgy, even participating in the sacred meal of communion. Jesus, it seems, poses little problem for these elders. They can respect him as having been a spiritual presence and even as a continuing spiritual presence in the world. As these people have expressed themselves, Jesus is much more acceptable than the church.

When traditional Indian people came to Living Waters' Sunday service—and many of our regular participants were traditional—they were faced with a choice when it came to the Eucharist, whether to participate or not. Many found Living Waters a comfortable place to pray with Indian people, yet they were not always ready to concede the efficacy of this important Christian ceremony. The political compromise and resulting disempowerment that come from participating in the conqueror's ceremony was and is simply too great. Abstaining from bread and cup became a final act of resistance and a clear political choice, even in a church that was clearly and more radically Indian.

On the other hand, many chose to go ahead and participate.[2] There were various reasons for their acquiescence: (1) traditional values often dictate that spiritual respect for another's ceremony supersedes one's political conviction; (2) for many, there is a recognition of spiritual power in Jesus that goes beyond ethnicity or culture and is similar to the spiritual power already experienced in traditional Indian ceremonial life; (3) there is a traditional valuing of shared hospitality (when in someone else's camp, one does what they do); (4) most important, many simply were expressing a sense of solidarity with those Indian people who have been converted to Christianity by participating occasionally with them. Among these elders there is a sense that those who have remained with the traditional ways or returned to them cannot abandon converted Indians as if they no longer belong to the community. Decolonization is a process that requires some patience, especially as those who have worked more consistently at the process extend their solidarity to those who are not yet at the same place in that process. The Indian concern for community will not permit the individual to exclude others from the group.

In any case, the distinction between these traditional people's response to Jesus and the church or Christianity as an institution is critical. They have largely screened out Christian language about Jesus and focused only on the mythic person. The second point concerning language about Jesus takes on importance, however, because so many Indian people have been missionized and continue as members of mainline denominations. One response to the problem of language, then, is to search for more culturally appropriate translations of metaphors. Thus, it has become axiomatic in third-world theological contexts to talk of contextualizing and inculturating theology. Likewise, culturally discrete interpretations of Jesus have become commonplace in world Christianity. In the interests of American Indian Christians, one might propose the development of an American Indian christology that would make Jesus more authentically accessible to Indian people. This process might begin by identifying existing Euro-Christian language that is unhelpful or even destructive. One example of the latter is the common Christian reference to Jesus as Lord.

Language and Lordship: Jesus as Conqueror

The scene was the 1990 World Council of Churches Consultation on Justice, Peace, and the Integrity of Creation in Seoul, South Korea. "Jesus Christ is Lord!" So read the huge banner above the dais, the last gasp of triumphalism at an anti-triumphalist event. The banner represents the bare-bones common confession of the great variety of communions who make up the World Council of Churches, the doctrinal glue that holds us all together. Yet as I sat in the assembly, the colonial oppressiveness of the proclamation began to weigh on me in ways I had never before considered. The cultural otherness of the language used in this common confession once again meant that American Indian peoples were being co-opted into a cultural frame of reference that necessitated self-denial and assimilation to the language and social structures of the conqueror. My reflections at that moment began a much deeper and longer-term reflection on issues of christology and conquest that resulted in a radical shift in my theological thinking and in the self-identity of the ministry project with which I have been affiliated for the past eleven years.

As foundational as this confession is for the World Council of Churches, it is the one scriptural metaphor used for the Christ event that is ultimately unacceptable and even hurtful to American Indian peoples. There was no analogue in North American indigenous societies for the relationship of power and disparity which is usually signified by the word *lord.* To the contrary, North American cultures and social structures were fundamentally marked by their egalitarian nature. Even a so-called chief had typically very limited authority, which even then depended much on the person's charismatic stature within the community and skill at achieving consensus. The American Indian experiential knowledge of lordship only begins with the conquest and colonization of our nations at the onslaught of the European invasion. What we know about lords and lordship, even today, has more to do with Washington, DC, the Bureau of Indian Affairs, and the modern tribal governments created by act of Congress. Unfortunately, by extension, even the church becomes a part of these new colonial relationships, with lords in the form of bishops and missionaries (both male and female) to whom we have learned as conquered peoples to pay lordly deference.

To call upon Jesus as Lord suddenly began to strike me as a classic example of the colonized participating in our own oppression. To call upon Jesus as Lord is to concede the colonial reality of new hierarchical social structures; it is to concede the conquest as final and to become complicit in our own death, that is, the ongoing genocidal death of our peoples.[3] It is an act of the colonized mind blindly reciting words that the colonizer has taught us which violate our own cultures but bring great comfort to the lordly colonizer and his missionaries.

Lordship and the Shaping of the Experience

It can be objected that the lordship metaphor for Christ is actually helpful for White, Amer-European Christians, because it puts many into a posture of humble surrender to another, a posture to which most are quite unaccustomed. Yet, I would argue that the metaphor does exactly the opposite and that it is ultimately not helpful for Christians any more than it is for American Indians. Rather, the metaphor seems to excuse White Amer-Europeans from any earthly humility or surrender, and often to facilitate a lack of consciousness with regard to the impropriety of relationships of exploitation. Since one has surrendered to an overwhelmingly powerful numinous Other, no other surrender or act of humility is called for within the human community. Indeed, many Christians seem to feed on a hierarchical view of the world that has historically privileged, and continues to privilege, White people on this continent and in other third-world colonial contexts. Thus, rather than being humbled in submission, they are empowered and emboldened—sometimes even explicitly empowered to impose their own brand of submission on others. Having submitted to the lordship of Jesus, there is no longer any earthly authority to which I must submit or pay homage. Indeed, humbled as vassal before Jesus, one becomes empowered as Jesus' champion in the world, a soldier for Christ. Unfortunately, this notion of White superiority and White privilege regularly serves White political and economic interests as well, defining those interests as somehow naturally concurrent with the interests of God.

Moreover, *Lord* is one of those biblical metaphors that seem to have lost all symbolic cognitive moorings in modern American society. The problem is that there are no *lords* in our society and no use of *lord* as a form of address that might conceivably give the metaphor content. Indeed, any use of the word in the United States today is an anachronistic metaphor requiring the hearer to summon up memories of historical uses of the word in English history and literature that predates the American Revolution, or it requires a cross-cultural understanding of the living anachronism in contemporary English society. Like the language of the *Kingdom of God*, these persistent metaphors from the first-century Mediterranean world require that modern North Americans must engage in enough of a linguistic-cultural history lesson to have some idea what the word might have meant in the past before they can appropriate any spiritual content from the proclamation of Jesus as Lord for the present.

Modern biblical exegesis is an ongoing attempt to recover meanings in the biblical texts from research in ancient biblical societies and languages. Thus exegesis would attempt to explicate the lordship metaphor in terms of the social and political arrangements that dictated the use of language in Palestine and the Greco-Roman world of the Christian gospels. This, however, does not solve the problem that the most accessible use of the word for Amer-Europeans (and undoubtedly for many of the rest of us because of our experience of colonialism in America) is not its use in the eastern Mediterranean world of Jesus' day, but rather its use in European cultures, which continues to some extent today—in places like England, for instance, which still maintains in Parliament a House of Lords. Yet the European use of the word, rooted as it is in the social structures of medieval feudalism, is in actuality a far cry from the Palestinian (Aramaic) use that would have been familiar to Mark or even the Hellenistic (Greco-Roman) use that would have been the experience of Luke.

What we are close to saying here is that to continue to use the metaphor in literal translation may be leading the faithful astray even in White, Amer-European churches, quite apart from the more complex issue of translating the culturally foreign term for American Indian hearers. Of course, it can be argued that it is the preacher's responsibility to interpret, to teach the correct meaning, to unpack the metaphor for the ecclesial community. Yet, it seems ludicrous to think that the only path to salvation is in a trans-cultural, ancient history lesson. Especially when one considers the needs of children in Amer-European churches, one must ask if it is fair to them to insist that they must come to understand something quite outside of their lived experience in order to engage the spiritual traditions of their families.

More to the point, what we are experiencing is a shift away from the useful, meaningful, experiential use of language to what can only be categorized as "religious language." And it can be further argued that religious language is, by definition and in actuality, language that has lost its meaning; that is, religious language has no currency of meaning in the day-to-day, real world use of language. Religious language is made up of old language usages that now continue to have meanings only insofar as they continue to function in that small slice of modern life reserved for religion.

NO OTHER NAME:
COLONIZER'S CLAIM TO UNIVERSAL TRUTH

Many would, of course, insist that the American Indian case for spiritual self-determination can and must be made on its own merits without recourse to discourse. While Indian peoples have a spiritual understanding of the world that is inherently amenable to some central Christian concepts, such as grace, we must understand Indian spiritual traditions in their own right and in their own uniqueness. They are not spiritual "puzzle pieces" that can be locked into a universal Christian truth but have their own meaning and vibrancy within each discrete Indian culture. On the other hand, for the sake of those Indian people who have made a lasting commitment to the colonizer's religious traditions and have converted to Christianity, it can be important to demonstrate the plausibility of Indian religious traditions on the basis of an interpretation of the colonizer's own texts. In this section I will interpret two of those texts with a different eye than most Amer-European or European biblical scholars would bring to the task. The first text is from the Acts of the Apostles 4:10-12:

> [9] . . . by what means has this man been healed?
>
> [10] Be it known to you all, and to all the people of Israel, that by the name of Jesus Christ of Nazareth, whom you crucified, whom God raised from the dead, by him this man is standing before you well.
>
> [11] This is the stone which was rejected by you builders, but which has become the head of the corner. [12] And there is salvation in no one else, for there is no other name under heaven given among human beings by which we must be saved.

"There is *no other name* under heaven given among human beings by which we must be *saved*" (Acts 4:12). The Rev. Harry Long, a legendary Muskogee Methodist pastor, a radical and troublemaker, asked me a couple of years ago if I would not give some attention to this particular text. I think Long had decided many years prior to our conversation to pay less attention to this text and lend his own affirmation to the revival of traditional native spirituality—both in our national (i.e., reservation or "tribal") communities and in the context of urban Indian communities. Yet, I think, the text continued to trouble him as an ordained Methodist minister, and he hoped that an Indian with some training in biblical studies might be able to clarify the text for Indian people in a new way.

For us, the question is indeed whether there is salvation in our traditional religious beliefs and ceremonies or whether the missionaries were right, that our old ways were mere devil worship that badly needed to be replaced by this Good News brought to us by the White missionaries, who all too often came with the colonizer army and paved the way for government treaty swindlers.

This is serious business. If the missionaries are right, then we Indian peoples have at least three problems. First of all, I can be saved now, because God sent us White people, but what about my Indian ancestors? They were directly accused of engaging in devil worship by the earliest European invaders of Indian lands, and, unfortunately, classical Christian doctrine holds out little hope for their rejoining any of us who have heard the Good News and have been converted to Jesus since then. According to the missionary gospel we have been taught, in heaven we will be separated from our ancestors and will live for eternity in a world ("new heaven and new earth") populated primarily by our conquerors and colonizers.

Second, and more immediately pressing, we will also be separated from many in our national communities (tribes) and many of our relatives because they have chosen not to convert from, or even to revert to, their old traditional belief systems. Discouraged by the dominance of White missionaries and the collusion of those missionaries with oppressive government and military subversions of our communities and our native economies, many of our relatives have decided that there is no good news in the Good News and have helped to fuel the revival. Thus, there is a distance placed between those who have become Christian and those who have as a matter of conscience decided that they cannot be Christian because Christianity represents the worst of the history of colonialism among Indian peoples in North America. The third problem has to do with many contemporary Indian clergy. While they genuinely want the healing of Indian peoples, they find themselves caught in a quandary between the claim of Christian exclusivity and the revival of traditional ceremonial life among our peoples.

Yet the biblical text at hand does not necessarily read as the missionaries have insisted. Is there salvation only in Jesus? This is the way we have been conditioned to read the story in Acts, but a closer reading makes interpretation much more complex. To begin with, the use of the noun *salvation* and the verb *saved* must be read in the context of the story itself and not merely read as if the author had the usual English language meanings in mind in verse 12. The story actually begins a chapter earlier in chapter 3 when Peter and John heal a lame man at the entrance of the Jerusalem Temple. They are taken to court because they have healed him on the sabbath, the traditional day of rest for Jewish peoples, on which no work was to be performed by divine law. Proceeding carefully, the lawyers wished to know, "By what means has this man been healed?" (Acts 4:9).

The use of the verb for healing is important. Indeed, it is the same verb that is translated as *saved* in verse 12. This verb carries a range of meanings that include medical healing and spiritual salvation. The question is, how have English translators moved from one meaning of the word to another in two verses with no explanation? The related nouns likewise carry a range of meanings, including savior and healer, salvation and healing. Before we offer another translation of the text, it is important to ask how the word was first used in the story. It would seem reasonable to think that the author would have used the words in the immediate context in not terribly disparate ways.

To understand these related words in their Greek cultural context requires a reading of several hundred years of Greek literature. Already, some six hundred years before Acts was written, the Greek poet

Pindar called Asclepios, the Greek god of healing, "the savior of his people." He was clearly a savior because he visited patients in his temples at night and brought to them miraculous, overnight healings of a great variety of physical maladies. There was as yet in Greek consciousness little attention to any notion that might be similar to the modern Christian notion of salvation. So *savior* clearly meant *healer.* Likewise, it is well-known that the word *salvation* originally referred to physical healing of an illness, and that the verb *save* referred to the action of *healing.* Luke clearly uses this meaning of the verb in the early part of this story. While Peter says to the man, "In the name of Jesus Christ of Nazareth, rise up and walk" (3:6), five verses later Luke describes the man as "the lame man who was healed" (3:11). That is to say, the lame man was saved not for eternal life, but from his lame leg. Surely, we cannot discount the possibility that there was also a spiritual saving that happened, but that is not a part of this story. In this context the verb means physical healing.

When the priests and lawyers ask Peter and John, "By what power or by what name have you done this?" (4:7), they are asking about the physical healing. Peter's response is equally clear. The physical healing (saving) of the lame man was done by "the name of Jesus Christ of Nazareth" (4:10): "By him is this man standing before you well." This seems clearly to imply a spiritual power for physical healing (saving) that can be summoned by using the name of Jesus. And here I say the name of Jesus because the rest of the identifying label is not name but title ("Christ") and geographical locator ("of Nazareth").

Hence, when we finally get to the key verse (4:12), there is little reason to shift the meaning of the words in a wholesale fashion. Peter must be saying, "There is *healing* [not salvation] in no one else, for there is no other name under heaven given among human beings by which we must be *healed* [not saved]." While this use of language can certainly carry a double meaning, it is important to understand that this whole story is about a healing–the miraculous, physical healing of a lame man. To change the story to meet our own needs for salvation language does an injustice to the author and to the meaning of the story.

We are still left, however, with Rev. Long's original question. What can the text mean when it says there is no other name by which healing can take place? At the surface level, this claim seems ludicrous if not patently false. Even in Peter's day there were trained (however poorly by modern standards) physicians who effected healing and gave healing care to the sick. There are numerous stories from the time of Jesus that attest to the miraculous healing work of other charismatic healers in Palestine. In our American Indian communities we have considerable experience with healing styles that use spiritual medicine and ceremony. What are we to say? That these healings did not occur?

I want to suggest that this verse, typically used by Amer-European missionaries to coerce our conversion to Christianity, has been consistently misread and misinterpreted in the missionary claims of Christian exclusivity and superiority. Commentators consistently miss the most obvious point of the story; namely, that the reader is supposed to know a bit more about the name of Jesus and to draw out the meaning of the story from the meaning of the name. Like many of the particularities of ancient Palestinian culture, this is not foreign to Indian hearers of the story, since we come from cultures where names still have meaning. In the world, however, names have largely ceased to carry any real meaning beyond euphony or family sentimentality. What do the names George, Betty, Bob, Kathy, Bill, Ted, and so on, actually mean? Eagle Elk, Red Eagle, Bacon Rind, Earth Walker, Crazy Horse: those names can be explained. They have meaning and are carefully given to the bearers because of their meanings.

I want to ask, then, can the meaning of the name Jesus help us to understand why Peter would insist that healing can only happen by means of this name? Few modern Christians remember that Jesus was a very common name in Palestine two millennia ago. Some will remember that it was actually a shortened form of the Hebrew Bible name of Moses' successor, Joshua. This Hebrew name was a combination of two elements, a noun and a verb, *ja* and *shua*. The first part of the name occurs also in the name Jonathan (*ja - nathan*), which is actually a similar name to Nathaniel (*nathan - el*). These last two names have a counterpart in two Greek names, one male and one female: Theodore and Dorothy, both combinations of the words for God (*theos*) and gift (*dor*). In Hebrew, *nathan* means gift, while *ja* and *el* are variant names for God, shortened forms of *yahweh* and *elohim*. All mean "gift of God." The name Jesus or Joshua includes this shortened form of *yahweh*. The verb or action part of the name (*shua*) translates "saves" or "heals." Thus the name Jesus means "God Heals (or Saves)." Here we have the meaning of the text clearly stated.

The focus, suddenly, is not on Jesus at all but on God! Jesus is not identified here as the only source of salvation or as the only savior. Rather, God is identified as the only ultimate source of healing. God is the Healer. This much every Indian person can readily acknowledge. So it has always been in our ceremonies and among our healing specialists since time immemorial. The power to heal always comes from the spiritual energy of *Wakonda*, even when particular individuals have been identified as the vehicles through whom certain kinds of healing or help can be facilitated.

Yet the missionaries have used this story to proclaim to us a self-serving untruth, that God has spoken only to them and communicated only through Jesus. And under the immense pressure of colonization and conquest, many of our ancestors felt they were left with little choice but to accede to the self-proclaimed superiority of the White invaders of our land, to convert to their religious belief, and to acknowledge the superiority of their God. The nature of colonization is such that it entices the strong to take advantage of the weak in all aspects of life: social, political and economic. Such domination in the sphere of religion serves as an essential reinforcement for these other modes of domination. And so the missionaries, whose minds were every bit as much colonized as ours, saw Indian vulnerability and used that vulnerability to advance their own cause quickly and decisively.

Perhaps now that the land is in their possession (or at least under their political control) the churches will leave Indian people alone to find our own way spiritually. Indeed there are signs that the mainline denominations intend to abandon Indian peoples and the churches they have created in our communities. Funds have been regularly cut back from reservation churches, and the growing urban Indian population, fostered by ill-intended government policies of forced assimilation, has been regularly ignored by the same churches that rushed into the missionary enterprise on the ever-expanding frontiers of Manifest Destiny a century ago. Unfortunately, the signs are not entirely positive. As the mainline denominations pull back from us, the even more doctrinally rigid pentecostal and right-wing evangelical groups have moved in like vultures to clean up the remaining scraps on the garbage heap of Indian colonized vulnerability.

We are not yet done, however, with the colonizer's texts. We must look at one other passage before we conclude. The beginning of the Gospel of John (1:1-4) is a wonderful, poetic statement that identifies the spiritual power that John associates with Jesus. That power he calls Logos.

CHRIST, LOGOS, PRE-EXISTENCE, AND CORN MOTHER

In the beginning was the Logos; and the Logos was with God; and the Logos was [a] God [or "divine"]. This one [It] was in the beginning with God. All things came into being through It, and nothing happened without It. What came into being through It was life; and life was the light of humanity [human beings]. And the light shines in the darkness, and the darkness cannot overcome it.

As American Indian readers of this important colonizer sacred text, we must first come to terms with the gender of this Logos concept in John 1. It is clear from John's telling of the story that he intends us to understand a personification of the Logos, but it is certainly not clear at all that he intends us to understand it as a male personification that should thereafter be referred to as "he," which is how English translations regularly translate the pronouns of verses two to four. The initial problem for English-speaking interpreters is that the Greek noun *Logos* does carry an assigned grammatical gender that is masculine. English speaking interpreters have regularly made the mistake of assuming that grammatical gender is necessarily a real indication of the gender of the object or person to which the noun refers. This is not, however, how human languages usually function, as any speaker of an Indian language knows already. In German, for instance, young men and young women are often referred to with a noun whose grammatical gender is neuter (*das Mädchen; das Herrlein*), yet no one would suggest that these people actually are genderless. Likewise, French can shift in its reference to God from *le dieu* (masculine) to *la divinité* (feminine) without substantially affecting the actual gender of God. Yet even the French pronouns will automatically shift to match the grammatical gender of the noun, so that after *le dieu,* God will be referred to as *il* (literally, "he") and after *la divinité,* the reference to God will change to *elle* (literally, "she"). The point is that we must carefully guard against ascribing gender to a person or object on the basis of the grammatical gender of the noun (or even pronoun) used to refer to that person or object.

Thus, I have chosen to play it safe and refer to the Logos as *It* with a capital initial letter to indicate Its divine status in John's mythic construct. This does not mean that I believe God to be a gender neuter any more than I believe God to be exclusively masculine. Rather, I know God to be both male and female, because my ancestors have always called on God as Grandfather and Grandmother together, as *Wakonda Monshita* and *Wakonda Udseta,* the Sacred Above and the Sacred Below. Philip Deere, the famous Muscogee medicine man, was fond of making the point that God, or the Sacred Other, is ultimately the Unknowable and, as such, has no gender until It makes Itself known. And in many of our American Indian cultural traditions, God, the Unknowable, makes Itself known in a reciprocal duality that is both male and female. Hence, I argue that to follow the missionaries by simply always ascribing maleness to God would be wrong and that to ascribe maleness to the Logos would be to fall into that trap. There is no compelling reason to interpret the Logos as male. Biblical interpreters have even entertained the possibility that the Logos is a metaphor for the Old Testament personification of Sophia or Wisdom as a female aspect of divinity.

Of course, the Logos does become manifest to humans as a male entity a few verses later when, implicitly, the Logos becomes incarnate and is identified as Jesus. This introduces a second and most interesting problematic in our interpretation. Namely, how are we, precisely and accurately, to make the identification between Jesus and the Logos or between Jesus and the Christ, ultimately, since John seems to clearly infer a philosophical or theological identification between Christ and Logos? While this topic has been explored with considerable finesse by biblical scholars over the past century, it has a particularly promising potential for American Indian Christians in their discrete interpretation of the gospel. This potential begins with an understanding not of the identity between Jesus and the Logos in John's introductory paragraph, but rather with a clear distinction between the two that must help to define the ensuing connection.

While most American Christians, especially more conservative ones, live with a simple notion of a one-to-one equivalency of the names Jesus and Christ, a majority of theologians and biblical scholars have, especially since Rudolf Bultmann, distinguished the two both as names and as concepts. Bultmann, for example, introduced the distinction between the "historical Jesus" and the "historic Christ." He found the historical Jesus to be very elusive and unrecoverable, arguing that the documents (primarily the gospels) were not written as or intended to be read as history. Rather, they were always intended to be generative of faith in Jesus as the Christ. Hence, they were written not to convey historically accurate information, but the story and each part of it were told in ways to enhance the faith of the believer and to teach the continuing importance of Jesus as the Christ of God. Thus, Jesus becomes the human vehicle for experiencing and for communicating the more mythic, spiritual, theological, and enduring function of the Christ of God.

To apply this understanding to the Logos hymn at the beginning of the Gospel of John means that we must begin to distinguish Jesus and the Christ of God in one very decisive way. Namely, it is clear from John 1:1-4 that the Logos–the Christ of God–is a pre-existent part of God. Jesus is not pre-existent in this same way. Rather, Jesus is a human being who has a birth, a beginning in time, and whose birth is identified by early Christians as a particular incarnation or manifestation of the Christ or the Logos. While Christians can claim that Jesus became the incarnation of the Christ, it would violate nearly two thousand years of European Christian history to claim that Jesus was pre-existent in the same way that the Logos is presented here as pre-existing all things and participating with God even in the creation of all things. This should already signal that the two terms, *Jesus* and *Christ*, have different meanings and functions in the biblical texts, that they are not just two names for Jesus like modern American first and last names.

Up to this point the text at hand has described the Logos as having had two functions only. It was a part of creation, and some millennia later It returned to action in Its incarnation in Jesus. Yet this seems terribly limiting of God on the part of human interpreters. Why would this Logos, which was so instrumental in the creation act, have lain dormant for so much of human history? Surely there must be another way of interpreting this text.

The first question we must raise, of course, is the functional one. What is it this Logos does? How does it function as a part of God? From the little bit that we have in the Gospel of John, it seems that the Logos is some aspect of God, perhaps the creative aspect of God's self, perhaps the creative, communicative aspect of God's self as God communicates with human beings. If this is plausible, then it is unlikely that we could defend any period of inactivity or dormancy. Rather, it would seem that John merely does not mention other occurrences where the Logos or Christ was functioning in the world. Indeed, nowhere does John claim that this is the only action of the Logos since creation. Jesus, it seems, is merely one, albeit very powerful, occurrence of the Logos in human history.

This, suddenly, is a notion of Christ that Indian people can begin to understand naturally within their own cultural experiences and knowledge, without having imposed upon us or inculcated in us new categories of knowledge that come from the colonizer's culture and history. If the Logos or the Christ is merely that aspect of God that communicates creativity and healing or salvation to human beings, then we can even add to Christianity's knowledge of salvation from our own experiences and memories of God's functioning among Indian communities throughout our history.

In this sense we can claim to have a history of many such experiences of the Christ and can even begin to name some of them and tell the stories that go with the naming. But this also means that we can never be trapped into saying that God has only spoken this Good News through Jesus, or that the only way to salvation is through a European or Amer-European message brought by the colonizer to the conquered.

In the final section I want to suggest the comparison between the mythic truths inherent in the gospel stories of Jesus and one of our American Indian traditional foundation stories.

CORN MOTHER AS CHRIST

Because of our experience of ultimate reality as a bi-gender duality, any Indian equivalent for the Euro-Christian notion of the Christ would include examples that are explicitly female. Thus, the revered mythic and historic figures of Corn Mother and White Buffalo Calf Woman, examples from two different Indian cultural traditions, would perhaps come close to functioning in ways that could be conceived of as christological. As narrative oral texts they certainly approximate the earliest Asian narratives about Jesus, and, as in Christianity, each of these figures continues to be significantly involved in the day-to-day well-being of the communities that tell these stories. Each recounts a salvific moment in the community's past yet continues to function to bring some element of "salvation" and wholeness to the people who honor the story today. This essay will focus on the Corn Mother narratives.

The story of Corn Mother is told in variant versions among Indian communities of different language families from the east coast of Canada throughout eastern North America to Florida and across the southern United States as far west as the Keresan Pueblos in New Mexico. The story is a part of the foundational mythic life of these different peoples, not only as an aetiology for corn, but for the sacredness of life and the sacredness of food. The story involves the willing self-sacrifice (vicarious suffering) of the First Mother (Corn Mother) on behalf of her children. While initially First Man was the hunter and alone provided for the sustenance of his family, as the family grew ever larger it became important to introduce new sources of vegetable foods. The details of the story work themselves out quite differently in different communities, with some variety in teaching emphases, but the central mythic themes are intact in all the tellings of the story.

In the Penobscot telling, the death of First Mother is actually requested by the woman herself, against the wishes of her husband, and only completed after he himself makes a long journey and consults with the Creator. In a variety of other tellings the woman is murdered by her own children, although in each of these tellings she nevertheless willingly agrees to the killing and even invites it. In some of these stories Corn Mother provides food in the absence of game by privately scraping or shaking the corn (and sometimes beans) off her own body. When two of her children sneakily discover where the food is coming from, they accuse her of tricking them into cannibalism, and this becomes the excuse for the murder. In a Natchez version two daughters accuse their mother of feeding them defecation and proceed to kill her. In another set of tellings the murder of the woman happens as a result of the foolishness of a powerful, mythic boy child called Blood Clot Boy, who entices the participation of his sibling. But in all these tellings the self-sacrifice of the woman is emphatically consistent and results in the enduring fecundity of the earth and production of vegetable foods.

In these stories First Mother's death is also the first human experience of death. Her burial is accompanied by ceremony and sometimes pronounced weeping. In a fairly typical telling the surviving family discovers that the clearing where she has been buried is miraculously filled with fully mature food plants, most prominently including corn. That is, First Mother, who is buried in the earth, becomes productive in ways that were unexpected and continues to nourish her children long after her death.

Common Theological Themes

There are a number of common theological themes in these stories. The first and perhaps most important is that food must henceforth be considered sacred. Eating becomes what Euro-Christian theology would signify as sacrament, because eating always involves the eating of the flesh of First Mother. She, in her dying, becomes identified with the earth, with Grandmother. In one telling of the story tobacco is provided by Corn Mother in the middle of the vegetative cornucopia that grew in what had been a clearing in the forest the day before. Her voice is heard as her children approach it, announcing the import of their discovery of this surfeit of food and adding that the tobacco is to be used as a part of their prayers. It is the breath of the Mother and is to add power to their prayers as the smoke is carried up to the sky.

There is more to this story than is conveyed in the simple telling of it. Out of this story emerges a considerable theology that includes the important teaching that all life—including that life considered un-alive by Euro-science, rocks, rivers, lakes, mountains, and the like—is interrelated. When one fully understands this teaching—a simple sounding notion that requires years (if not generations) of learning—one finally understands the sacramental nature of eating. Corn and all food stuffs are our relatives, just as much as those who live in adjacent lodges within our clan-cluster. Thus, eating is sacramental, to use a Euro-theological word, because we are eating our relatives. Not only are we related to corn, beans, and squash, since these things emerge immediately out of the death of Corn Mother, but even those other relatives like Buffalo, Deer, Squirrel, and Fish ultimately gain their strength and growth because they too eat of the plenty provided by the Mother—eating grasses, leaves, nuts, and algae that also grow out of the Mother's bosom. More than that, when we eat, we understand that we are benefiting from the lives that have gone before us, that all our human ancestors have also returned to the earth and have become part of what nourishes us today. Thus, one can never eat without remembering the gift of the Mother, of all our relatives in this world, and of all those who have gone before us. Indian people are not cannibals. Indeed, the idea is so abhorrent, even at the mythic level, that the Seminole version of the story has the two boys deeply offended to the point of murdering their mother because they fear that she has forced cannibalistic practice on them in the eating of foodstuffs from her own body.

Another key theological theme and a continuing cultural value among Indian peoples of different tribal backgrounds is the concept of vicarious self-sacrifice. In all these stories Corn Mother sacrifices herself willingly for the sake of her children. And so it is that individuals in our communities have lived with the notion of both ceremonial and very real physical sacrifice for the people. Ceremonially, this is lived out in our communities in rites like the Rite of Vigil (vision quest), the Sun Dance, and even the Rite of Purification (sweat lodge).

The first experience of death by the people in the death of Corn Mother teaches also the truth of the old saying attributed to Seattle: "There is no death; only a change of worlds." More important, in terms of our day-to-day existence in Indian communities throughout North America, we understand that our ancestors continue to live in very real ways. This happens in two important ways. First of all, they continue to live in a spirit world where we hope to join them at the end of our life here. But just as important, these ancestors continue to live in us, both in our memories and in our physical lives as we continue to eat the produce of the earth to which they have returned in one way or another.

Finally, these stories contain some ethical/theological content, as well, focused especially toward our young men. In those variants of the story in which Corn Mother is killed by male offspring, there is an implicit warning to men about the potential for male violence in society. Men are to pay attention to the results of immature male decision-making, especially when it leaves women out of the decision-making process. We are particularly to be attentive to the potential for inherent male strength to explode in foolish, unpredictable, and irreparable ways against the females in our midst. Moreover, we are to pay attention to the inherent valuing of female gifts and wisdom in our communities. We are to remember forever that healing in the form of both food and spiritual sustenance has come to us traditionally not through men but through a woman, whether it is White Buffalo Calf Woman or Corn Mother. This wisdom is a constant temperance of male dominance, aggression, and assertiveness in our communities.

CONCLUSION

The story of Corn Mother is one example of the power and cosmic balancing of American Indian mythic traditions. Eventually, the healing power of it and stories like it and the ceremonial ways that they undergirded caused a more interesting and persistent rephrasing of my brother's initial question. Why should Indian people be coerced to give up God's unique self-disclosure to us? Why ought Indian people learn to identify after the fact with God's self-disclosure to some other people in a different place and time in a mythic tradition that is culturally strange and alienating? To many in our contemporary American Indian community the answer to these questions is obvious. Our traditions, they will argue, are ancient and precious and are to be revered and lived. To the modern Indian traditionalist, there is little need to pay any heed to the colonizer's churches or doctrines.

On the other hand, many who have been converted to those churches may also find these ancient traditions to be precious. Indian Christians will want to struggle in the coming generation to understand their Christian commitments increasingly on their own terms in ways that incorporate their own cultural traditions of the sacred. The Christian Indian interpretation of Jesus as the Christ will eventually differ considerably from the interpretation offered in the colonizer churches and hierarchies. This process of nativizing Indian Christianity began with the first Indian ministers in the seventeenth century and continues in the bold and energetic work of modern Indian ministers like Harry Long.

In terms of an emergent communal vision of healing for a people that has been long abused and marginalized by the colonial relationships in North America, it seems that more and more Indian people are making the former choice. They are insisting that the relationship between Indian peoples and the churches is so fractured as to be irreconcilable from the vantage point of American Indian liberation. The spiritual hope today for Indian nations, they argue, is to recover their historical and traditional ceremonial forms. A great many Indian families have been evangelized into the churches, of course, and the churches will continue to be some force in every Indian community. Yet, those congregations and missions have long ceased to grow and are rather in decline these days. The younger members of churched families have tended to be among those who have made the transition back to traditional ceremonies and religious traditions.

In any case, it would seem that the colonizer churches themselves will necessarily have to rethink their notion of Christian exclusivity and make room for American Indian religious traditions as being potentially as powerful and salvific as the best vision well-intentioned peoples have for Christianity. I hope that my interpretation of two important texts will make it possible to understand the notion of Christ with much greater inclusivity and parity of power between colonizer and colonized. Likewise, it should be possible today for a mutual respect to emerge that will allow Christians to acknowledge the inherent spiritual power and goodness of American Indian religious traditions. My brother came to the end of his life having forsaken his early Christian connection in favor of a more traditional religious life. Yet he maintained a respect for the churches and never hesitated to dialogue with the colonizer in the hope of healing, not only for Indian people, but for the colonizer people of North America as well.

Notes

[1] This ceremony is persistently and wrongly signified in anthropological and religious literature as quintessential evidence for the radical individualism of plains Indian societies.

² For White, Amer-European Christians there is a curious aspect. Whether an Indian participant in Eucharist is Christian or not, they came to Living Waters' communion with a belief (even faith) in the presence of Jesus in the sacrament. I would even go so far as to say that there was a stronger or more lively sense of the "real presence" of Jesus in the sacrament than there is in most suburban Lutheran congregations.

³ For a description of missionary participation in injustices committed against Indian peoples, see George Tinker, *Missionary Conquest: The Gospel and Native American Cultural Genocide* (Minneapolis: Fortress Press, 1993).

13.

From Medicine Man to Marx

The Coming Shift in Native Theology

RT. REV. STEVEN CHARLESTON

Gramsci showed that socialism was freedom, absolute freedom against every dogma, every revealed truth, and every preconceived schema. . . . Marxism, Gramsci stated, shows how every theory is derived from a particular social and economic situation. But if this statement is true, we must also apply the same yardstick to Marxism itself and believe that not even it will be the "last" theory. . . . Indeed, one can extend this so far as to believe that in a communist of the future, Marxism might vanish and leave the field to religious or idealistic conceptions which will find in that very world and society their liberation and their real freedom.

Alberto Pozzolini, *Antonio Gramsci*[1]

This chapter has a very simple premise. I believe that in the next generation of Native Christian theology we will experience a significant shift from spirituality to economics. The reasons for this shift are already in process, but fundamentally they arise from the context of colonization, particularly the context of Native People[2] as a small indigenous community resident in one of the declining centers of capitalist hegemony. As new economic realities force the hand of both rich and poor in the century to come, Native leaders, Christian and Traditional, will have to take a stand: either for the status quo of colonialism, or for a reform of church and society that will introduce a radically different model of relationships into the future. To meet this challenge, Native theology needs a new sense of balance in how it speaks. It needs a new vocabulary, a new code of ideas and words, to communicate its vision around the world. To develop this language will require a commitment to the truth that intentionally opposes the assumptions of consumerism. It will demand a level of response that will shake Native America out of its marginal role in capitalist culture and into prominence as a leading force in the Second Reformation: the watershed event of the next century that will change the nature of Christianity for the next one thousand years.

THE QUESTION OF CONTEXT

In his latest work on the nature of religious community, *Who Are the People of God?: Early Christian Models of Community,* Howard Clark Kee offers a concise summary of the importance of context in the development and articulation of any cultural/historical theological worldview. While Dr. Kee is concerned with tracing the development of community models in the early centuries of Jewish-Christian contact, I am persuaded that his use of the analytical tools of contemporary social sciences are equally applicable to more modern sociocultural situations— in this case, the situation of Native People as we enter the final historical stages of American culture from an industrial to an information/service corporate state. Consequently, it is helpful to quote Kee's approach at some length:

> In the latter decades of the twentieth century, developments in the social sciences and philosophy have had implications that call for reappraisal and reconstitution of the tasks of historical, literary, and theological analysis of human culture, including the biblical world. Certain sociologists, in addition to assessing concrete social phenomena and trends in the social structures of human life, have given attention to the social nature of linguistic communication and even of knowledge itself. This has given rise to the concept and procedures of what is called sociology of knowledge. Concurrent with this epistemological development has been the recognition among philosophers as well as sociologists that historical inquiry must take into account as fully as possible, not merely so-called facts as isolated phenomena, but the symbol systems in terms of which life is lived in any culture and which provide meaning and value for the members of the society under investigation.[3]

The "society under investigation" in this instance is the contemporary Native society of North America. Looking from the inside out, I would focus on those "facts" of our theological life that have become the symbol systems we use in our own internal sociology of knowledge as Native People and which we broadcast from our culture to articulate our worldview to others. Like Howard Clark Kee, I believe the time has come for a "reappraisal and reconstitution" of that reality in light of major changes that are already in process and that are most likely to continue occurring well into the next century.

To underscore the value of examining our theology as an expression of linguistic symbol systems, I begin by suggesting that the fundamental context of any Native People's theological discourse is the context of colonialism. We are a colonized people. This basic fact itself has profound implications for all that we say and do in constructing intellectual systems for ourselves and in communicating those paradigms to a larger ethnic audience.

In essence, we have been a culture which has had one symbol system, one entire cultural construct, overlaid and replaced by another. The process of colonization is more than the exchange of economic, social, and political power from a militarily weaker community to a stronger; it is also the exchange of the intellectual and spiritual worldview of one people for that of another. This violent stripping away of cultural norms and the forced mutation into new paradigms is the formative social experience of the colonized. It has shaped our intellectual language as Native People in subtle and subversive ways.

Consider Kee's analysis of the act of translating from one set of symbol systems to another:

> These features of the socially constructed understanding of the world do not determine in any absolute sense what one thinks or does, but they do predict how one is likely to respond to the world. Those who decide voluntarily to adopt another "knowledge" must learn and appropriate it. Members of the out-group, however, do not regard the articles of faith and the historical tradition of the in-group as self-evident, since their own central myths, as well as their process of rationalization and institutionalization are different. Lacking a translation code or refusing to use one, they consider another group's natural attitude—even when it in many ways overlaps with their own—as perverse and hostile. The members of one group may try to educate or convert the benighted, or declare war on them.[4]

In microcosm, this statement summarizes the Native experience, both historical and contemporary, in this sense: Native People were colonized by a foreign culture whose values and worldview could not be easily accepted as self-evident because they contradicted the mass of the ancient symbol system developed by Native civilization over centuries of social development. The dominant culture, Western European culture, tried to both "educate and convert" Native People into its own process of rationalization. Its members sought to force or entice Native

People into learning and appropriating this alien construct, and when those strategies failed, they declared war on Native communities and attempted to exterminate them. This is the historical fact of European colonization in North America. However, the process described above continues. While it may not occur on the battlefields or in the boarding schools, it certainly continues in the social, political, economic, and intellectual exchange between Native and European peoples.

My central concern is with this ongoing process as it continues to affect the Native People of North America, particularly in their expression of religious/spiritual values. My argument is that while Native People have maintained a posture of resistance against assimilation into the "knowledge" of Western colonialism, they have done so only to a certain degree. That is, as a People, we have responded with the use of certain symbol systems and the values they embody, but we have not yet used our full vocabulary as a culture. We have been speaking of our Tradition, but only in its most esoteric form; while this has been a noble effort and one that should be advanced in the years to come, it is time to extend that effort to a wider range of Traditional Native cultural values that speak even more authoritatively to the contemporary and future situation of our People on a global scale.

THE LANGUAGE OF SPIRITUALITY

Building on our understanding of the context in which we live as a colonized community, we can ask this simple question of ourselves as Native theologians: If Kee is right and the "facts" that we communicate are indicative of our deeper sociology of knowledge, then what are some of the "facts" under which we presently operate as a sub-society in contemporary North America?

The limits of space in this chapter don't allow us to give a very detailed answer, but I do think we can sketch a fairly accurate sociological portrait of Native theological reality at the end of this century by reference to a single symbol system (almost to a single word) which has come to epitomize Native tradition, thought, and culture. We can say that the rough parameters of that reality are the boundaries we have established for ourselves through the use of the linguistic symbol system called *Native spirituality*.

The words we use as Native People when we speak theology are the words of *spirituality*. They are words that speak in the poetic cadence of mysticism. We have created a symbolic language using evocative images, such as Mother Earth. We have identified ourselves as spokespersons for an indigenous, traditional spirituality that emerges from the ancient matrix of our tribal past. This identity allows us an internal connection with our own history (which is the sociological as well as the theological ground for our identity as a sub-culture within the context of American society) and it has given us a persuasive presence in communicating our symbols (the metaphorical "facts" of our culture) to a larger audience. The construct we have come to call Native spirituality has been the *translation code* we have used in defining ourselves through the use of our unique set of history, myth, and philosophy, and it has become the operative medium of theological exchange as we seek to translate those cultural realities into the foreign language of Western mindsets.

In other words, our context has worked well for us over the last years since the Civil Rights movement brought us into prominence once again in the popular consciousness of postmodern (but, as I will suggest, pre-colonial) America. We have used our own past effectively to reconstitute ourselves (to touch on Kee's analysis) as a visible minority presence in American society and to articulate those facts about ourselves that we believe serve us best in relation to others.

Our success can be measured in some ways by our own struggles to control these facts from being completely co-opted by others. As we come to the close of this century, we have once again become popular icons in the self-generated mysticism of Western civilization. Scores of suburban dwellers are attached to the shamanism they believe is Native; groups of non-Native people gather regularly to "drum" and to call on their "spirit-helpers"; putative Native spiritual leaders appear at retreats and workshops guiding others through rituals and ceremonies designed to link them with the Native spiritual past; Native images and words are constant touchstones for the global ecological movement; various flavors of Native spiritualities have become staples in the New Age cafeteria of religions and sects; the proliferation of popular books, tapes, and videos "by or about" Native spirituality has been steady and profitable for major publishers as well as the many small presses and distributors who cater to the exotic market of American religious interest; we have even witnessed a minor surge in Native spiritual-centered motion pictures that have gained wide audiences in mainstream, adult America (for example, "Dances with Wolves") and in young America (for example, "Pocahontas").

All of these indicators demonstrate the increased awareness of Native spirituality over the last thirty-something years. At their best they are genuine examples of how the realities of Native tradition have entered the cultural vocabulary of North America. For this we can be truly grateful and proud. But at their worst they are painful examples of what Michael Harrington, perhaps the last great figure of his generation of American socialists, called "the chic primitivism of a bored affluence."[5]

The context for our theologizing, therefore, has worked fairly well over these many years, but it has given us some mixed results. Now, as we look ahead to the next generation of Native leadership, we must give these results the reappraisal they so obviously demand as we strive to reconstitute ourselves in alignment with the major shift already in process in the dominant American culture.

DANCES WITH ELEPHANTS: THE NATIVE DILEMMA

The latest census figures for Native America show that we are roughly 1 percent of the population of the United States and 2 percent of Canadian culture. In other words, we are sociological mice living among the ethnic elephants of North America. In simple terms of size, we are a small community in our own homeland, far smaller proportionally than most other global indigenous peoples. It may be sobering to realize that as a tiny sub-group of the United States, we have more in common with the Ainu of Japan than we do with the Inca of Peru. Consequently, our context is more than just an analysis of our impact through our self-identification with Native spirituality or our ability to translate these images into the consciousness of other populations. It is also a basic factor of the sociological consequences of being a minuscule minority in a rapidly shifting majority: the mouse may capture the attention of the elephant far beyond its relative size, but when the elephant begins to move the mouse had better be ready to move, too.

Our dilemma is in anticipating that move.

While I do not pretend to be an expert in the field of the social sciences, I believe there are clear indicators that Western-style colonialism will reappear in the next century far beyond the limits it has already manifested in communities of poverty around the world. The phenomenon of economic exploitation by a few nation-states over against the mass of humanity has been masked over the last many years by a Cold War psychology that saw any critique of capitalism as a communist plot. Consequently, the discussion of contemporary colonialism occurred largely through the channels of liberation theology, particularly in its Latin American and African-American variations. However, while Native People offered a creational spirituality, our own voice in analyzing the economic realities of the poor in this hemisphere remained fairly quiet. We spoke eloquently of Mother Earth, but without consistency when the dialogue shifted to a theological critique of class structure, economic theory, and global exploitation. Liberation theologians from many communities have spoken powerfully on these central issues of concern to the world's poor. Our own contribution to this dialogue has been important but one dimensional. Now, I believe, Native People need to speak with a new voice. We need to speak up against the worldview that swept over our People and left us impoverished as a free nation. More than this, we need to join our voices with those of all communities who cry out for justice and mercy in the cold silence of technological consumerism.

What we once considered only Western European colonialism has become international technological consumerism. We are continuing to evolve into a global culture of consumers, a new elite of the international class of wealth and privilege, over against those millions of others who support this habit through their own poverty and hard labor. The export of the capitalist economic paradigm has reached almost universal levels. With the collapse of other European-based theoretical alternatives (such as socialism in its many forms, but especially the deviant socialism of Soviet Russia and Eastern Europe), the field has been left to the exponents of capitalist exploitation economic theory without an effective challenge, even from the ranks of liberation theology. In short, critics of capitalism are in disarray and struggling for a new language to use in rallying humanity to some standard against continuing ecological ruin and economic exploitation. The struggle is now much more than a single-front war. The forces of corporate oligarchy, which see the planet largely as their competitive chess board for global control and profit, are centered not only in Europe and the United States but in Japan, Korea, Taiwan, and Singapore as well. Multinationalism is capitalism evolving into a hydra which clearly outdistances the old arguments of classical Marxism, grounded as it was in the nineteenth-century European experience. The rules have changed. The realities have shifted. But the demands for some effective response are more urgent than ever.

A few of the bell-wether signs for Native People in North America should be apparent to cultures who already have an experience with exploitation; for example, it has become axiomatic to speak of the diminished role of a democratic electorate in the United States, just as it has become common to refer to the "special interests" and "lobbies" of major corporations as the power behind the throne of Western states. The demarcation line between the poor and the affluent in North America and Europe can be measured by the graphs of a decline in public assistance and affirmative action, just as there is a corresponding rise in statistics of social dislocation and crime. The quick-draw use of American military power in interventionist policies is standard. The confidence of the people in almost all branches of government falls just as the demands for law and order increase. Finally, the basic mathematics of global debt and national deficit predict a radical financial default as certainly as if they were the tectonic plates beneath the superstructure of global capitalism.

While these opinions might have seemed radical even twenty years ago, today they are the common discussion on C-SPAN and CNN. These are not apocalyptic visions of some imaginary future but only garden variety data that anyone can pick up and analyze. What do they tell us?

I am not a politician or a prophet. I am speaking here only of the fundamental context to which Native theologians are going to have to respond in the next generation. My thesis is that this context will cease to be the relatively benign atmosphere we have known in the last years of this century; if things continue to emerge along the channels already charted by simple economic policies among international capitalist nations, and if the present rates of consumption within those nations also continue as they have at current levels, then the bottom line for the poor of the world will be reached by the middle of the next century. This is not a difficult equation to factor. It is, sadly, common sense and simple experience.

LISTENING FOR THE SHOE TO DROP

In March 1996, *Smithsonian Magazine* ran a feature article entitled "How to Succeed in Business: Follow the Choctaw's Lead."[6] While this glowing picture of one Native tribe's economic recovery may have been only mildly informative and encouraging to most readers, it was deeply interesting to me personally. I am a Choctaw. And while I could feel the warmth of the glow coming from the pages of the article about how members of my tribe were benefiting from the mini-miracle of economic development on a few reservations, I could not prevent myself from wondering what I was reading between the lines.

Consider the sampler of statistics offered in the article of only a few resources left in North America: Between 50 percent and 80 percent of all uranium, between 5 percent and 10 percent of all oil and gas reserves, and 30 percent of all coal is on land currently controlled by Native tribes or communities. In addition, many tribes have rights over water sources that are increasingly needed for urban development. More than ninety tribes have land that is still heavily forested, while millions of acres of "Indian land" are leased for food production. Admittedly, these resources, as abundant as they may appear in the postmodern age, are only a tiny fraction of what Native People once claimed as their birthright. That original inheritance was lost or, to be more precise, stolen by Western state-capitalism over years of violent exploitation. Now, in the twilight years of Western industrial society, the question becomes this: What will happen when Western societies begin to become desperate for more resources to continue maintaining their affluence over against the needs of the rest of the world? What real counterweight is there to the power of multinational corporations as they increase their use of the poor as cheap labor and seize even more of the Earth's declining resources? Given the clear direction of a widening gulf between rich and poor, what does the future truly hold not only for indigenous peoples but for all the world's poor?

Optimists might say that an enlightened "kinder, gentler" colonialism will simply voluntarily reduce its needs to provide for the whole of a hungry humanity. My ancestors, even those ancestors of the Choctaw middle class, might say: *Good luck.* As dark as it may seem, as uncomfortable as it may seem, this fact of Western-style colonialism's pervasive history must be raised by Native People, even in the midst of our honeymoon relationship with liberal New Age America.

While the drumming and the loving between us continue, it is important that we begin to speak with different words than *spirituality.* We need to adopt the language of sociological, economic, political reality, especially as we look ahead to our common future. We need to acknowledge that the demons of our past may have been lulled to sleep by the full stomachs of capitalist America, but they have not been done to death. They can (and I believe will) be revived when the need for more resources becomes acute in the next century. Those resources will be required by Western-style powers (including not only Taiwan, but the much more powerful emerging capitalist state of mainland China), if they are to maintain their comfort level. And as much as it may disquiet us in this generation to admit it, the historical facts of our shared experience leave us with only the most appeasement-obsessed hope that things will be different the next time around. While some Native People in North America may be enjoying the last afterglow of capitalist enrichment in this generation (which, after all, we were the first to pay for and the last to receive), the vast majority of our cultural siblings in Central and South America go to bed hungry. While we may be insulated from the hidden dimensions of contemporary colonialism (child labor, sweat-shop manufacture, substandard conditions, poverty wages, and so on), our cousins in other indigenous societies live with these realities on a daily basis. The economic truth is that most poor nations wait for the other shoe to drop as Western-style capitalist societies continue to absorb the planet at an alarming rate.

When Archbishop Desmond Tutu of South Africa attended the 1994 General Convention of the Episcopal Church, his vision of the major issue facing the church of tomorrow had little to do with ordaining homosexual clergy or adopting inclusive language (which were favorite Western topics); rather, his primary concern was the issue of international debt. As a Christian heir to the experience of Western colonialism in Africa, he understood implicitly that the symbol systems we use can appear benign only as long as they are shared in the embrace of affluence. In the end, in the realities of power politics and economic necessity, the patterns can and do change dramatically and quickly. Global debt means that the poor must mortgage their own future to pay for the comfort of the rich. In time, as this burden becomes intolerable for whole sections of the world, then some exercise of power will result. That exercise is what I describe as colonialism. Consequently, the power shift between "haves and have-nots" is the future. It is the future for the nations of Africa. And it is the future for the Choctaws of the United States. As the trends of economic displacement graphically illustrate for any who have eyes to see the writing on the wall, the forces that can revivify colonialism are already at work, and the clock is running.

While I know that my opinions will be disturbing to many, perhaps especially to other Native People who have adopted the "knowledge" of Western colonialism, I believe that the searing experience endured by my ancestors, as well as those of many other indigenous peoples, will be revisited on future generations of Native People unless we act now to rechannel history into new paths. Therefore, the overriding concern I have as a Native person, as a theologian, and as a Christian is in hastening the coming of the Second Reformation: the global reappraisal and reconstitution of religious sociology, of community, to protect not only resources, but people; not only Natives, but all populations; not only spirituality, but survival.

NATIVE ECONOMIC THEORY: A NEW TRANSLATION CODE

As a Native theologian, my response to the changing realities of the context in which I live is to stand for a clear and powerful affirmation of Native tradition over against the rise of international corporate colonialism. I stand in the historic experience of my People. I call on the People to speak once again with a united voice for economic justice, ecological sanity, and political freedom. These are our birthright and our legacy as the indigenous People of this hemisphere.

I believe that the time has come for us to use the best analytical tools at our command to construct a new *translation code* for our dialogue with our peers in other ethnic communities. If solidarity is our goal, then we must find the common language we need to unite our voices in the proclamation of a Native economic theory that challenges colonial assumptions and that advances human dignity and liberation in the century to come. In other words, we must create the climate for the Second Reformation now so that our grandchildren may breathe that free air in their lifetime.

In his landmark work *Prophesy Deliverance!*, Cornel West began this process of creating a new theological language in the best analytical traditions of the African-American People. He adapted the elements of classical Marxism to craft a theology that expresses the Black agenda with clarity and individuality. West uses the traditional language of Marxism (particularly the progressive Marxist views of Antonio Gramsci) to illustrate how concerns raised by Howard Clark Kee can appear when translated into the hard world of power economics. Following Gramsci's use of "hegemonic cultures," which I suggest is a linguistic symbol system for "colonial powers," West offers this interpretation that sounds strikingly similar to Kee's description of competing societies and their "knowledge" exchange:

> A hegemonic culture subtly and effectively encourages people to identify themselves with the habits, sensibilities, and worldviews supportive of the status quo and the class interests that dominate it. It is a culture successful in persuading people to "consent" to their oppression and exploitation. A hegemonic culture survives and thrives as long as it convinces people to adopt its preferred formative modality, its favored socialization process. It begins to crumble when people start to opt for a transformative modality, a socialization process that opposes the dominant one. The latter constitutes a counter-hegemonic culture, the deeply embedded oppositional elements within a society. It is these elements the hegemonic culture seeks to contain and control.[7]

Let me be clear about what I believe this means for Native America: My goal is to reconstitute our culture as the original and continuing oppositional force to Western state colonial capitalism in North America. We are the original "counter-hegemonic" culture of this hemisphere. Our "socialization process" opposes the dominant one. We have, inherent in our tradition of the Tribe, a clear alternative to Western-style economic capitalism as the only option for the future. In fact, I would submit that true American history in relation to our People is the history of a hegemonic culture's consistent attempts to "contain and control" the Native alternative, precisely because it so obviously contradicted European colonialism and so powerfully offered the poor of all cultures a living alternative to oppression and exploitation.

Cornel West has said that "Christianity and Marxism are the most vulgarized, distorted traditions in the modern world."[8] I would add to that short list "Native tradition." Our tradition (that is, our process of socialization carried out historically over centuries of Native cultural development) stands in sharp distinction to the economic principles and theories, as well as the vertical social organization, imported to our shores by Western colonialism. It has been denigrated and distorted by historians, anthropologists, and theologians precisely to contain its message of liberation for others, including the many others of African, Asian, Hispanic, and Anglo descent who are as marginalized by capitalism as we historically have been. While we have been permitted recently to self-describe this reality through the careful language of *spirituality,* we have yet to speak clearly of it in its other traditional manifestation: *commonality.*

The fundamental economic theory that runs as an unbroken thread throughout Native tradition is symbolized in the term *commonality.* It is as central to our tradition as spirituality. Perhaps more so. And while it is unique in its cultural expression, it mirrors many of the categories common to what Cornel West describes as progressive Marxism. It is not by accident that classical Marxism sought its antecedents in the ancient social-economic organization of Native America. Frederick Engels, in his essay "The Origin of the Family, Private Property, and the State," displays the nineteenth-century approach of early Marxism as it gropes to find its "roots" in the cultures of Native America. And while the search was in the right direction inasmuch as Native People had evolved a sophisticated "socialist" nation long before the coming of the Europeans, it is also true that Engels's approach is flawed by the inherent racism of European-Native relations, which dictated that indigenous cultures must be viewed as "primitive"; therefore, ironically, even nascent Marxism participated in the colonial paradigm of Europe by its continuing denigration of Native peoples (in fact, even "progressive" Marxists like Gramsci held these distorted, racist views). However, the fact remains that if we are searching for a *translation code*–a linguistic methodology that will allow us to articulate a theological perspective across cultural boundaries while remaining authentic to the core values of our unique tradition–then the fundamental praxis of Marxist economic theory is as solid a bridging tool as we are likely to find in the near future. Our task, like that of African-American people, is to take our best intellectual/spiritual values and translate them over the bridge of liberation theology to form a new network with other men and women who share our commitment to cultural equality, economic justice, and ecological balance. In short, we must speak to be heard, and as St. Paul reminds us, our words must be open to interpretation, to analysis, to solidarity with others if they are not to be unintelligible. Before, however, we refer to the Native economic theory I believe will be the basis for a stronger theology in the next generation, we must face the issues of prejudice against any use of Marxist thought as West has cautioned us to do.

First, we ought to assert that while the mutant socialism of Stalin deserved to pass from human history for the oppressive model of coercion that it was, the essential categories of socialist economic theory and their continuing benefits for the poor and oppressed must never be allowed to disappear from legitimate discourse among Christian thinkers, especially those dedicated to economic justice and ecological balance. What West calls "progressive Marxism," especially the cultural analysis of Marxists such as Gramsci, is a valuable *translation code* (linguistic symbol system) that can help us to articulate the Native alternative in ways that communicate to Western thinkers and theorists (not to mention African, Asian, and Latin American communities). The demonization of Soviet-style Marxism must not be allowed to interfere with our ability to speak of issues of class and exploitation without fear or prejudice.

Second, while this language may seem odd for Native People themselves to adopt, especially since we have confined ourselves to the soft syllables of spirituality, it is as much a part of our traditional vocabulary as *Mother Earth.* What I have described as *commonality* is the definitively Native paradigm of our intellectual, social, and economic history. It is the ground of our economic theory and, therefore, the complement to our spirituality. It is, in fact, the material out of which that spirituality is fashioned.

Third, the economics of both capitalism and colonialism, and even of what I describe as the Second Reformation (as a global community effort to preserve human freedom and natural life), demand that we use economic and social terms that speak clearly and directly to the realities of the poor and the oppressed. To avoid using any categories that originated in Marxist philosophy simply for fear of offending the hegemonic sensibilities of the dominant culture reduces us at best to parroting a language not our own and at worst to silence in the face of our own cultural holocaust.

COMMONALITY: THE NATIVE ALTERNATIVE

As Native theologians, if we truly want to honor our cultural heritage and spiritual tradition, we must begin to speak about the economic and social principles that shaped our civilization and set it apart from the Western European models that were forced on us by armed aggression. To honor the "Tribe" and to honor "Native tradition" mean honoring the essential aspects of what I call Native *commonality.*

Let me be clear about my intent in using this new language, this new symbol system, for the advancement of a Native theology for the next century. It is not my purpose to mimic Marxist thought. It is not my intention to simply reclothe Marxism in Native dress. Semantics alone is not the issue. Rather, I am looking for the kind of linguistic reference points that will allow Native People to speak authoritatively of their cultural tradition in ways that form a strong *translation code* to other cultures. I am convinced that the time is long overdue for us, in the Native community, to do this, and I am equally convinced that the time is growing short when we have the luxury to build bridges with our experiential peers before the weight of economic dislocation collapses even the bridges that now exist in such tentative form. When Christian activists such as Jim Wallis, the editor of one of the leading progressive magazines in the United States, says "socialism is a dead word" and when he asserts "if we care about radically Christian transformational politics–Gospel rooted vision that puts the poor, community and women's rights at the center–then I want to shed the old Left, socialist tags," then those of us who would make common cause with Christian progressives need to sit up and listen to our choice of words. Language counts. The use of codes, of systems, that communicate our theologies must be given careful consideration. Moreover, in this process of watching our tag-words, those of us from the Native community enter the dialogue with a fresh perspective. Because we have not been as active in verbalizing our economic theory, and because we have such a deeply rooted history in what the West would describe as formative socialism, we have something very helpful to contribute, if only we choose to speak of it with the candor and vision that Christians like Wallis need in order to hear us.

What I call *commonality* is Native *spirituality* as it takes concrete shape in the secular social-economic-political lives of the Native culture. It embodies the most traditional elements of that culture. It arises from the unique perspective of Native America. It is the distillation of the principles that guided and fashioned most Native societies in North America prior to the arrival of Western colonialism. It is the implicit social fabric of Native People that still exists in both rural and urban native communities. It has parallels throughout the indigenous world and in the theoretical cultural understandings of many other communities worldwide. Therefore, it is well suited to be a bridging mechanism for our People to others internationally. It speaks our language, but in a way that others can easily translate.

What are the "basics" of Native *commonality?* I will make only a partial response, because in raising this concept I am openly inviting Native leaders, both Christian and Traditional, to enter the conversation and define the ground of our theology as a communal exercise. However, I will highlight these six simple principles formative to *commonality* as the essential framework for the economic/social basis of a Native People's liberation theology:

- the foundational understanding that land may not be owned;
- the communal use of land and the means of production;
- the intentional sharing of resources in an equitable manner among all those in need;
- the use of kinship modalities rather than class structures;
- the exercise of consensus in governance as a guarantee of democratic institutions;
- the philosophical embodiment of community through individuality rather than individualism.

My suggestion is that these basic six points contain the rough parameters for the articulation of a liberation theology that is rooted in traditional Native culture. Under each category there are ample cases of practical experience within the Native community from which to draw; there is a wide range of tribal models to illustrate the economic and political theory inherent in each one; there are spiritual/religious connections that ground these principles in the sacred worldview of our tradition throughout North America; and finally, there are obvious points of reference to the theologies of many cultures, not the least of which is the "Marxist culture" of most international forms of liberation theology itself.

Of course, I am not suggesting that these are the only six points available to us, but they are a place to begin. Moreover, I believe they are strong starting points for us because they impel us to global discussion of economic reality as equal participants in the literal life-and-death struggle of the world's poor. As Christian theologians, to adopt even these simple principles of Native *commonality* means envisioning the Kingdom of God not just as an ideal for some distant supernatural future but as the Tribe brought into existence in the everyday lives of real people here and now. It also means returning our talk about Native *spirituality* to the original context where it always resided in traditional Native life—in the bottom-line realities of how people live, work, and relate as common citizens in a shared community.

Finally, if we are to herald the reform of the church as an intentional counterweight to resurgent colonialism, if we are to inaugurate a truly international Second Reformation, then we are going to have to do that with global language that makes sense to a global community. A valuable part of that dialogue from the North American Native perspective will always be the spiritual language of Earth, Creator-Creation, and the Sacred Circle of Life. All of these mystical, evocative, poetical images are to be maintained, even to be protected from the spiritual strip-mining of the New Age. But for all of their value, they are only half of the equation.

We will not succeed in offering people a way into community against capitalist colonialism unless we succeed in offering them a genuine *alternative*. That alternative is the Tribe. It is precisely the ancient models of state and society, of economics and production, of giving and receiving that were the hallmarks of Native civilization. In other words, we have something to offer people other than just our spirituality. We have concrete, solid, foundational models of community handed down to us by our ancestors (preserved by them even at the cost of their own lives and liberty); these are the true alternatives to Western state capitalism in North America. Speaking of these alternatives means speaking in the harder language of economics. It means speaking in ways that will sound like Marxism (although it means being critical of Marx just as we are critical of all Western philosophies). It also means being prepared for the anxiety, the fear, and even the hostility that will arise (both within our own community and among others) when we begin to voice a challenge to the Cold War assumptions of infallible capitalism and demonic Marxism. We must accept that as the cost we pay for breaking the modern stereotype of the complacent Indian, who is content to get the leftovers of the European banquet. But our critique will not be constructive unless we have something else to offer. And that something else is our own brand of liberation theology, our own vision of the Kingdom turned upside down to become the Tribe, our own definition of community grounded as firmly in the communal history of our people as it is in their spiritual tradition.

The other half of the spiritual equation for Native America is the economic theory of justice. We are not just a creation-based community of spirituality. We are a *justice-based community of Native commonality.* We ought to consider the meaning of this identity as it translates into theological perspective. For example, it means we have remained true to our ancient values as tribal people. It means we continue to reject the alien philosophies of any form of colonialism that would violate the principles of our theology. It means that as a proud part of the world's poor, we are announcing our intention to stand with any others who wish to join us in speaking freely about alternatives to Western-style consumerism and capitalist exploitation. And finally, it means that if we have to be considered renegades once again in American history, because we bring forward a spiritual agenda of liberation and because we threaten the status quo with our traditional critique of oppression, then so be it. Small in numbers though we may be, our voice is crucial because it is able to speak with such moral depth and visionary clarity. The Native principles of *commonality* declare a return of Native America to its historic identity as one of the leading counter-hegemonic cultures offering an alternative to Western-style capitalism. If our theology has any resonance at all, then it echoes an alternative form of social structure based on kinship that takes classical Western socialism and moves it beyond Marxism. As Antonio Gramsci envisioned: The real locus of reform (of revolution) is not just in "class struggle" between categories of rich and poor, but in *cultures* of economy that compete for hegemony in the realm of the spiritual.

This simple but fundamental realignment in Marxist theory opens the door for Native America to take a formative role in liberation theology for the next century. The building blocks are all there. Native People have an unprecedented opportunity to become a leading community in shaping the global response to colonial capitalism. The fact is: Western alternatives (classical socialism/Marxism) have faltered because they are rooted in the artificial soil of nineteenth- and twentieth-century

European industrial economic theory. Like a house built on sand, their foundations have been flooded away by the tide of consumerism that has swept over the planet through technological and multinational corporate channels. There is, however, an alternative left intact, even in the midst of the perceived triumph of capitalism. Like small islands after a storm, the Native communities of this hemisphere remain, anchored to the bedrock of Native tradition. To shift the metaphor only slightly, these small arks of culture have preserved the essential ingredients of a new life for the poor.

To release this potential, we must assert that what we have described as the social/economic theory of *commonality* is not a "primitive" form of socialism as defined by the West. Instead, it is the unique cultural form of socialism evolved independently by Native People over centuries of Native social and religious development. If the European forms of socialism have been washed away, the indigenous forms remain, exactly because they are grounded in the cultural anchor of tribal communities. The sophistication of Native *commonality* has allowed it to survive five hundred years of colonialism. Our vision is at once both deeply spiritual and utterly pragmatic. It is also enormously hopeful for all of humanity. Native America can support the cause of international liberation by helping European Marxism shed its last attachments to a bogus Western "scientific" theory. We can free Marxist thought from the constraints of "class" analysis alone and introduce the "cultural" analysis that theorists like Gramsci were only beginning to explore before the Cold War. In short, Native People can take the lead in articulating a new theological vision of economic justice that can translate older and more limited European ideas into the next century. We can speak in a language that all of the world's poor can understand. We can transcend the labels of Marxism and socialism by developing a truly indigenous economic theory to support the spiritual vision already so powerfully associated with our culture. In fact, the cultural analysis (rather than the class analysis) of a Native People's theology can prepare the way for a renewed movement of liberation-style theologies, grounded in the lives of people throughout the world, which can become the counteractive force against colonialism in the coming years. If we choose to speak in these terms, we can be a major partner in the Second Reformation. We can, quite literally, shift authority to the hands of the poor.

As jarring as that may sound to ears grown accustomed to the softer talk of spirituality, and as threatening to those conditioned to fear liberation theology and its Marxist theories, I believe we must shake ourselves free of the smothering silence of an imaginary triumph of capitalism before it lulls us into a false sense of security. Colonialism is not dead any more than socialism is dead. They are the perennial categories, the symbol systems, the translation codes of our global economic reality, whatever names or language we employ. They are the symbols of our reality as that reality is lived out in the everyday world of economic necessity. Like all systems and codes, they can be translated just as they are transformed. The context in which we live is the catalyst for that act of translation and transformation. As realities change, codes change. As codes change, languages change. As languages change, cultures change. As cultures change, reality changes.

The axis point of history occurs within these time-joints we call change. Gramsci was one of the first to see these flexible links as opportunities for the poor to effect change by injecting themselves into the moment with radical new symbols and codes that could shift hegemony from one culture to another. His vision broadened the base of Marxism. Now, that base must be broadened again. It must be broadened even beyond the foundation laid by Western or Asian Marxists. It must be extended beyond the range of traditional liberation theology. It must be made to include the original expression of socialist hope—the communal life of economic justice, spiritual tolerance, and ecological care that are the hallmarks of Native civilization.

Spirituality is the heart of that civilization. Commonality is its mind. This intellectual symbol system, set in place by Native People centuries ago and lived out by them over generations, even through the most severe attacks of colonialism, remains as the fulfillment of a promise made long ago to the world's poor. It is a religious vision of real life where the last shall be first and the poor shall inherit the Earth.

Notes

[1] Alberto Pozzolini, *Antonio Gramsci: An Introduction to His Thought* (London: Pluto Press, 1970), pp. 65-66.

[2] The term I use for Native American/American Indian/First Nations cultures in North America.

[3] Howard Clark Kee, *Who Are the People of God?: Early Christian Models of Community* (New Haven: Yale University Press, 1995), p. 11.

[4] Ibid, p. 9.

[5] Michael Harrington, *The Politics at God's Funeral: The Spiritual Crisis of Western Civilization* (New York: Holt, Rinehart and Winston, 1983), p. 149.

[6] "How to Succeed in Business: Follow the Choctaw's Lead," *Smithsonian* (August 1996).

[7] Cornel West, *Prophesy Deliverance!: An Afro-American Revolutionary Christianity* (Philadelphia: Westminster Press, 1982), p. 95.

[8] Ibid., p. 119.

14.

Black Robes

Native Americans and the Ordination Process

TWEEDY SOMBRERO

Growing up in a Navajo family on the reservation in northern Arizona in the late 1950s and early 1960s gave me a deep sense of belonging–to the earth, to a family, to God. From my parents and grandparents I learned the customs and traditions of the Navajo people. Although my mom took us kids to a Presbyterian church a couple of times and to a smaller nondenominational church just so we could have that experience, I did not grow up in the church, and being in ministry never entered my head. Nor do I consider myself a traditional Navajo, though my beliefs have been shaped by Navajo culture and traditions.

My family moved to Utah when my father took a job at the Intermountain Indian School in Brigham City. I entered the sixth grade there and lived in Utah until I graduated from high school and moved to Lawrence, Kansas, where I enrolled in Haskell Indian Junior College (formerly Haskell boarding school). It was in Lawrence that I first became aware of The United Methodist Church.

Until then, my knowledge of the church was very limited. I knew about God and God's love for us all, but I knew very little about the church. During my last year of junior college I met a young Native American who invited me to participate with him in a project. When he told me that he was a United Methodist pastor, I was surprised. My image of clergy had always been that they were white and getting up in years; yet he was a Native American, and he was young. As we talked, I shared with him some of my beliefs about God that I had learned from my grandfather. He encouraged me to hold on to those beliefs.

I had never heard of The United Methodist Church, so I questioned him about it. I was impressed that he did not pressure me to go to church. Nor did he tell me that I would have to give up Navajo beliefs to belong to his church. About two months later I decided to attend worship, and in 1973 I joined the church and immediately got involved in a lot of activities sponsored by the church on campus. It was a time I will never forget.

A few months before I graduated the pastor asked me if I would be interested in a church position. I immediately said no because I could never do what he did—especially on Sundays. He laughed and told me that there were other jobs in a church besides clergy. Then, about two months before graduation, he had some people come talk to us about church and community workers, mission opportunities, and other positions available to us. I became interested in the community worker job because my major was social work.

Upon graduation, however, I moved back to the Navajo reservation to work for my tribe as a social worker. I had done this for two years, when, out of the blue, I received a call from the minister in Lawrence saying he remembered my having expressed an interest in becoming a church and community worker. He told me about a position that had opened up at a church on my reservation in New Mexico. He had even called the pastor there to discuss me with him. Once again, I was impressed that this young clergyman had not forgotten what I had said and that he saw in me something worthwhile.

Unfortunately, the job offered by the church was not as a church and community worker but rather as a director of Christian education. At the urging of this young pastor I interviewed for it anyway in order to gain experience. I took the position, and my troubles began.

This particular church looked down on Navajo beliefs and culture. It taught Navajo people that in order to be good Christians, Navajos must give up being Navajo. This was neither my belief nor my understanding of God's love for everyone. Nonetheless, I gave my all to this congregation and started to feel a tugging at my heart that there was something else God had in store for my life. It was there that I met an African-American couple who kept saying to me that I should think about the ordained ministry. I talked to my father about this and his response was, "Absolutely not!"

I went through a whole year questioning the "tug" I was feeling. Then, in the summer of 1980, I was attending a camp meeting in Michigan, and the evangelist called me forward and told the people that he was going to pray for me because he knew I had a decision to make. He prayed that my ministry would always be blessed by God. I returned from that encampment knowing that I had been called by God to enter the ordained ministry. The next step was to tell my parents. But when? I entered seminary at Iliff School of Theology in Denver, and it wasn't until my second year that my parents found out what I was doing.

The following years involved a great deal of pain and struggle. My parents almost disowned me, and there was a lot of pressure from within the church to give up being a Navajo. The day finally arrived when I had to go before the Conference Board of Ordained Ministry. As I sat facing the four elderly white men, my heart sat in my throat. The interview went on for four hours, and it seemed every other question was, "Are you sure you want to be an ordained minister?" Once the ordeal was over, I had to wait two long days before I received word that I, in fact, had been accepted for ordination. Everyone I knew—except for my parents and some of my relatives—was excited that I was to be ordained. There were very few Native American women in the ordained ministry, and I knew I was making history.

Looking back, I realize that it took me over ten years to complete the ordination process. Was that because people were against me and were placing obstacles in my way? Was the process itself difficult? Whatever the answers, it shouldn't be like this. No wonder there are hardly any Native American ministers available for Indian churches. The process fights against who they are as Native people and puts them in a very vulnerable state that belittles their very essence as human beings.

I remember feeling very intimidated by those four elderly gentlemen on the Board of Ordained Ministry when they constantly asked me if I was sure I wanted to be in the ministry. One of them even suggested that no church would want me because I was a "divorced, single mother, Indian woman!" I remember telling him that those were the chances I was willing to take, "for if God is for me, who can be against me?"

As the date drew near, I approached the Board of Ordained Ministry for permission to wear Indian dress at my ordination. To my surprise, they turned down my request, saying that I would have to wear the traditional black robe. It was then that I learned that two of my friends—women who had been supportive of me as an Indian woman—were members of the Board of Ordained Ministry, but for some reason they had not been present at my interview. One was a Hispanic woman, and the other was white. I told them that I would like to wear my Indian clothes, and they said they would talk to the other committee members about it.

The day of ordination, while I was at dinner in the cafeteria, the chair of the committee came to me, very angry, saying, "I told you not to bring this business of your native dress to anyone else because we had already made a decision that you will wear a black robe." Later, I learned that the women had been sent on an errand while the four men met and decided I was to wear the black robe.

I arrived at the service of ordination wearing the required black robe over my Indian dress. As I stood in the processional line, I unzipped my robe so my Native dress could be seen. The chair of the Board turned to me and told me to zip it up. As we began to process in, he and I fought like children–him yelling at me to zip the robe and me saying no. Just before we were to enter the main hall, the chair stopped the line and told me that I would not be ordained. Exasperated, I said, "Fine," and left the line to take the robe off. At that point the bishop, who was leading the procession, realized that no one was following him and came back to determine the cause of the holdup. He firmly told the chair that the decision to ordain me had been made, and it was too late to change that. He then turned to me and told me to get back in line because we were going through with it whether I was tired of the battle or not.

What should have been an exciting and fulfilling day for me was now a very sad day. I felt that I would never be accepted and would probably never be given a church. Ironically, my ordination was good publicity for the conference and for the church that took credit for recommending me in the first place.

Were my parents right? Was the conference right? The difficult questions did not go away after my graduation from seminary and my ordination. There have been many rough spots, though I am now a member of another annual conference and have been appointed to a small inner-city congregation. My parents finally realized that I did not enter the ministry to tell them that they were devil worshipers because they continued to follow their Navajo ceremonies.

I try very hard to be like that young pastor in Kansas, who believed in me and did not push me to give up what I am in order to be a Christian. If anyone should get credit for my ordination, it should be that young man, along with the African-American couple and the two women who supported me wholeheartedly. The young minister became one of my best friends and confidants. All through seminary and the entire process of ordination, he was there. My sister was also there with me when I finally faced my parents with my decision to go into the ministry. Since that time, I have grown stronger in my faith, and I have my support system intact.

So where do we go from here? How do we help Native Americans through the process of ordination? There seems to be a lack of support for Native people wanting to pursue ordination. When I first expressed interest, everyone in the church was happy but did not give the support I needed to take the next steps. My pastor knew the process but did not offer any help. After my candidacy was approved by the local committee and the charge conference, I was put in touch with the Conference Board, which was neither supportive nor helpful. The supervising pastor to whom I was assigned not only lived in another town but was primarily interested in his impending retirement. We met twice, after which he withdrew and left me alone to figure out future steps. There was no interest shown in how I was doing or where I was in the process.

Is there a better way to assist Native people who are struggling with a call to the church's ministry? Surely ways can be found to guide and support Native candidates, especially when they start to question their identity as Natives. Native people like me, who grew up in the tradition, find a cold world in the church in terms of process. United Methodists claim connection among themselves, but when and where does it take place? Navajos claim the same kind of connection through their clan system, and it works much better because Navajos do take care of each other and are supportive of one another. The church needs to follow this example and provide a candidate with nurture and encouragement. Maybe then we would have more Native Americans as clergy. It's a dream and a dilemma that we as Native American Christians face.

15.

Walking in Balance

The Spirituality-Liberation Praxis of Native Women

ANDREA SMITH

> Doing theology, thinking theologically, is a decidedly non-Indian thing to do. When I talk about Native American theology to many of my Indian friends, most of them just smile and act as if I hadn't said anything. And I am pretty sure that as far as they are concerned I truly hadn't said anything.
>
> William Baldridge[1]

William Baldridge (Cherokee) points to one of the difficulties faced by Native Americans trying to write theology—we are always writing to a non-Native audience. Because there is virtually no Indian middle class, because Native people have an 80 percent high school drop-out rate, and because Native cultures are oral rather than written, any theologian in an academic setting, if she is honest with herself, knows that very few Indian people will read her work and that she will have very little direct impact on Indian communities. Not surprisingly, few Native people find themselves in academic theological professions. This notwithstanding, Native people *do* engage in a spirituality/liberation praxis. This is most obvious in our struggle to engage in Native spiritual practices, given that, even today, Indians find it difficult if not impossible to protect their religious traditions under the laws of the United States.[2] Since, however, Native peoples do not split the sacred from any aspect of life, Native activism tends to be grounded in spirituality. Certainly at the forefront of our struggles for spiritual/political liberation are Indian women. Native women have always received less media attention than men, and even in feminist circles indigenous women rarely get proper credit as the first to resist patriarchy in this hemisphere. Nevertheless, among Indian activists it is widely acknowledged that women do much, if not most, of the work. In order to gain access to women's perspectives, however, it is necessary to go elsewhere than to standard theological texts.

METHODOLOGY

The methodologies of Asian feminist, womanist, and mujerista theologians offer possibilities for uncovering Native women's perspectives on spirituality/liberation praxis. As a matter of principle, feminist theologians focus on the experiences of women as a starting point for theology, but here a host of methodological questions arises: Whose experiences are being represented and by whom? What counts as "accurate" representation? How does the theologian claim to "know" the experience of the collectivity, and what authorizes her to be its voice? Ada María Isasi-Díaz calls upon theologians to account for their methods: Are they rooted in the day-to-day experience of the people they write about? She states, "Often we have seen the experiences of other marginalized groups, including Hispanics . . . used as examples to illumine answers to questions determined by those who control the systems, while never allowing the marginalized groups to pose the question. . . . Mujerista theologians discovered that we need the voices of Hispanic women themselves to be present in the theological discourse."[3] But how can the "voices" of non-academic women "be present in the theological discourse" when that discourse takes place in an unfamiliar or inaccessible—which is to say, an academic—arena? As womanist theologian Dianne Stewart pointedly asks, "How can womanist theologians actually develop a theology that will be informed by, and synthesized with, the religious life of ordinary black women who never read books published by Orbis Books and other elite publishing houses?"[4] If, as Korean theologian Chung Hyun Kyung argues, the point of liberation theology is to close the gap between religion and politics so that "the community becomes the theologian," any conversation that excludes the voices of the community is pointless.[5]

Many womanist, Asian feminist, and mujerista theologians use stories to represent Black, Asian, and Latina women's voices. Because slaves were not allowed to read the Bible and learned it by word of mouth, Black communities have tended to experience the Bible through the flexibility of an aural culture. According to Renita Weems, the protean nature of oral tradition has given Black communities the freedom to modify and retell stories from the Bible to suit their changing needs.[6] Katie Cannon claims that Black women's literature is a crucial link to the oral traditions of the past as a mode of ethical instruction and cultural dissemination: "This literary tradition is the nexus between the real-lived texture of Black life and the oral-aural cultural values implicitly passed on and received from one generation to the next."[7] Gloria Ines Loya similarly describes the literature, music, and arts of Latinas as a source for theology, "a mirror of the lived experience of women."[8] Chung looks to Asian women's activism and storytelling—and not just to their Bible stories—as resources for theology.

Like African-American culture, Native cultures are orally based. Consequently, storytelling is a critical resource for uncovering Native women's experiences. The burgeoning literary tradition of Native women provides a window into how story maintains community. Such literature is generally more accessible and more likely to be written with Native people in mind—unlike theological texts, which are written primarily to a non-Indian audience. Consequently, I will look to Native women's literature as well as to the more academic writings of Native women as a resource.

Of course, using storytelling and literature as theological resources does not answer Dianne Stewart's problem with the inaccessibility of scholarly presses. Instead, it raises yet another question about the politics of method: At what point does using literature as a representation of "authentic voices" from the community become a way of ignoring actual people? Isasi-Díaz uses meta-ethnography as a way of including women at the grassroots level in the development of mujerista theology. She interviews Latina women from different communities in the United States about their lives and their spiritual practices and then draws from their interviews generative themes for mujerista theology. In this way she hopes to undermine the division between the theology done in academic circles and that done on the grassroots level. Similarly, Stewart insists that womanist theologians remain connected to the everyday experiences of Black women. She writes, "If womanist theologians are committed to understanding and analyzing black women's social and religious experiences, we cannot talk about black women without talking *with* black women."[9] The problem that this general meta-ethnography presents for a theology *of liberation* is that most people, even most women, are not activists for social change. Therefore, to identify women's spirituality/liberation praxis, the theologian-cum-historian and ethnographer must focus on the lives of activists specifically. Marcia Riggs does this by looking at the women's club movement of the early twentieth century, but she tends to ignore the activism of today's Black women.[10] I will look most to contemporary Native women's activism, based on my own history of activism, as a source for identifying spirituality/liberation praxis.

This essay is not meant to be a definitive account of Native women's spirituality and political activism. It reflects my particular perspective as an urban-based activist, but there are certainly diverse experiences among Native women, depending on tribe, geographic location, age, whether one is urban- or reservation-based, and so forth. Rather, this chapter is meant to be suggestive of what Native women might contribute to theological conversations about liberation, particularly among women-of-color theologians. More extensive and thorough research among the diverse forms of Native women's organizing is necessary for a more exhaustive account.

Before continuing, however, I should make two interpretive points that are not, properly speaking, questions of methodology, but which will frame the rest of this discussion. First, because Native religions, like Native cultures in general, are orally based, they are quite flexible. Indians tend to give less weight to an orthodoxy of religious belief than to spiritual centeredness and ethical behavior—what Native people call "walking in balance."[11] Second, Indian spiritualities tend to be more practice-centered than belief-centered; that is, what makes one Indian is not simply holding the proper set of core beliefs but behaving like an Indian. Vine Deloria, Jr. (Standing Rock Sioux), notes that, in a Native context, religion is "a way of life" rather than "a matter of the proper exposition of doctrines."[12] Of course, this should not be taken to mean either that Indian religions have no content or that anyone gets to be Indian who "decides" to "behave like one." Rather, these points suggest that, in looking at Native women's activism as a source for spirituality/liberation praxis, standard theological categories do not have much relevance. New categories come to the fore. As Chung argues, "Doctrinal purity or religious boundaries [are] not of concern. . . . What matter[s is] the life-giving power of justice in whatever form it comes."[13] The "meanings" of Native political and spiritual practices refract through culturally specific lenses, and in the sections that follow I will discuss a few of them.

RELATIONSHIP TO TRADITION

Aloysius Pieris calls upon the Asian church to lose itself in "the *non-Christian experiences* of liberation."[14] Native liberation also requires a de-centered Christianity. This post-Christian approach is not a wholesale rejection of Christianity, although some do reject it entirely and try to reclaim the traditions of their particular nations. Haunani Kay Trask (Native Hawai'ian), for example, calls Christianity "the most vicious religion in the world."[15] Since many Native people can trace the abuse in their families to within a generation or two of mission boarding schools, they have had to reject Christianity to heal their trauma. Some indigenous women also reject Christianity to recover their more woman-centered indigenous traditions. In some respects, however, the neo-traditional rejection of Christianity is a legacy of Christian dualistic thinking. Vine Deloria notes that neo-traditionalist attempts to reclaim Native spirituality occur within an either/or logic system foreign to Native cultures. Ironically, however, Deloria himself maintains an either/or stance, writing, "We cannot reject the Christian religion piecemeal. . . . The whole religion has been misdirected from its inception."[16]

It is possible to critique the oppressive practices of the Christian church without wholly rejecting Christianity itself. Belief systems that seem mutually inconsistent to the dominant culture, like Christianity and indigenous religions, can coexist in indigenous cultures. To illustrate with a real-life example: At a conference several years ago I heard a story about an Indian man who gave a speech in which he claimed that the next speaker was going to say things that were completely wrong. When his turn came, the next speaker, also Indian, began, not by attacking the preceding speaker, but by announcing that everything he said was completely true. He then went on with his talk. The event is notable because it struck no one present—not the speakers, not the Indian audience—as odd.

Consequently, even Natives raised with a more traditional worldview do not always feel the need to reject Christianity outright, even as they criticize its abuses. Many Indians tend to relate to both Christianity and to their Native traditions along a continuum. (Of course, there are Native women who choose to embrace a variety of other foreign traditions, from Judaism to Zen Buddhism, but Christianity has long been the colonizing religion of Native women.) Some define themselves as wholly Christian, others as wholly traditional, but probably most relate to both in some degree or fashion. For instance, someone who is primarily traditional may occasionally attend church. This flexibility can lessen the need for many Native Christians to "reinterpret" Christian concepts that they find oppressive; they simply may ignore what they find inadequate or offensive in Christianity and look elsewhere, usually to Native traditions, for what they need. For example, in contrast to White Christian feminists like Elisabeth Schüssler Fiorenza, it has been my experience that Indian people generally do not try to "re-envision" scripture because they often do not read it in the first place. At one sermon at an Indian church I attended, for example, the pastor noted, "Obviously reading the Bible is not necessary for salvation, because otherwise no Indians would be saved." When Native people do grapple with the biblical text, as Robert Warrior does in "Canaanites, Cowboys, and Indians," they tend to produce critiques directed toward non-Indians and their oppressive approaches to the Bible. Indians who are not theologically trained generally do not concern themselves with the Canaanites. In fact, at one gathering of Native seminarians that I attended, one pastor challenged us to find out who in our communities knew what seminary was. Thus, attempts to "re-envision" scripture in response, for instance, to Warrior's work may be evidence of what Isasi-Díaz describes as an academic theologian's impulse to answer questions that those at the grassroots are not asking.[17]

The capacious, flexible, and essentially pragmatic worldviews of indigenous peoples run completely against the grain of mandates like Elisabeth Schüssler Fiorenza's to produce a universally applicable feminist discourse:

> Those discourses that advocate christological "regionalism" in turn serve the interests of liberal pluralism. Studies written from a professedly "ethnic local point of view"–like "white" European, Australian, American, African American, Asian, African, or Latin American articulations of feminist christology [Fiorenza seems typically unaware of Native Americans]–are also in danger of postmodern co-optation. They turn into the "reverse" of malestream readings and become "regionalized" whenever they grow into exclusive articulations that belong only to a discrete ethnic group. Such discourses are in danger of reinforcing the oppressive divisions of class, race, gender, religion, nation, and age that have been articulated by western colonialist powers. . . .
>
> . . . Feminist christological articulations that do not argue for their theoretical significance but rather relinquish claims that their insights are valid for everyone unwittingly foster such a regionalization and privatization of emancipatory political struggles.[18]

In this passage Fiorenza seems to reduce all difference claims to self-inflicted wounds ready to be exploited by "western colonialist powers." To think, however, that one can make claims that are "valid for everyone" presupposes something strikingly similar to the coercive, "malestream" worldview of "western colonialist powers" against which Fiorenza pits herself. In other words, she seems unaware that the most oppressive structural feature of would-be totalizing discourse is its very claim to universal applicability. In contrast to Fiorenza's absolutist mandates, "most tribal religions make no pretense as to their universality or exclusiveness. . . . They integrate the respective communities as particular people chosen for particular religious knowledge and experiences."[19] Without doubt, such a pragmatic worldview prevents Native people from making universalist claims about spirituality or liberation; it also suggests, however, that no other discourse, including Christian discourse in any of its manifestations, is in a position to do so either.

Until recently, this radical de-centering of foundational truth-claims, especially of Christian truth-claims, has had no counterpart in European thought. According to the European positivist grammar of truth, if proposition *p* is true, then *not-p* must be false. Indigenous peoples have never thought this way. Even their creation stories take no epistemological precedence over those of other cultures. Europeans always have found this paratactic thinking maddening. Charles Eastman (Sioux) illustrates with the following story:

> A missionary once undertook to instruct a group of Indians in the truths of his holy religion. He told them of the creation of the earth in six days, and of the fall of our first parents by eating an apple. The courteous savages listened attentively, and after thanking him, one related in his turn a very ancient tradition concerning the origin of maize. But the missionary plainly showed his disgust and disbelief, indignantly saying: "What I delivered to you were sacred truths, but this that you tell me is mere fable and falsehood!" "My Brother," gravely replied the offended Indian, "it seems that you have not been well grounded in the rules of civility. You saw that we who practice these rules, believed your stories; why, then, do you refuse to credit ours?"[20]

Of course, while Indian liberation may not necessitate the wholesale rejection of Christianity, the revitalization of indigenous traditions probably will be at the heart of Indian liberation with Christianity playing, at best, a supporting role. Those with a vested interest in White Christian hegemony find such de-centering even more threatening than absolute rejection, because it changes Christianity from an ontological foundation to an appropriable resource. That means, among other things, that Christianity, and White culture in general, no longer have to be at the center of every conversation. As Menominee poet/activist/maid Chrystos says in her poem "Rude as 2:29 A.M.," "I don't have time/ to hate white folks/ which offends you because it means you aren't/ the center of the world as your whole life/ has conspired to teach you."[21]

CONTINUITY AND CHANGE

Unlike mujerista or Jewish feminist theologians, Native women activists seem less preoccupied with grappling with the oppressive features of their own traditions. The reason is that, prior to colonization, Indian societies for the most part were not male-dominated. Women served as spiritual, political, even military leaders. Many societies were matrilineal and matrilocal. Violence against women and children was infrequent, unheard of in many tribes. Native people did not use corporal punishment against their children. And, although there existed a division of labor between women and men, women's and men's labors were accorded similar status.[22] As Winona LaDuke (Anishinaabe) states, "Traditionally, American Indian women were never subordinate to men. Or vice versa, for that matter. What native societies have always been about is achieving balance in all things, gender relations no less than any other. Nobody needs to tell us how to do it. We've had that all worked out for thousands of years. And, left to our own devices, that's exactly how we'd be living right now."[23] Concerned with "balance in all things," Native societies were far less authoritarian than their European counterparts. Seventy percent of tribes did not practice war at all. When societies did wage war, their intent was not to annihilate the enemy but to achieve honor through the bravery of their warriors. A warrior accrued more honor by getting close enough to an enemy to touch him, and then leaving him alive, than by killing him.[24] Consequently, most Native women regard sexism within indigenous communities as a result of colonization rather than a feature of indigenous cultures themselves. While not perfect, pre-contact Native societies were relatively free from systematic oppression.

Like Jewish women, Native women struggle with issues of change and transformation within their traditions. In times of genocidal danger, the idea of transforming traditions to meet current needs can seem particularly threatening. Blu Greenberg raises this issue for Jewish women, stating:

> Antagonists' charges take many forms. . . . While these specific emendations [concerning women's status] in Halakah in and of themselves may be fine, all this tinkering ultimately will undermine Torah, tradition, mitzvot, Halakah, norma, faith stability, rootedness; in short, everything we hold so dear. One aspect of that reality is that the status quo, as we have inherited it, has not been totally static. Surely there are risks involved whenever tradition undergoes change. But Halakah is not to be treated as a *goses*, a rapidly failing body that one cannot move lest it give out its final death rattle. Halakah was intended to be preserved, and there is a healthy difference between preserving and freezing solid.[25]

Change is an issue that Native women also have been forced, albeit in different ways and for different reasons, to contend with. Patriarchy is now firmly entrenched within most Native societies, although nonpatriarchal worldviews on gender relations still persist. Consequently, women (like former Principal Chief of the Cherokee Nation Wilma Mankiller) who strive for political leadership are accused, ironically, of not being traditional. Rayna Green (Cherokee) tells the story of an Indian conference on development at which a man gave a speech condemning the breakdown of traditional Indian values. He attributed this to the increasing number of Native women leaving home and assuming leadership positions. An elderly woman responded, "You know, I'm very interested in speech about the old days–your old days must have been really different from our old days, because in our old days, women were at the seat of power. . . . In our old days, women were at the center of knowledge and understanding about leadership, about distribution of power, about the distribution of goods and about the allotments of roles and power. . . . Let's talk about the old days; I say, 'Bring on the old days.'"[26]

There are many controversies over changing gender relations in Indian communities, ranging from whether or not women can sit at drums to whether or not women should be tribal chairs. At issue is how much change can a community, Indian or otherwise, accommodate and still be traditional. And who decides what tradition is, anyway? "At what point in the reinterpretation of Judaism," asks Judith Plaskow, "does the Jewish tradition cease being Jewish and become something else?" Her answer:

> Such anxieties misunderstand the nature of fundamental religious change, which is both slower and less manipulable than the question of limits assumes. . . . The Jews of the past, drawing on the religious forms available to them, created and recreated a living Judaism, reshaping tradition in ways consonant with their needs. What determined the "Jewishness" of their formulations was not a set of predetermined criteria, but the "workability" of such formulations for the Jewish people: the capacity of the stories and laws and liturgy to adapt to new conditions, to make sense and provide meaning, to offer the possibility of a whole new life.[27]

Similarly, the Colorado Sisters (Chichimec) wrestle with these issues in their performance piece, "A Traditional Kind of Woman: Too Much, Not 'Nuff." In their depictions of contemporary Native women who struggle with domestic violence, AIDS, substance abuse, and identity, they ask, can an urban woman be traditional? What is traditional anyway? Muriel Borst (Kuna/Rappahannock), in the title of her one-woman show, points out that "tradition" for contemporary Native women is "More Than Feathers and Beads."

Native cultures have always changed to meet current needs. As Marilou Awiakta (Cherokee) notes, one attribute of an oral culture is the ability to adapt rather than to try to maintain itself against a written, fixed set of principles.[28] The only cultures that *never* change are the dead and petrified kind; however, after the damaging transitions forced upon Native cultures by colonization, now virtually all change is regarded with suspicion. The challenge, then, is to find a way of welcoming change that may be helpful but to root it firmly within tradition. As Leslie Silko (Laguna Pueblo) writes in her novel *Ceremony*:

"There are some things I have to tell you," Betonie began softly. "The people nowadays have an idea about the ceremonies. They think the ceremonies must be performed exactly as they have always, maybe because one slip or mistake and the whole ceremony must be stopped. . . . That much is true. . . . But long ago when the people were given these ceremonies, the changing began . . . if only in the different voices from generation to generation. . . . You see, in many ways, the ceremonies have always been changing. . . .

"Things which don't shift and grow are dead things. . . . That's what the witchery is counting on: that we will cling to the ceremonies the way they were, and then their power will triumph, and the people will be no more."[29]

SPIRITUAL/CULTURAL APPROPRIATION

Native women also practice a version of what Chung calls a "survival-liberation centered syncretism" (though this may not always be the appropriate term in that they might also practice multiple traditions without blending them, as in syncretism). Unlike Korean Chung, however, Native women are concerned more centrally with issues of cultural/ spiritual appropriation, and, as a result, are reticent about sharing this process of "syncretism" with outsiders. In fact, Indian spiritual and cultural appropriation—a form of thievery that activist Justine Smith (Cherokee) calls "spiritual racism"—has become so pervasive that indigenous people are declaring war against it. Most Indian activist groups have written position papers condemning the use of their cultural traditions by outsiders. Hopi and Lakota elders have issued similar statements.[30] One Oakland-based group known as SPIRIT exists only to expose such theft. Indian nations are even using the legal theories of intellectual property rights to file lawsuits against those who make a profit by stealing their culture. Natives who write openly about Indian spirituality are generally viewed with suspicion, and many are exposed as "plastic medicine people."[31]

Even Native theologians like Steven Charleston (Choctaw) and George Tinker (Osage), who write defenses of Native spiritual practices in the interest of showing that they are not "satanic," risk encouraging the long-standing propensity of non-Natives to commit what Pieris calls "theological vandalism"—that is, the adoption of "exotic" foreign practices in isolation from the culture to which they rightfully belong.[32] The issue of appropriation calls into question the value of writing defenses of Indian spirituality for non-Indians. Fumitaka Matsuoka sheds some light on this problem. He notes that the important battle to be fought is not for cultural validation. The dominant culture is prepared to accommodate a little "multiculturalism"—a pow wow here, a pipe ceremony there—as long as the structures of power are not challenged. As he states, "The central problems . . . have to do, ultimately, not with ethnic groupings or the distinctness of our cultural heritages as such, but with racism and its manifestations in American economic policy, social rule and class relations."[33]

During my four years in Chicago I found that whenever Native people agitated for something big, like restoring "minority" status to American Indians for affirmative action purposes or eradicating the Columbus Day parade, the powers that be invariably said, "No, but why don't you hold a pow wow, or come in regalia to this or that public event?" At one session on Native women at the 1995 annual meeting of the American Academy of Religion, an audience participant suggested that future panels on Native issues include singing, dancing, and other forms of cultural "sharing." Inés Hernandez-Avila (Colville/Nez Perce) responded that she is reluctant to do so because providing entertainment would contribute to the stereotype that Indians are not capable of critical intellectual activity.

It is unquestionably true that there is much intolerance toward, and ignorance about, Native religions and cultures in the United States. We still do not even have freedom to practice our traditional religions. But as activist/scholar Gabrielle Tayac (Piscataway) notes, intolerance toward Indian religions cannot be addressed by educating White people about our spiritual beliefs, because our religious oppression is not based on ignorance but on the seizure of Indian lands upon which Indian spiritualities are based.[34] It is not an accident that Congress allows the use of peyote by the Native American Church but will not pass a law protecting Indian sacred sites, since the latter would entail a threat to U.S. government corporate control over Native lands. Writing defenses of Indian spirituality outside of a discussion of land claims not only leaves us open to cultural appropriation but diverts attention from the central issues of sovereignty over our lands and resources. Thus many Natives have joined with Chrystos in declaring to non-Indians: "While I am deeply spiritual, to share this with strangers would be a violation. Our rituals, stories, and religious practices have been stolen and abused, as has our land. I don't publish work which would encourage this. . . . My purpose is to make it as clear & as inescapable as possible, what the actual material conditions of our lives are."[35]

In response to the problem of spiritual appropriation, the Traditional Elders Circle has issued a communique on what is appropriate to share with non-Indians. The simple message is that all of creation is connected; people must live in balance with each other and with the earth to ensure our collective survival; abuse, repression, and exploitation of the earth's resources are not part of "the natural law."[36] These values are probably common to all indigenous cultures. Gay and lesbian theologians also seem to have adopted some version of them, although they do not stress the need for a balanced relationship between humans and the earth. Carter Heyward, for example, calls God "our relational power"; Gary Comstock likewise refers to God as "mutuality-in-relationship" and describes sin as "the violation of mutuality and reciprocity."[37] Spirituality, then, is not something to be purchased by paying $300 for a pipe ceremony. Instead, it is a way of living in "right relation" with the awareness that everything one does affects everything else. As Chrystos writes in her poem "Shame On":

> We've been polite for five hundred years
> & you still don't get it
> Take nothing you cannot return
> Give to others, give more
> Walk quietly
> Do what needs to be done
> Give thanks for your life
> Respect all beings
> simple
> and it doesn't cost a penny.[38]

In feminist theology, cultural appropriation has become a hot topic. The article "Appropriation and Reciprocity in Womanist/Mujerista/Feminist Work" in the *Journal of Feminist Studies in Religion*, based on a panel at the 1991 annual meeting of the American Academy of Religion, highlights much of what is at stake. Most of the authors cited in this essay have stressed the value of cross-cultural education. They have not questioned intercultural "borrowing" per se; rather, they have attempted to formulate guidelines to ensure that such borrowing remains respectful. Native people question the value of this kind of "education" for Native liberation. Certainly Native women want others to be informed about our scholarly analyses, political struggles, and intellectual work; however, the contributors to the *JFSR* article do not distinguish between these forms of sharing and cultural or spiritual sharing. It is these latter kinds that Native women find most suspect.

In addition, contributing writers describe cultural appropriation as an important problem but not a survival issue. Delores Williams also has remarked that appropriation, while annoying, is perhaps not the most pressing topic on the discussion agenda of feminists, womanists, and mujeristas.[39] Among Native women, however, appropriation *is* widely regarded as a matter of survival. As Chrystos says, "There are many forms of genocide, and this is one of them."[40] At the United Nations Conference on Women in Beijing, indigenous women from around the world identified combating spiritual and cultural appropriation as a primary concern. The Beijing Declaration of Indigenous Women condemns "the appropriation and privatization of our community intellectual rights . . . [and] the piracy of our biological, cultural, and intellectual resources and heritage." It further demands "that our inalienable rights to our intellectual and cultural heritage be recognized and respected. We will resist all processes seeking to destroy this heritage and alienate our resources and knowledge from us."

Non-Indians tend to downplay appropriation as a political and spiritual concern. If, however, appropriation is really as trivial as non-Indians suggest, why are Native people subjected to such violence when they condemn it? For example, when a mere handful of Native students began a peaceful campaign to eradicate Chief Illiniwik as the mascot of the University of Illinois, they and their children received death threats, dead animals were left at their doors, they were beaten by police, a White student union formed at the university, the Ku Klux Klan organized a chapter nearby, and the FBI began recruiting Indian students on campus. Most Native students found the situation intolerable and were forced to leave. Then the state legislature passed a resolution—the first of its kind—in support of the mascot. Anti-mascot campaigns have led to similarly violent and reactionary displays around the country.

LAND-NATIONALISM

As Gustavo Gutiérrez (Quechua) states, "Sinfulness occurs . . . in oppressive structures created for the benefit of only a few."[41] Although liberation theologians locate sin in social oppression rather than in individual agency, they identify the basic structure of oppression differently. White feminist theologians like Mary Daly locate "original sin" in patriarchy.[42] Black theologian James Cone's early works center on racism.[43] Latin American liberation theologians, including Gutiérrez, tend to emphasize class structure. Womanists call for a multivalent approach to oppression. Unlike feminist/womanist/mujerista theologies of the United States, Native women's spirituality/liberation praxis is centered in a national land-based struggle. Native women activists have often been reluctant to call themselves feminists because they generally experience colonialism, rather than sexism, as their primary mode of oppression. As mentioned above, Native women remember pre-contact Native societies as egalitarian. It was colonization that introduced the structures of homophobia, racism, capitalism, and sexism into most Native nations. Because Native women regard themselves as members of autonomous indigenous nations, the struggles they face are not those of civil rights, in terms of either racial or sexual equality. Rather, Native women concur with Malcolm X that the real fight is a land-based, national one: "Revolution is based on land. Land is the basis of all independence. Land is the basis of freedom, justice, and equality."[44]

Mary Crow Dog (Lakota) articulates the difference between Natives and most other racial and ethnic minorities in the United States: "They want *in*. We want *out*."[45] This is something of an over-simplification, of course. Other feminist theologians also stress the importance of community self-determination and the limits of civil rights. The eventual self-determination of the community in question, however, often is envisioned as taking place within a larger, diverse society. For instance, according to Judith Plaskow, the Jewish civil rights struggle assumed that "in the absence of persecution and enforced segregation, Jews and Judaism would assimilate to the prevailing social and cultural norms of the environment." While she is critical of the aims of "civil rights," she nevertheless asks at the same time, "Is communal identity and cohesion really at odds with participation in a wider society? . . . Is it not possible that the interaction of distinctive subcommunities could enrich a total community?"[46] Native nationalists, in contrast, are not interested in interacting with "a wider society," especially if that society is the United States or Canada. "Never forget," admonishes Chrystos, "america is our hitler."[47] Many indigenous people do not consider themselves citizens of Canada or the United States and refuse to vote in non-tribal elections or to be counted in the census. Some reservations have their own license plates and passports.

Even in urban settings many Indians tend to reject the authority, if not the coercive power, of the government. I once conducted an informal survey among Indian women in Chicago, asking them what barriers would prevent them from accessing the U.S. legal system if they were the victim of a crime. Even though several of the respondents have always lived in the city rather than on the reservation, the most common answer was that doing so would be tantamount to dealing with a foreign government. Even in diverse urban areas Indians often emphasize community autonomy. For example, when the Indian agencies of Chicago meet together to strategize how to access various foundation monies, they inevitably clash with representatives of those foundations over the issue of "diversity." At one meeting the foundation spokesperson emphasized that Indian agencies could receive a lot of money to develop programs that would help overcome the segregation of Chicago's ethnic communities. This advice ran directly counter to the agencies' own plan, which was to raise enough money to buy housing in one area of the city so that all Indians could live together. Often Indians do not identify with the umbrella term *person of color*, either you're Native or you're not. In fact, not all Indians even identify primarily as Indians; many identify exclusively by nation.

Such community solidarity has led Native women activists to argue that fighting colonization is such a priority that there is no need to address the issue of sexism at all. Women of All Red Nations (WARN) founder Lorelei DeCora Means (Lakota) once stated:

We are American Indian women, in that order. We are oppressed, first and foremost, as American Indians, as peoples colonized by the United States of America, not as women. As Indians, we can never forget that. Our survival, the survival of every one of us—man, woman and child—as Indians depends on it. Decolonization is the agenda, the whole agenda, and until it is accomplished, it is the only agenda that counts for American Indians."[48]

At the United Nations Conference in Beijing, the indigenous women's caucus began formulating a statement criticizing the struggle for gender equality as oppressive to indigenous women. Winona LaDuke explained that attempting to be "equal" with men under the current capitalist and imperialist world order will do nothing to liberate most women. "It is not, frankly, that women of the dominant society in so-called first world countries should have equal pay and equal status, if that pay and status continue to be based on a consumption model which is not only unsustainable, but causes constant violation of the human rights of women and nations elsewhere in the world."[49] The statement, still in process, does denounce sexism but calls for its eradication *within* the context of self-determination for all peoples.

Spirituality is integral to this anti-colonial struggle because Native spiritualities depend upon the land base that gave rise to them; they cannot easily be transplanted to another geographic area. Many ceremonies must be performed at specific locations. As Vine Deloria states:

> The structures of their traditions is taken directly from the world around them, from their relationships with other forms of life. Context is therefore all-important for both practice and understanding of reality. The places where revelations were experienced were remembered and set aside as locations where, through rituals and ceremonials, the people could once again communicate with spirits. . . . The sacred lands remain as permanent fixtures in their cultural or religious understanding.[50]

This close relationship with the land makes environmental issues central to indigenous liberation struggles. Like Rosemary Radford Ruether, Sallie McFague, and other ecofeminist theologians, Indians "envision a healed society, in the sense of nondominating relations between human beings in interrelation with the rest of nature."[51] Both Ruether and McFague, however, only peripherally analyze environmentalism in relation to colonialism, imperialism, and capitalism. McFague states, "The nuclear issue and issues of political and social oppression are intrinsically related, for at the heart of all these issues is the question of power: who wields it and what sort it is." She, however, seems startlingly unaware of environmental racism when she says that

"as a threat rather than a reality, nuclear doom requires an act of imagination if it is to become part of our reality, part of our 'world.'"[52] Native
people require no such act. They are living currently with the "reality"
of "nuclear doom" because *all* uranium mining and nuclear testing take
place on or near Indian land. Consequently, Native communities face
60 percent birth defect rates in some areas, 80 percent cancer rates in
others.

   Ruether similarly states, "The issue of poverty, of the growing division between misery and affluence, will thread through this whole
account [of environmental destruction]." But then she writes, "The challenge that humans face . . . is whether they will be able to visualize and
organize their own reproduction, production, and consumption in such
a way as to stabilize their relationship to the rest of the ecosphere and
so avert massive social and planetary ecocide." She seems to assume
that all contribute equally to ecological disaster, that all are equally
affected by population policies, that all have the same power to organize their production and consumption.[53] Native activists more precisely
locate the environmental crisis in the question, "Who controls the land?"
The majority of energy resources in the United States are on Indian
land, and thus Indian people are generally the first to be affected by the
destruction caused by resource extraction. Their lands also are targeted
for dumping of toxic waste. Many Indian activists believe that treaty
rights are the best protection against environmental devastation wrought
by rampant capitalism.[54] Multinational corporations believe it, too. That
is why they fund anti-Indian hate groups to fight treaty enforcement.
"Naming reality" in light of the ecological crisis we face, as McFague
argues, is important.[55] Changing personal consumption patterns, as
Ruether suggests, is also important. Native women activists recognize,
however, that the struggle to protect the earth entails a long, hard battle
against the United States government and multinationals. As Mililani
Trask (Native Hawai'ian) argues, "We cannot stand by the stream and
say our chants and beat the drum and pray that the river people will
survive. . . . Natural resource management is a tool, a skill, and a weapon
that the women warriors of today need to attire themselves with if they
are going to be prepared for battle. Prayers are the foundation, but . . .
[we need] to seize control and political power. We cannot go out and
fight America with the spear and a prayer; we need to do more."[56]
Native women are prominent in these struggles.

HEALING

   While in the past, indigenous struggles were almost entirely land
based, it has become increasingly clear that Native people, and particularly Native women, also must heal from the psychological effects of

colonization. Sexual abuse, domestic violence, alcohol abuse, and teen suicide–the legacy of colonization and particularly of boarding schools– have devastated Indian families. In response, there is a growing "wellness" movement, largely spearheaded by women, which stresses healing from abuse, both on the individual and the community level. The University of Oklahoma holds two national wellness and women conferences each year, which over two thousand Indian women attend. These conferences help women begin their healing journeys from various forms of abuse and teach them to become enablers for community healing. The Indigenous Women's Network also sponsors gatherings that tie together the healing of individuals and communities from the trauma of this nation's history. At a 1994 conference each of four days had a different focus: individual healing, family healing, community healing, and political struggles in North America and the world.

Spirituality is an integral part of this movement because mainstream paradigms for dealing with abuse–for example, the Twelve Step model of Alcoholics Anonymous–tend to be less effective for Native communities than traditional spiritual practices. Deloria notes that, in contrast to Christianity, healing is a central motif of Indian religious traditions.[57] In her short story "Keeping Pace with the Rest of the World," Wilma Mankiller contrasts traditional approaches to healing with Western medical models: "[The doctor] did not know how to heal an illness, only how to cut it out. . . . More to herself than to Pearl, Ahniwake added, "He did not know my clan, my family, my history. How could he possibly know how to heal me?"[58]

Because indigenous spiritual traditions are land based, healing necessarily involves restoration of a proper relationship with the land. Beth Brant's (Mohawk) collection of short stories, *Food and Spirits*, illustrates this connection. Her characters come to terms with abuse while reestablishing their relationship to the earth and creation. In "Swimming Upstream," for instance, Anna May overcomes her desire to commit suicide when she identifies with a salmon with a torn fin trying to swim upstream. When the salmon makes it, she throws away her bottle of liquor and begins life again.[59]

While liberation theologians like Gutiérrez and Pieris have properly stressed the political structure of evil, Native activists have found that it is impossible to maintain the fight for liberation without a simultaneous movement to heal the damage done by colonization. Much of the American Indian Movement's drug and alcohol abuse and its mistreatment of women can be attributed to the fact that its male leadership did not deal with the impact of colonization on their psyches. Steve Old Coyote, Squamish spiritual leader, notes that the first priority facing Indian communities is the abuse of women and children: "As long as we are destroying ourselves from within, we don't have to worry about the outside."[60] Mililani Trask further notes that the fight against oppressive structures means nothing without the commitment to "building a strong nation."[61]

The growing recognition of sexual and domestic violence in Indian communities probably has been one of the primary factors in the increasing number of Native women who either identify as feminists or at least more fully address issues of sexism. As Gail Small (Northern Cheyenne) of Native Action has stated, abusers need to be held accountable for their misdeeds before being restored to community.[62] Loretta Rivera (Seneca) of the Minnesota Battered Women's Justice Project has declared that if sovereignty is going to be used to cover up the victimization of Native women, then we need to rethink what sovereignty means.[63] Frances Wood, in her discussion of violence against women in the Black church, says, "Misogyny against Black women did not begin with their enslavement in the United States."[64] While most Native women activists might say that misogyny in Indian communities did begin with colonization, this can no longer serve as an excuse to ignore the misogyny that does exist now. They are beginning to see the truth of Woods's words: "We do not serve the best interests of women, children, or men when we refuse to hold men accountable for oppressive behavior."[65] Whereas Native women activists once tended to view the struggle against sexism as standing at odds with anti-colonial struggles, increasing numbers now see the fight against sexism as consonant with, even necessary to, sovereignty movements.

CONCLUSION

I have attempted to echo the spirituality/liberation praxis of Native women who fight for Indian sovereignty. One pitfall for theologians who attempt to "reproduce" the voices of their community, however, is that they inadvertently appoint themselves community spokespersons. Particularly in the celebrity-driven culture of the United States, the predominantly non-Indian readers of theological texts inevitably fixate on the author rather than the Native communities the author is discussing. Clearly, good intentions are no substitute for a strategy. Perhaps theologians can stop signing their own names to their books, or use their clout to push through collaborative, community-based publications. Further discussion on such strategies is a pressing need for Native people, as well as all liberation theologians in academic circles. Because Native women are constantly battling the forces of genocide, they cannot afford to waste time on academic efforts that have no real relevance for the community. The challenge liberation theologians face today is not just to devise sophisticated theological analyses that reflect the needs of our communities but actively to be part of a grassroots-based movement for social transformation. Our job is to be engaged in the task of eliminating the oppression our communities face, not making a living from it.[66]

Notes

[1] William Baldridge, "Toward a Native American Theology," *American Baptist Quarterly* (December 1989), p. 228.

[2] See Jace Weaver, "Losing My Religion: Native American Religious Traditions and American Religious Freedom," herein.

[3] Ada María Isasi-Díaz, *En la Lucha* (Minneapolis: Augsburg, 1993), p. 63.

[4] Dianne Stewart, "An Approach to Womanist Theology," unpublished paper, Union Theological Seminary, May 6, 1994, p. 11.

[5] Chung Hyun Kyung, *Struggle to Be the Sun Again* (Maryknoll, N.Y.: Orbis Books, 1993), p. 103.

[6] Renita Weems, "Reading Her Way through the Struggle: African-American Women and the Bible," in Cain Hope Felder, *Stony the Road We Trod* (Minneapolis: Augsburg, 1991), pp. 60-61.

[7] Katie Cannon, *Black Womanist Ethics* (Atlanta: Scholar's Press, 1988), p. 5.

[8] Gloria Ines Loya, "The Hispanic Woman: *Pasionaria* and *Pastora* of the Hispanic Community," offprint, p. 127.

[9] Stewart, p. 11.

[10] See Marcia Riggs, *Awake, Arise and Act* (Cleveland: Pilgrim Press, 1994).

[11] This is one reason why Native people in an urban setting are more likely to attend an Indian church regardless of denomination than to go to a predominantly non-Indian church of their own denomination. Native people are also notorious for not attending church regularly. Consequently, Indian ministries generally focus on community action.

[12] Vine Deloria, Jr., "A Native American Perspective on Liberation," *Occasional Bulletin of Missionary Research* 1 (July 1977), p. 16.

[13] Chung, p. 95.

[14] Aloysius Pieris, *An Asian Theology of Liberation* (Edinburgh: T & T Clark, 1988), p. 86 (emphasis added).

[15] Haunani Kay Trask, speech, Sisters of Color International, 5th Annual Conference, Hamilton College, Clinton, N.Y., April 21-23, 1996.

[16] See Paula Gunn Allen, *The Sacred Hoop* (Boston: Beacon Press, 1986); Deloria, p. 17; Vine Deloria, Jr., *God Is Red*, 2d ed. (Golden, Colo.: Fulcrum, 1992), p. 265.

[17] Robert Allen Warrior, "A Native Perspective: Canaanites, Cowboys, and Indians," in *Voices from the Margin*, ed. R. S. Sugirtharajah (Maryknoll, N.Y.: Orbis Books, 1991), pp. 294-95; Isasi-Díaz, p. 63.

[18] Elisabeth Schüssler Fiorenza, *Jesus: Miriam's Child, Sophia's Prophet* (New York: Continuum, 1995), pp. 9-10.

[19] Deloria, *God Is Red*, p. 210.

[20] Ibid., p. 86.

[21] Chrystos, "Rude as 2:29 A.M.," in *Fire Power* (Vancouver: Press Gang, 1995), p. 49.

[22] See, for example, *A Sharing: Traditional Lakota Thought and Philosophy Regarding Domestic Violence* (South Dakota: Sacred Shawl Women's Society, n.d.); *Sexual Assault Is Not an Indian Tradition* (Minneapolis: Division of Indian Work Sexual Assault Project, n.d.); Paula Gunn Allen, "Violence and the American Indian Woman," *The Speaking Profits Us* (Seattle: Center for the Prevention of Sexual and Domestic Violence, n.d.), pp. 5-7; see also Annette Jaimes and Theresa Halsey, "American Indian Women: At the Center of Indigenous Resistance in North America," in *State of Native America*, ed. M. Annette Jaimes (Boston: South End Press, 1992), pp. 311-44.

[23] Winona LaDuke, quoted in Jaimes and Halsey, p. 319.

[24] Jaimes and Halsey, p. 315; Tom Holm, "Patriots and Pawns," in Jaimes, p. 355.

[25] Blu Greenberg, *On Women and Judaism: A View from Tradition* (Philadelphia: Jewish Publication Society of America, 1981).

[26] Rayna Green, "American Indian Women: Diverse Leadership for Social Change," in *Bridges of Power: Women's Multicultural Alliances*, ed. Lisa Albrecht and Rose Brewer (Philadelphia: New Society Publishers, 1990), p. 63.

[27] Judith Plaskow, *Standing Again at Sinai* (San Francisco: Harper & Row, 1990), pp. xvi, xvii.

[28] Marilou Awiakta, *Selu: Seeking Corn-Mother's Wisdom* (Golden, Colo.: Fulcrum, 1993), p. 16.

[29] Leslie Marmon Silko, *Ceremony* (New York: Penguin, 1986), p. 126.

[30] See Marilyn Masayevsa, "Cultural Appropriation: A Hopi Response," *Indigenous Woman* 2 (1995), pp. 35-36.

[31] See Traditional Elders Circle, *Communique No. 9* (June 21, 1986).

[32] Steven Charleston, "The Old Testament of Native America," in *Lift Every Voice: Constructing Christian Theologies from the Underside,* ed. Susan Brooks Thistlethwaite and Mary Potter Engel (San Francisco: Harper & Row, 1990), pp. 49-61; George Tinker, "Spirituality, Native American Personhood, Sovereignty, and Solidarity," in *Native and Christian*, ed. James Treat (New York: Routledge, 1996), pp. 115-31.

[33] Fumitaka Matsuoka, *Out of Silence* (Cleveland: United Church Press, 1995), p. 93.

[34] Gabrielle Tayac, "Native Struggles for Freedom under the Law," respondent, American Academy of Religion, Philadelphia, Penn., November 1995.

[35] Chrystos, *Not Vanishing* (Vancouver: Press Gang, 1988), preface.

[36] Traditional Circle of Indian Elders and Youth, *Communique No. 12* (June 14, 1989).

[37] Carter Heyward, *Touching Our Strength* (San Francisco: Harper & Row, 1989), p. 24; Gary Comstock, *Gay Theology without Apology* (Cleveland: Pilgrim Press, 1993), pp. 28, 30.

[38] Chrystos, *Dream On* (Vancouver: Press Gang, 1991), p. 101.

[39] Delores Williams, lecture, December 5, 1995.

[40] Chrystos, *Dream On*, p. 101.

[41] Gustavo Gutiérrez, "Liberation Praxis and Christian Faith," in *Frontiers of Theology in Latin America* (Maryknoll, N.Y.: Orbis Books, 1983), pp. 21, 1-2.

[42] Mary Daly, *Beyond God the Father* (Boston: Beacon Press, 1973), p. 2.

[43] James H. Cone, *A Black Theology of Liberation* (Maryknoll, N.Y.: Orbis Books, 1986), p. 7; see, Allen, pp. 30-42.

⁴⁴ Malcolm X, "Message to the Grassroots," in *Malcolm X Speaks*, ed. George Breitman (New York: Grove Press, 1963), p. 9.

⁴⁵ Mary Crow Dog (with Richard Erdoes), *Lakota Woman* (New York: HarperCollins, 1991), p. 77.

⁴⁶ Plaskow, pp. 92, 94.

⁴⁷ Chrystos, "Winter Count," in *Dream On*, p. 13.

⁴⁸ Lorelei DeCora Means, quoted in Jaimes and Halsey, p. 314.

⁴⁹ Winona LaDuke, keynote address, UN Conference on Women, Beijing, China; reprinted in *The Circle* 16 (October 1995), p. 8.

⁵⁰ Deloria, *God Is Red*, p. 67.

⁵¹ Rosemary Radford Ruether, *Gaia and God* (San Francisco: Harper & Row, 1992), p. 9.

⁵² Sallie McFague, *Models of God* (Philadelphia: Fortress Press, 1987), p. 15.

⁵³ Ruether, pp. 87, 47.

⁵⁴ See Rudolph C. Ryser, "Anti-Indian Movement on the Tribal Frontier," Occasional Paper #16, Center for World Indigenous Studies, April 1991.

⁵⁵ McFague, p. 3.

⁵⁶ Mililani Trask, "Indigenous Women Are the Mothers of Their Nations," *Indigenous Woman* 2 (1995), p. 26.

⁵⁷ Deloria, *God Is Red*, p. 250.

⁵⁸ Wilma Mankiller (and Michael Wallis), *Mankiller: A Chief and Her People* (New York: St. Martin's Press, 1993), p. 233.

⁵⁹ Beth Brant, *Food and Spirits* (Vancouver: Press Gang, 1991), pp. 117-25.

⁶⁰ Steve Old Coyote, speech, Seattle Urban Indian Ministry Conference, Seattle, January 1990.

⁶¹ Trask, p. 24.

⁶² Gail Small, speech, Native American Reproductive Rights Conference, Rapid City, April 1993.

⁶³ Loretta Rivera, interview with author, December 8, 1995.

⁶⁴ Frances Wood, "Take My Yoke Upon You," in *A Troubling in My Soul: Womanist Perspectives on Evil and Suffering*, ed. Emilie M. Townes (Maryknoll, N.Y.: Orbis Books, 1993), p. 43.

⁶⁵ Ibid., p. 45.

⁶⁶ Special thanks to Justine Smith, Tom Reisz, Delores Williams, Judith Plaskow, James Cone, Debbie Landsberg, Dianne Stewart, Jace Weaver, and all the women of WARN.

16.

Politicizing HIV Prevention in Indian Country

CRAIG WOMACK

I want to tell a couple of stories and see what it arouses in you, the reader. When I taught in Omaha, I was the only full-time Native faculty member in the entire university. Consequently, schools, libraries—even people throwing parties—were constantly asking me to come tell "Indian stories," except of course they said "Native American" rather than "Indian." And by "Native American stories" they meant creation, hero, trickster, coyote stories. My own biased view makes me strongly suspicious that they really wanted children's stories, nice stuff that presents white people with images of themselves, all mixed together in a highly palatable pan-tribal stew. My concern has to do with the way we play into colonial discourse with these stories, the way we depoliticize our own literatures in an oral tradition that was once highly nationalistic, and the way significant tribal differences are blurred and a sense of specific sovereignty diminished. I am concerned about what happens to the political intent of the stories when they are separated out of their tribal contexts, removed from a total existential situation. For example, in the case of Creek (or Muscogee) stories, a pan-tribal context might cause a divorce from a sense of "Creekness"—knowledge of what it is to be from a clan, a town, a nation where these narratives are contextualized with other stories, songs, and ceremonies from within the Creek Nation rather than performed as isolated fragments alongside a confusing array of tellings from other tribal traditions. Would these stories better serve our own folks in the context of the passed-on, tribally-specific traditions, histories, religious practices, and political thought that create their meanings?

My purpose in this chapter is to move literature closer to activism and politics rather than farther away, and, for those reasons, the two stories I have chosen are not of the creation-hero-trickster ilk (which isn't to say that these stories are apolitical, but that they are often presented as if they are). Trickster is probably here somewhere, anyway, struggling in this "postmodern" age, if such a thing really exists, with the damn nuisance of a latex condom—an unnatural barrier at very best, a snag in serious snagging.[1]

The first story begins at a conference on AIDS issues in Indian country; the name of this gathering: "Sharing the Vision: Native American Survival in the Age of HIV and AIDS." The conference was held September 23-27, 1996, in Portland, Oregon. My partner (a Nahuatl guy from Mexico) and I had gone on our own funds since neither of us works for an AIDS organization or social agency, though we have both done AIDS work. The Portland Area Indian Health Board, after we arrived, very graciously paid for our hotel, for which I want to say a heartfelt *mado*,[2] since we didn't have a place to stay and a Blackfeet friend of mine only had room for one of us, given that he himself was staying with friends.

My interest in the conference was as a Creek-Cherokee man who is gay and seeking ways to become more involved in HIV prevention in Indian communities, including the one I now live in. Further, as an Indian writer (and, yes, I *do* want to be called an Indian writer, thank you very much; I do *not* feel this limits my work or my audience), I have been trying to make HIV issues affecting Native men a more central concern in my essays, stories, and poems, given the fact that European-introduced diseases have historically had drastic effects on the populations of tribal nations. Well, in addition to all this serious stuff, I always enjoy hanging out with other Native gay guys, like to see old friends, and need to get away with my partner every now and then. And, hell, Portland's a beautiful city; the motel ended up being right on the Columbia River (there was a blood-red lunar eclipse over the river the last night of the conference).

One of the workshops my partner and I decided to attend was on the subject of spirituality in relationships. Since we were a fairly new couple and had only been together a couple of months (take note, this is like decades in heterosexual years), I was thinking like a newlywed, I reckon, along the lines of "hey, this will be good for us."

When we got into the workshop, the first thing the presenters did was announce that they were a divorced heterosexual couple, then turned off the lights, and while the guy in braids either played the flute or a tape of one—it was plumb dark in there, so I'm not sure—the other half of the divorced couple sang a song in English about doing things the "Indian way."

And that was *before* it got weird.

In fact, if the session would have just stayed whacked, we would have been OK. The Native couple next commenced telling about their failed relationship with all the psycho-babble at their command (they were best friends now, and they could call each other up without enabling). They told us that the session "wasn't about homosexual or heterosexual." I guess this was supposed to make us queers feel better, but I wondered why it *wasn't* about Native gay guys, given that we were at a conference that seemed to me to have something to do with Native gay men, since we were gathered around the issue of AIDS in Indian country. Men having sex with other men is, by far, the largest cause of transmission of HIV in Indian communities. The 1995 data from the Center for Disease Control (vastly underestimated, by the way, because of under-reporting and lack of knowledge in terms of identifying Native people with HIV/AIDS) report that of the 1246 cases of Native AIDS transmission reported to them that year, 618 were from men having sex with other men, while only 80 were from heterosexual sex. The other means of infection were 219 from IV drug use, 175 men having sex with other men *and* using IV drugs, 87 hemophiliacs, 16 blood transfusions, and 51 unknown. So, it seemed to me that a session on spirituality in relationships, presented at a Native American AIDS conference, did in fact have something to do with Indian gay guys.

All right, maybe I'm being a petty, histrionic queen on that score, but let me move on. The workshop quickly catapulted from irksome to catastrophic. In order to liven things up, we were handed cards, some blank, some with various symbols on them, and told we were going to participate in an exercise. The meaning of what we were doing was never explained before, during, or after the exercise, but we were instructed to walk around the room and hug people. I don't exactly come from a hugging bunch, but I acted like a good sheep and followed the rest of the herd. I had fun watching all those who, like me, had to mask the grimaces behind smiley faces. After we hugged one another for five minutes, the presenters called the exercise to a halt, and everyone was told to show his or her card. The husband, or ex-husband, went around telling various people they were dead, infected, or clean, depending on the symbol on their card. The dead and infected folk had to point out all the people they had hugged, pointing and calling them out one by one. These others were pronounced infected or dead. To my horror, one of the people pronounced dead was a Navajo friend with AIDS, who, literally, that spring, had almost died from opportunistic diseases yet had made a strong rally over the summer, and one of those pronounced infected was his partner who, also literally, had AIDS.

The point of the exercise must have been about the chances of transmitting the disease (though none of this was explained at any point), but the problem, of course, was the symbolism used to make the case. Rather than symbolically exchanging fluids—the contact of blood and semen—we had passed on the disease by hugging!!! Surely to God this was not what the presenters believed or meant to imply, and the exercise was probably conveying the opposite meaning of what they had intended. At this point, as the beaming heteros were killing us off faster than General Sherman, I wanted to scream at the top of my lungs–and I should have; this is my failure and responsibility–"HIV is not transmitted by hugging people!" There were many older straight people in the room who may have left confused or wondering if they could get HIV by touching their infected loved ones, kin, and friends in their respective tribal communities.

I kept assuming that the exercise would evolve into some form of civilized discourse, that the Indian killing would eventually stop, and that we would be allowed to ask questions and raise concerns about the incredible implications of what we had all just witnessed. Such a moment never came, however, just more psycho-babble about self-esteem. In the next exercise we all had to go around the room and rate our self-esteem on a scale of 1-10. The presenter said his was off the scale, somewhere around 25. I believe him.

I kept trying to catch the eye of the presenters to indicate that I wanted to ask a question about the AIDS exercise, but they'd have none of it, and they next launched into a discussion of "spirituality" in which every single reference to sexuality was made in the context of addiction, alcoholism, and recovery from addiction. I hadn't felt quite as beat up since I was a kid in the Southern Baptist Church, and, by the end, we'd been pummeled to death with a bloody war club on the good Red Road to recovery from sexual addiction. If what was presented to us during the workshop was healthy spirituality, relationships, and sexuality, please let me keep my addictions, and I'll let you all have fun at your meetings. Of course, none of this is the real intent of recovery programs; I want to say that before all my clean and sober friends read this and stop speaking to me.

I mean, *puh-lease.*

Since when did our own traditions place sexual relationships in the category of addiction and disorder?

Before I go much farther, let me say that this was a low point in an otherwise useful conference where a broad range of Indian people–gay and straight, urban and reservation, tribal employees and social agency representatives–were gathered together to learn better ways to generate positive prevention messages in Indian communities, which have had a higher per capita infection rate than other minorities. One emblematic statistic along these lines is that of the eighty founding members of Gay American Indians in San Francisco, a young organization founded before the onslaught of the epidemic, only twenty are still living.

During the day that followed, my partner and I, traumatized and in need of recovery from the workshop on recovery, discussed a general lack we see in the presentation of AIDS-prevention messages for Native people. We talked about the tendency to ignore the political aspects of AIDS, a disavowal of the reality that AIDS, like other issues in Indian country, has to do with the relationship between colonizer and colonized, and how he related experiences in Mexico that make evident the need to discuss the political dimensions of the disease.

It is not my intention to negate the importance of the conference or the agency that hosted it; I don't want to be one of those naysayers who bad-mouth those trying to do good work in difficult circumstances. The National Native American AIDS Prevention Center (NNAAPC) is the major case management service for Native people with AIDS, serving five hundred clients at eleven project sites in Oklahoma City, New York, North Carolina, Kansas City, Milwaukee, Minneapolis, the Navajo Nation, Phoenix, Seattle, Anchorage, and Hawaii. I am part of the National Leadership Development Workshop that has worked with NNAAPC on targeting Native gay men for services and training.

My wish is to contribute somehow to a discussion of the epidemic in Indian country. Given our history of population decimation due to European-imported diseases, it seems to me that AIDS is directly related to discussions of sovereignty and national survival. I want to talk about the irony of the narrow focus that tends to characterize AIDS as merely a medical concern, or a matter of personal healing, rather than including the political ramifications of the disease.

The purpose for contextualizing HIV/AIDS in terms of politics and history is not toward the end of creating a sense of victimization—poor Indians trampled down by whites—but to point out that Indian people have often led resistance movements and that these might be analyzed for strategies to face modern assaults against sovereignty, from whatever directions they come. What worked, what didn't, how might we improve? We need a theory of resistance and sovereignty, developed through an analysis of our own cultures, our own speakers, writers, teachers, intellectuals, and warriors.

Yet much of HIV prevention in Indian country gives little attention to these issues of politics and history. To use a corollary, if one looks at lesbian sexual identity, it is interesting to note that lesbianism is often discussed in relation to feminism and patriarchy. It is seldom singled out as an individual matter, a matter of mere sexual orientation or personal identity; it retains its political roots. Might we learn something from this more holistic treatment of lesbianism that might be consistent with our own traditions where gayness is part of a larger tribal context? If we want to find ways to convince tribal communities and tribal leaders that we're not just "one-issue" folks—the gay guys, the AIDS guys—how can we have dialogues that do not include discussion of tribal sovereignty?

In addition to the politics of the United States government, the white gay community itself contains strong elements of racism, homophobia and self-hatred, and exclusionary tactics. Simply put, white gay culture can be racist, cruel, and mean-spirited, not a helluva lot of fun for Native gay people. To see evidence of this, one need only peruse the personal ads in any gay periodical and note how many of them are marked specifically for race, requesting white partners and, further, asking for "discreet" encounters with guys who don't look or act gay, many going so far as to exclude fats/fems and a whole long list of other undesirables. Few groups can best the white gay community for its elevation of white racial purity and exclusionary tactics for those who don't meet white-defined standards of perfection. A Native gay guy has a tough row to hoe in the white gay community. Obviously, the ads do not represent the entire gay community, but they certainly, at the very least, indicate a strong area of sickness within it. In some communities, perhaps many of them, acceptance of Native gay men in the larger gay community is impossible. Yet these issues of blatant, overwhelming racism often are left undiscussed in regard to AIDS prevention, and they seem directly related to issues of low self-esteem, which contribute to substance abuse and more risky behaviors that increase one's chances of contracting the virus.

The need for a discussion of colonialism also becomes apparent when one examines prevention messages themselves. Although the tactics of the couple at the Portland conference were extreme, to say the least, the idea of sex as dysfunction comes through all too often in prevention when the messages are voiced in the language of prohibition and retribution, that is, as Christianized puritanical discourse. The couple merely may have been an extreme reflection of this problem within the prevention community itself. For instance, one pamphlet I have seen that is used in Indian country has one word on its cover in big, bold letters: **ABSTINENCE**. I've never read the pamphlet, because the cover is so personally offensive to me, but I am guessing that, if one opens it up, it takes a more moderate tack inside, presenting abstinence as a choice along a range of possible choices. Yet this pamphlet disturbs me deeply. Since when did abstinence become normative sexuality in Native cultures, past or present? The title of the leaflet is offensive to me because it presents an impossibility, and, further, it is antithetical to my understanding of my own cultural traditions. I always thought it was the guys in the white collars who believed in that. Certainly there are instances where individual Native gay men, for reasons important to them, choose to be celibate for a time, often because of a prior period of promiscuity and unhealthy behaviors that reflected low self-esteem.

Depicting abstinence as any kind of norm, however–acting as though it is natural and the way things ought to be–presents young Native people with the kind of unattainable lifestyle, inconsistent with their own world views and experiences, that forces them to say, "Oh f–k it. I might as well have a good time before I get sick, if the only choice is to live a long life like a monk." As Neil Young says–not that anybody but old curmudgeons like me listen to Neil Young– "It's better to burn out than it is to rust." Quality of life is seldom brought into the discussion. Reducing risk to zero is presented as a possibility. This is ridiculous. If we look at our own oral traditions, which of our narratives teach us that the world is a risk-free place?

Instead of teaching kids what the risks are for particular behaviors and allowing them to decide what levels of risk they wish to take, we often present AIDS messages to the tune of "Onward, Christian Soldiers"–once again, that is, as apocalyptic Christian discourse rather than as trickster/survival strategies. Over and over again, on AIDS posters and pamphlets, is the recurring theme, in various guises: "sex kills," "God's gonna get you for that," "if you play, you pay," "just say no." Jonathan Edwards and other Puritans must be grinning from their New England graves, assuming they ever grin.

What are we going to do when some combination of therapies, such as protease inhibitors used with AZT and other drugs, changes AIDS from a terminal disease to a chronically manageable one? Will we still couch our messages in retributive Christian language even when the disease is no longer life-threatening and the message that sex kills isn't true? By taking up the fundamentalist Christian messages of abstinence, celibacy, addiction, disorder, and inherent sinfulness, we've confused self-abnegation with self-discipline.

As Curtis Harris, project director of the American Indian Community House in New York City, has been saying recently at AIDS meetings, we have failed to point out that condoms are unnatural barriers, that they are not the way things are meant to be, even though they are necessary at the current time. Along similar lines, abstinence, though one possibility along a spectrum of choices involving risk-management, certainly isn't a normal state of affairs. Although it usually isn't presented as the primary means of prevention in AIDS messages, the language of abstinence and prohibition rather than the language of managing risk still is often employed.

The next story I would like to tell occurred after returning home to Omaha after the Portland conference. My partner and I had a great time at the conference, saw many old friends, and learned a lot in spite of the tragi-comic workshop. A couple of weeks later we attended National Coming Out Day, October 13, 1996, at the student center on campus where I taught. There was an outstanding speech given by Melinda Parras, executive director of the National Gay and Lesbian Task Force, in which she summarized the current state of legislation affecting gays and lesbians and emphasized the importance of issues like affirmative action as part of the broader issues of civil rights that the gay community needs to recognize.

Just before the speech I saw something that was like one of those "no this can't really be happening" deals. The new Gay, Lesbian, Bi-sexual, and Transgender Center in Omaha had decided to name itself the "Berdache Center," and there was its banner waving proudly for all to see. When I asked the director of the center if they'd consulted with any Indian people regarding their feelings concerning the name, given that the name so directly refers to Native cultures, he 'fessed up that not a single Native person's opinion had been sought out because "we didn't know how to find any of *them*" (my emphasis). The GLBT Center argued that it was honoring Indian people, since the term *berdache* refers to the fact that many tribes had special roles for gays and lesbians. The word, however, is of Arabic origin; it refers to male slaves who acted as anally receptive prostitutes; it was prescribed by white anthropologists to describe Native cultures; and it is a name that is generally disliked by Native gays and lesbians.

In addition to writing a letter to this man and including information written by Native gay men regarding the highly problematic nature of the term *berdache*, I sent an editorial to the *New Voice of Nebraska*, the state's monthly gay and lesbian periodical. In it, I detailed the multiple problems and many levels of offense encompassed by the term. What I failed to say in the letter, though I certainly made these comments in subsequent letters to the GLBT Center and to the campus newspaper, was that there is also a central issue of cultural appropriation. (The whole thing became an issue on campus when an article about me appeared on the front page of the paper, filled with statements I'd supposedly made, written by a guy I'd never spoken to in my whole life, and they were forced to print a retraction—an interesting debacle, given that being spoken for rather than being allowed to speak for one's self is at the heart of the debate.) Regarding cultural appropriation, there is a problem with the notion of universality—often accepted in the dominant culture. This lies in the automatic assumption that a concept such as two-spiritedness—the word Native gay men often use to describe themselves rather than the derogatory term *berdache*—is universally available to those who are outside the culture, not part of the passed-on religious, ceremonial, and cultural traditions that provide the meaning for such roles through a complicated social, religious, and political matrix in tribes that have their own terms for gays and lesbians. There is something quintessentially American in the supremacist assumption that one has the right to own and claim for one's own every damn thing in the universe.

In an essay like this present one, I'm probably preaching to the choir, so what I'd like really to get to is a phenomenon that came out of this experience and that has continued to fascinate me. In my correspondence with the GLBT Center, we kept going around and around in an endless loop. I kept saying, "Did you talk to any Indians?" and they would reply, "No, but we got a lot of information off the Internet." Then I'd say, "Yeah, but did you talk to any Indians?" And they'd go,

"No, but we contacted the Berdache Research Center" in Wichita (evidently there really is such a place!). And then I'd go, "YEAH, BUT DID YOU TALK TO ANY INDIANS?" Well, you get the picture . . .

I realized something from these conversations. Not only is it the *norm* in the dominant culture to assume that what white folks say about Indians is inherently superior to what Indian folks say about Indians, but Americans carry a deep investment in that assumption—that they *prefer* whites' accounts of things Native. (Some of you are probably thinking, no kidding, it took you this long to realize *that*. OK, I'm a little slow. I'd known this before, but I started seeing it in a new light.) The assumption that everything begins and ends with the white version of reality has everything to do with the suppression of sovereignty, the violation of treaty rights, the belief that European literary theory is inherently superior for explicating texts written by Native people, and a number of other issues revolving around the presence of an Indian viewpoint. Subsuming or erasing an Indian voice is central to these endeavors.

I've always believed that one of the key functions of Native Studies is to present an Indian viewpoint, but this caused me to see *why* doing so is so central to our mission. Violations of sovereignty and treaty rights depend on white control of discourse about Indians. If we start thinking, speaking, and writing for ourselves, we might, for example, imagine a more radical version of sovereignty than as "domestic dependent nations,"[3] which has been defined for us already in disregard of our own experience of full nationhood, evident in our oral traditions, and corroborated in our earliest dealings with Europeans, where we were recognized as nations in every sense of the word.

So, I learned a lot from my dealings with the "Berdache Center" in terms of the way AIDS work is directly related to issues of colonialism and the dominant culture's need to define other cultures and speak for them. There is a literary sidelight that I wish to explore in this regard. It relates to a book entitled *Native*, written by William Haywood Henderson.[4] Henderson, a non-Indian, is widely praised by Edmund Wilson, a popular white gay author, who describes him as "quite simply the best young writer I know about in America right now." Henderson's Indian character in *Native* is a genericized "Native American" living in Wyoming, whose tribe is never named in the novel.

In addition to constantly using the B word (*berdache*), the Indian character, Gilbert, reports Native ceremonies involving ritualized gang sodomy:

"I have things to give you, boys." He danced, soft and spinning, dead still, chanting, silent. "See me? You think I'm drunk? No. Magic." Sam tapped his fingers with Gilbert's beat. "Screw. Screw up your courage." Sam leaned back toward me, leaned away, his shoulders starting to tilt. "You can hear the music. Smell the sweat

stirred up by the firelight. Some young warriors. Screw the berdache. Make the rain. Luck. Heal something. Berdache." He did
a fancy turn, arms out, one hand up, one hand low. He chanted at
us. He blocked everything behind. "Tell me I can't dance. Tell me
I'm not something you could prize."[5]

Hard to believe, isn't it? This is the best, we're told, America has to
offer. White's praise of the novel leads us to believe there *is* something
in a name.

We see Indian as totally Other, as sexualized erotic, as object. Ceremony and religious practice rendered in the same breath as gang sex
for the prurient pleasure of whites. Blasphemy presented as cultural
authenticity. Gilbert, believe it or not, expands on his disrespect some
pages later, and none of this is presented to the reader ironically but
rather is rendered as Native cultural norms:

> He ordered another beer, cupped the mug in his full hands when
> it arrived, drank deeply. "You see," he said, "to get right down to
> it, there was this thing called a berdache, not a thing, a person, a
> sort of male squaw, and they were nothing odd, they were even
> kind of sought out, and they'd dress like they weren't male and
> they weren't female, and a man would take this berdache as a
> wife as if it were something special, a real honor, a real thrill in
> the crotch. . . .
>
> "These berdaches weren't just different. They were magic, the
> center of ceremonies, making rain, healing, spiritual power. You
> see, if you want a good crop or some rain showers, you take a
> berdache, at night preferably, knowing that darkness always adds
> to even the dullest events—but this isn't dull, it's great in the dark—
> and you light a fire and put this guy in the center of a circle and
> you bring out the warriors, start the drums, young warriors, and
> they start dancing around the berdache, and then they screw the
> berdache to make the magic." He shifted far over toward me,
> held a finger across his lips, removed it, sat up square again.
> "Not like I've ever made it rain or gotten banged by a war party
> or brought anyone luck. It's not like that anymore, not since
> berdache became faggot." His voice trailed off, and he finished
> his beer, reached for mine and downed the last inch in the bot-
> tom.[6]

I hope Gilbert never meets any of the Indian women I know, who'd
kick his White Indian ass for calling them squaw. And maybe there's
something to be said for cultural decay, since Gilbert reports that it put
an end to the happy ole days of rape by war parties.

In an interview Henderson claims to have known an Indian gay guy in college. Now there's an interesting claim to authenticity! According to the interview:

"One of my biggest concerns with the character of Gilbert is that people will misperceive it as a racist characterization," Henderson states. "But the entire Native aspect of the book comes from a friend of mine [to whom he dedicates the novel] from college. He's not from a mountain tribe but he told me all these *berdache* stories. The problems in *Native* don't come from Gilbert, they come from the response of white people."[7]

It's not white people, however, it's Gilbert who totally negates his own culture, turning it into a "real thrill in the crotch," a sex orgy meant to titillate his listeners (and the author's readers) if they are dumb enough to believe this junk.

Although the author's talents are immense in regard to his evocation of the Wyoming landscape and his minimalistic prose style that reflects the white characters' unspoken desires, this is a guy, no matter what Edmund White says about the superlative quality of the novel, who shouldn't be writing about Indians. This is not an argument that non-Indians should never write about Native culture. Henderson, however, in addition to rendering one of the most stereotyped depictions of Native people in recent history, also reveals an incredible naiveté in some of his scenes that places them in the realm of the laughable. In the bar scenes in the novel Gilbert sashays around these white heterosexual cowboy bars, spouting off crap about *berdaches* straight from an anthro text, stuff that is totally unconvincing as dialogue and uncharacteristic of any Native gay guy I've ever known. He physically flirts with these cowboys and gets up in their faces.

Now, let's imagine this little scene. We're in rural Wyoming. We're in a white cowboy bar. Gilbert is the only skin in the place, and he's telling everyone that he's a fag and that he wants to have sex with them. What do you reckon the life expectancy of this poor bastard is going to be? My guesstimate is that it would take somewhere between thirty and forty-five seconds for some redneck Indian hater to get his buddies together, take Gilbert out into the parking lot, and line him up in the sights of their deer rifles. And if I was there that night, I might be tempted to help them. Anybody who knows anything about white/Indian relations on or near reservation communities can easily see the absurdity of Henderson's book. On the rez, *Native* could be read as slapstick.

In fact, it would be hard for me to name a novel with less of a Native American sensibility. Gilbert is nameless (he has no last name), rootless, tribeless, landless, and he goes about telling genericized stories with a corresponding lack of any specific connections or slightest degree of authenticity and performing generic "ceremonies" as well. In this novel this isn't rendered as psychotic displacement but as normative. Gilbert, in fact, is depicted as a powerful character with spiritual gifts, who sees through the white protagonist, Blue, by recognizing his unspoken desire for Sam. The author himself, in the above-quoted interview, indicated he does not see Gilbert as problematic. Gilbert is not a minor character in the novel; he is omnipresent, making his misrepresentations even worse.

Perhaps Henderson's intentions, like the good guys in the white hats at the GLBT Center, were to honor Indian people through his depiction of Gilbert as a *berdache*. It's hard to say; we can only guess. Unfortunately, well-intentioned individuals can make disastrous decisions, especially when they are misinformed. Much damage can be done, and the consolation that the offender's intentions were good may not be of much use after it is too late to repair the situation. Henderson got way out of his league when he took on the responsibility of writing about Indian people. Judging by his work, Henderson does not have sufficient grounding in Native culture, or the history of colonialism that Indian people have endured these last five hundred years, or any knowledge of specific tribal traditions, to understand the implications of his decision to write about Indians.

Yet he decided to write his book anyway, and Edmund Wilson decided to claim that it's the best thing since frybread—not that White knows what frybread is—without any inclusion of an Indian perspective whatsoever. Henderson writes well about Wyoming landscapes, but his portrayals, thus far, of Native people leave much to be desired in their genericized, tribeless representations and speech rooted in anthropological texts rather than in an ear for dialogue. Perhaps a more fitting title for the novel would be *Non-Native*.

Books like *Native* raise central issues. Why didn't the gay periodicals ask any Native critics to review Henderson's book? Maybe they couldn't find any of "them." Let Edmund Wilson talk the thing up all he wants, let Henderson write ten more bad books if he insists, but, at the very least, let us have a few Indian voices invited to participate in the evaluation of such materials when the works themselves so directly reference Native people's cultures. Again, I see connections here between literature and sovereignty, as illustrated by the response to *Native* and events at the GLBT Center. A people's right to define themselves in their own terms, to explicate their own cultures and histories, and to choose their own aesthetic criteria are central concerns of the idea of sovereignty. This too is self-determination.

AIDS-prevention messages need to be evaluated in light of this colonialist impulse to subsume, bury, misrepresent, ignore, and/or erase tribal voices. Formulating positive prevention messages rooted in tribal values, worldviews, and the joyful expression of Native identity, rather than in prohibitive/retributive Christian discourse, depends on our ability to analyze and critique this colonizer/colonized relationship and the ways in which we sometimes unknowingly endorse the oppression ourselves.

Now, let's build on the two strands we've developed from telling stories. In terms of the way we internalize colonialism, we've talked about (1) the prohibitive and retributive language of fundamentalist Christian discourse that sneaks into our messages; and (2) the failure to allow a group of people to speak for themselves, the tendency to silence their voices and erase their presence.

Instead of messages that name what people *can't* do, what about messages that make Native gay guys feel good about being Native gay guys, that confirm their place in the circle of tribal life *as gay men*, that argue that the Creator has blessed them with two-spiritedness? When we look at the posters and the pamphlets, few take into account an incredibly important issue, the issue of audience. Thus far, not many of the messages have been targeted at the group that is most affected by the disease–Native gay men–nor have they dealt with an important aspect of these men's identity–their gayness. I don't know if this is for fear of the homophobia in Indian country, an attempt by prevention agencies not to be labeled by tribes as "the gay folks," or a recognition that AIDS affects other groups besides gays, but totally leaving gay guys out of prevention messages is a really weird approach. I suspicion (this is my grandmother's word, and I love it; she's always suspicioning things) this erasure of gay male presence from prevention messages is an endorsement of colonialism that we don't even realize. We've accepted, without knowing it, the politics of silencing the Other.

For several years now we've had a growing interest in the concept of two-spirited roles in traditional cultures and a resurgence of pride among Native gays and lesbians, but we haven't brought these powerful metaphors into prevention posters, flyers, and other kinds of information enough yet. What about a prevention message that runs along these lines: "As a Native gay man, you are blessed and gifted *because you are gay.* . . . Your talents are needed in our community. Among many ways you can help us out, one is staying healthy. Another is educating your friends and relatives about HIV and AIDS. As a gay man, you probably have knowledge about HIV and AIDS that they do not, and you can pass this information along. You can tell them how you have stayed strong. . . . " I'm just brainstorming here, but I think you can see how this differs from the abstinence pamphlet in its avoidance of characterizing sexuality as sin and in its recognition of the very real presence of gay men in Native communities.

Among Creeks, there was a tremendous resistance movement that fought Oklahoma statehood at the turn of the century. It was led by

Chitto Harjo. The dissidents, who met at Hickory Grounds, one of the stomp grounds in eastern Oklahoma Creek country, were called Snakes because one of Harjo's names means "snake" in Creek and he was seen by whites as the leader of the movement, though in reality the resistance was broad in scope and fostered by many men and women. What is fascinating about the Snakes is that in total defiance of the proclamation of dissolution of the tribes at statehood in 1907, they elected a tribal government, a tribal court, a bicameral legislature, and a police force, and continued to insist on the reality of tribal sovereignty—as well as to practice it—even when the official Creek government in Okmulgee had been forced to shut down and the Creek Nation was considered by whites to be nonexistent. In fact, their Lighthorsemen, a tribal police force, traveled the countryside, posting the laws of the continued nation, and punishing Creeks who accepted allotment certificates or leased their lands to whites. The Snakes' vision of government transcended, therefore, a mere act of imagination. They followed up words with deeds, continuing their government out at Hickory Grounds into the 1930s.

A study of the Snakes and other Indian resistance leaders, writers, and intellectuals might add insights for critical/literary/activist strategies. Learnings from the Snakes might include but not be limited to the following possibilities:

Chitto Harjo and other Creeks of his time were talented intellectuals. Harjo's understanding of Creek history, government, treaties, and culture, and their relationship to U.S. history, was intimidating to white senators and members of Congress. He knew a lot more than they did about the history of their country and Indian relations. We have tremendously talented Native gay men in our communities, and we need to trust our own knowledge, our own cultures, our own histories, and allow these men to generate ideas in order to formulate our own HIV-prevention messages rather than looking to the outside or applying frameworks like Christian apocalyptic discourse. Many of these men are talented political strategists with lobbying experience who have a lot to add to HIV prevention.

Harjo was able to explain the Treaty of 1832 and Creek history, spreading out his copy of the treaty year after year on the desks of senators and representatives, with more knowledge at his disposal than any of the bureaucrats he encountered, making arguments for its continued validity. He went around telling legislators how the treaty made Oklahoma statehood illegal. Whether or not they listened, Harjo did manage to get their attention, perhaps due to the bold manner in which he advanced arguments for full nationhood and his demand for answers, making the argument that the treaty still stood and that its intent was clear—Creek government held the same status as any other nation.

"The Creek country west of the Mississippi," the treaty reads, "shall be solemnly guaranteed to the Creek Indians, nor shall any State or Territory ever have a right to pass laws for the government of such Indians, but they shall be allowed to govern themselves." Harjo posed simple questions like, why were these words no longer true? He reminded the politicians that Creeks had rejected the General Allotment Act of 1887. Congress had then passed the Curtis Act without the tribes' approval, knowing that the nations would never agree to allotment. Harjo was unswerving in his convictions, and so much more sophisticated in his knowledge of law and history than the politicians that they would hide from him when he was in Washington. Their secretaries had special instructions to turn him away, claiming their bosses were out of their offices or back home with their constituencies. Once, Harjo had even seen the president, handed him the treaty, and told him that if he could explain how the treaty allowed for allotments, he would believe it was so. Harjo, when telling the story, would say, "He just shook hands with me and that was all."

Harjo combined head and heart in fascinating ways, giving speeches without any scripts and speaking from an internal conviction about the sacredness of words, especially with regard to promises made.

Harjo also had radical notions about sovereignty, believing Indian nations to be on an equal footing with European nations, and his statements went far beyond the status quo of "domestic dependent nations." In the fall of 1906 Harjo and a delegation of Snakes showed up at the Old Elk's Lodge Hall in the Seaman Building on West 3rd St. in Tulsa. The meeting was a special Senate Investigating Committee reporting on the state of affairs in Indian Territory during its transition into the State of Oklahoma. The Secretary of Interior was there, along with senators from Colorado, Montana, Connecticut, and Kansas.

Since the construction of the railroad in the 1870s, white people had been pouring into Indian Territory and settling along the railroad route, even though this unauthorized immigration was expressly forbidden by the Indian Trade and Intercourse Act of 1834. Twenty years after the construction of the railroad, the white element composed two-thirds of the population of Indian Territory. These very senators sitting in the meeting secretly had fostered this indirect method of taking over the territory, knowing that the immigration would build a strong momentum for eventual statehood, a ploy that had been successful earlier in adding Texas and Oregon to the United States.

When the senators came into the meeting and saw Harjo, an old familiar face who had stood before them with the treaty of 1832 spread out on their desks, they didn't dare ask him or the Snakes to leave. Harjo was imposing, and he had so much presence in Washington that they felt obliged to let him address the gathering. They knew that they could question him after his speech, thus giving them the opportunity to repair any damage if Harjo made nationalistic claims, which he was sure to do. At least there, on their own turf, they had some control over him, which wasn't the case when he was among his own people.

In contrast to the senators' boring repetition of things as usual, the effect of Harjo's speechmaking was electrifying. While the secretary and senators had stood up and read from prepared speeches that they didn't even have the intelligence to write for themselves, Harjo spoke from a different text, one inside himself that came from a sense of what was sacred, the very meaning of words themselves, and from the Creek Nation's historic relationship with a particular landscape. Harjo, speaking from memory and conscience, never lacked for language to express himself, and, even with an interpreter, the words in English conveyed a spirit of resistance. In his speaking and thinking abilities, Harjo carried forward the long line of well-known Creek warriors from which he was descended. Witnesses at the meeting reported that one could hear a pin drop in the hall, so intent was the focus between Harjo and the audience.

His speech covered contact with the first European explorers, their promises to respect Indian land-holdings and governments, the treaty of 1832 and the fact that his nation had "carried out these agreements and treaties in all points and violated none," the Civil War and his own participation on the side of the Union out of respect for the treaty, and the allotment process, which flew in the face of everything sacred that the Creek Nation and the United States had ever agreed upon.

The amazing thing about Harjo's speech was not simply the way he covered five hundred years of history and still stayed focused on the issue of full Creek nationhood but his understanding of the implications of this nationalism. At the end of his speech Harjo asked the senators what they thought, and they replied that things had changed and that the treaties no longer applied because of modifications by later agreements. They claimed that any attempt to resist would be useless. This didn't stop Harjo for one second, though, and he rejoined, "I think I have the privilege of appealing to the other tribes and notifying them in response to the disagreement between you and me in reference to the allotments." When the chairman of the committee said, "Do you mean the other four civilized tribes?" Chitto's response caused a stir in the meeting place: "I do not mean the other four civilized tribes, but I can call on the Spanish government, the British government, and the French government. I can call on four of the civilized governments across the mother of waters to come in and see that this is right. That is all I have to say."

He understood that the Creeks had international recognition as a nation of people that had treated unilaterally with other governments; the Creek Nation was on an equal footing with European nations. His was a much more radical stance than Chief Justice John Marshall's definition of domestic dependent nations in the 1830s. Even if the United States had refused to recognize the legality of the Creek Nation, the Snakes had determined to keep nationalism alive in their imaginations and spirits and in practice by continuing to hold councils and legislatures at the Hickory Grounds, no matter what happened in Oklahoma. No matter what this committee said to them, no matter what the political realities were, the Snakes continued as a nation. One of the songs at the stomp grounds, translated into English, says, "Long after I'm dead, this dance will continue." That was the faith of the Snakes, that they would continue to dance, take medicine, hold councils, and exist as a nation no matter what the whites said about the dissolution of the tribal government.

Perhaps Harjo can teach us that we need not accept limited definitions in our imaginings of ourselves, in our actions, or in our prevention messages. Maybe tribal sovereignty, rather than a repeat of European nationalism based on triumphalism and supremacy, can be more flexible, rooted in dynamism rather than "staticism"–looking to change as culture evolves. Maybe sovereign nations can make part of their concern homophobia and the lack of AIDS services in their own homelands, so that sick people can come back home instead of moving off to San Francisco or some other city. Communities need some of the next generation of Elders to stay home so the culture can be passed on. What a loss for young people if they were all to move away. Maybe sovereignty can combine head with heart, become a compassionate, larger circle that keeps our folks within the circle instead of sending them away.

Finally, the ceremonial ground was the center of political resistance for the Snakes, and maybe they could teach us that good politics depends on good religion. The famous Red Stick War of 1813-14 was a fight strongly driven by a religious revival, a war against American oppression led by spiritual leaders and medicine people, planned according to patterns in sacred stories out of the oral tradition. There seems to be a balance here: in recognizing the political nature of formulating AIDS messages, we can never abandon this spiritual center, and in recognizing the role of personal growth and healing in prevention, we should not be naive about the politics of colonialism.

Notes

[1] "Snagging" is Native slang roughly equivalent to "scoring" in common argot (as in "scoring on a date").

[2] "Thank you" in Muscogee.

[3] The term was coined by Justice John Marshall in the case of *Cherokee Nation v. Georgia* (5 Pet., 1 [1831]) to describe the clipped, limited sovereignty of Native nations.

[4] William Haywood Henderson, *Native* (New York: Dutton, 1993).

[5] Ibid., pp. 18-19.

[6] Ibid., pp. 52-53.

[7] William Haywood Henderson, interview, *Lambda Book Report* (March/April 1993), p. 22.

17.

Losing My Religion

Native American Religious Traditions and American Religious Freedom

JACE WEAVER

The summer of 1993 was a particularly hopeful one for those of us interested in Native American religious freedom. In Congress, amendments were introduced to the American Indian Religious Freedom Act of 1978 that would reverse the negative positions taken by the United States Supreme Court regarding sacred sites in *Lyng v. Northwest Indian Cemetery Association*[1] and ceremonial use of peyote in *Employment Division v. Smith*.[2] Provisions were also included restoring the "compelling state interest" test as the standard in religious freedom cases, permitting free exercise of Native religious traditions by prisoners, ensuring access to sacred sites and the availability of eagle feathers for religious practice, and providing enforcement mechanisms. These amendments, known variously as the Religious Freedom Restoration Act (RFRA), the Native American Free Exercise of Religion Act (NAFERA), and the American Indian Religious Freedom Act of 1993, were endorsed by every major religious organization in the country, in addition to legal, human-rights, environmental, and Native groups. Easy passage was predicted.

In June of that same year the Supreme Court decided *Church of Lukumi Babalu Aye v. Hialeah*.[3] The unanimous decision, in an action brought by practitioners of Santeria, struck down a ban by Hialeah, Florida, on animal sacrifice. Although the Court's opinion did not retreat from the Smith case's virtual abolition of the compelling state interest test as the standard for religious freedom claims under the First Amendment, it did find unconstitutional a prohibition the dominant culture had sought to impose upon a minority religion. In addition, two justices, Harry Blackmun and Sandra Day O'Connor, who had dissented (at least in part) in *Smith*, took the opportunity to reaffirm their opposition to its principle. And David Souter, who had not been a member of the Court at the time of *Smith*, authored a separate, carefully crafted opinion in which he called upon his colleagues to reconsider the decision in that case.

The summer of 1993 was a hopeful time. Yet as autumn came, hopes began to fall like the leaves from deciduous trees. Although RFRA was passed (thus restoring the compelling state interest test in free-exercise cases), as was the NAFERA provision relating to use of peyote, other necessary provisions, including that related to sacred sites, remained mired in Congress. With the sweep of the "Republican Revolution," Native issues dropped from the public agenda, and it is doubtful that they will receive much attention for some time to come.

Further, in the ensuing years, there have been 288 cases under RFRA, and even many supporters admit that the law has been abused. No fewer than six constitutional challenges to RFRA have found their way into the courts. The Supreme Court has agreed to hear one of these, involving whether the landmark status of a Catholic church in Boerne, Texas, represents a "substantial burden" on its ability to carry out its mission. In the Boerne case, a brief on behalf of the church by Douglas Laycock, a law professor at the University of Texas, contends that if RFRA is overturned "the entire body of law on congressional enforcement power" would be "called into question, and much of it would have to be overturned." Other legal scholars, such as Ira Lupu of George Washington University, argue that the law is unconstitutional inasmuch as it went "way beyond what the Supreme Court has said the Constitution requires of the states."[4] As for the High Court itself, four of those who took part in the *Smith* decision, including Justice Blackmun, have left the Court. The views of their successors on these matters remain uncertain, and, even if they were so disposed, their presence probably does not create a majority for a strong position in favor of free exercise of religion.[5]

From my location both as a lawyer and one involved in both religious and Native American studies, my central point is that as vital and correct as I believe passage of the congressional bills to have been, I do not for a moment believe them to be a panacea for Native land and religious freedom claims. There will continue to arise conflicts between the dominant culture and Native religions, and these will continue to be decided in the courts against Native interests. From the inception of the American Republic, there has been a tension between the obligation of the United States to protect Native rights and its policy of forcing their relinquishment. As Justice Thurgood Marshall declared in *Choctaw Nation v. Oklahoma*, at least since the Indian Removal Act of 1830, it has been "apparent that policy, not obligation would prevail."[6] This, however, is not simply a story of naked power, of a state's ability to impose its will upon those less powerful.

Yale law professor Stephen Carter in *The Culture of Disbelief* writes of both *Lyng* and *Smith*:

> Religions that most need protection seem to receive it least. . . . Native Americans, having once been hounded from their lands, are now hounded from their religions, with the complicity of a Supreme Court untroubled when sacred lands are taken for road building or when Native Americans under a bona fide religious compulsion to use peyote in their rituals are punished under state antidrug regulations. (Imagine the brouhaha if New York City were to try to take St. Patrick's Cathedral by eminent domain or if Kansas, a dry state, were to outlaw religious use of wine.)[7]

Carter attributes this to a trivializing of religion in American culture and an attempt to ban religion from public discourse in response to the Christian right's attempt to reshape society along lines it favors. In fact, neither *Lyng* nor *Smith* nor their progeny, as repugnant and offensive as they are, are incomprehensible and (with the exception of the elimination of the compelling state interest test) would have been highly unlikely to come out otherwise, because American jurisprudence, as currently contoured, is incapable of understanding, let alone taking cognizance of, Native land and religious freedom claims in their full scope.

Native religious traditions are very different in character from Christianity and Western religions. First, they are not primarily religions of ethics, or dogma, or theology. Rather, they are religions (if one may even use such a term with regard to Native traditions) of ritual practice. Further, they are not only religions of ritual observance, but they also permeate every aspect of daily life and existence. Natives, as is commonly said, draw no distinction between everyday life and their spirituality. There is not, as there is in Western religion, a sharp bifurcation between sacred and secular or profane spheres. Finally, Native religious traditions are intimately and inexorably tied to the land and often cannot be practiced merely anywhere, as can Christianity. For this reason, Native land claims, whether or not they are advanced in this manner, carry in themselves an explicitly religious claim.

The First Amendment guarantees that "Congress shall make no law respecting an establishment of religion, or prohibiting the free exercise thereof." Though it speaks in absolute terms ("make *no* law") and refers to "exercise" of religion, a word that on its face would seem to refer to practices, it in some sense does not mean what it says. The legislative history and subsequent interpretation both make clear that the concept of religion it embodies is a very Western, Enlightenment ideal. It is the flip-side or, if you will, the perfect corollary to freedom of speech and freedom of the press, also protected by the First Amendment. One is free, within certain defined parameters, to say or print whatever one wishes. Likewise, one is free to *believe* whatever one wishes. One is not free, however, to *do* whatever one wishes, even if one feels compelled by religious belief to do so. As Vine Deloria, Jr., and Clifford Lytle put it in *American Indians, American Justice,* "Beliefs are beyond the reach of the government no matter how unorthodox, but religious *practices* can be regulated by the state."[8] What Stephen Carter fails to say is that Kansas has *always* had the power to prohibit sacramental use of wine if it can demonstrate a compelling state interest in the subject matter and relate the ban to a valid secular purpose, such as Prohibition or the protection of alcoholics. Similarly, perhaps with slightly more difficulty, the City of New York *could* exercise its eminent domain power over St. Patrick's Cathedral, just as it landmarks churches, such as the one in Boerne, Texas, and requires them to maintain edifices that may have outlived their usefulness and for which the churches, as non-taxpayers, receive no tax breaks, the usual compensation for such interference. The only thing that makes the sacramental wine or condemnation of St. Patrick's examples so inconceivable is that they deal with a majority religion rather than a minority one or a new religious movement, making it unthinkable that a legislative body would ever attempt such a thing.

The First Amendment and the concept of religion it embodies thus can never afford full protection to Native religious traditions. It cannot encompass religions of ritual practice, or those that cannot be separated from other aspects of life into their own distinct sphere, or those that depend upon a particular place for their performance. It cannot do so, I argue, because, as intimated by historian James M. Washington in his article "The Crisis in the Sanctity of Conscience in American Jurisprudence," although it has a particular conception of religion, it lacks a concept of the sacred or the holy.[9]

Early on, law in North America absorbed into itself the doctrines of discovery and conquest used to justify colonial claims. It also sought to impose upon the land British concepts of land tenure and ownership, concepts totally foreign to the indigenous population. In 1828, Chancellor James Kent, the so-called father of American jurisprudence, wrote in his seminal work, *Commentaries on American Law*:

> When the country, now within the dominion of the United States, was first discovered by the Europeans, it was found to be, in a great degree, a wilderness, sparsely inhabited by tribes of Indians, whose occupation was war, and whose subsistence was drawn chiefly from the forest. Their possession was good and perfect to the extent requisite for subsistence and reasonable accommoda-

tion, but beyond that degree their title to the country was imperfect. Title by occupancy is limited to occupancy in point of fact. Erratic tribes of savage hunters and fishermen, who have no fixed abode, or sense of property, and are engaged constantly in the chase or in war, have no sound or exclusive title either to an indefinite extent of country, or to seas or lakes, merely because they are accustomed, in search of prey, to roam over the one, or coast the shores of the other. Vattel [Swiss legal theorist Emerich Vattel] had just notions of the value of these aboriginal rights of savages, and of the true principles of natural law in relation to them. He observed, that the cultivation of the soil was an obligation imposed by nature upon mankind, and that the human race could not well subsist, or greatly multiply, if rude tribes, which had not advanced from the hunter state, were entitled to claim and retain all the boundless forests through which they might wander. If such people will usurp more territory than they can subdue and cultivate, they have no right to complain, if a nation of cultivators puts in a claim for a part.[10]

So the concept of "aboriginal rights" entered the law in North America. While initially it took a treaty to create legally cognizable title in the courts, a concept of "aboriginal title" evolved and was refined in *Otoe and Missouria Tribe of Indians v. United States*. Begun in 1939, this was the first case to deal with the question of compensability for aboriginal title. To establish such title, the Otoe and Missouria had to prove that they "had lived in their ancestral homeland to the exclusion of all other Indians, and that the neighboring tribes recognized their claim to the ownership of their land."[11] Though the Otoe and Missouria prevailed in their claim almost thirty years later, that they were required to meet such a test at all displays scant understanding of Native cultures and the centrality and sacrality of land to them.

This standard would receive perhaps its harshest application in Canada in the case of *Delgam Uukw v. the Queen*, decided in 1991, in which Chief Justice Allan McEachern of the Supreme Court of British Columbia dismissed the land claims of the Gitksan and Wet'suwet'en people. McEachern rejected Native claims that the Creator had given them the specific land in question at the beginning of time. ("While I have every respect for their beliefs, there is no evidence to support such a theory and much good reason to doubt it.") Echoing Chancellor Kent, he went on to state, "Aboriginal life, in my view, was far from stable and it stretches credulity to believe remote ancestors considered themselves bound to specific lands."[12]

The clash of cultures with radically different epistemologies was evident as McEachern delivered his decision. He stated that "the Gitksan and Wet'suwet'en civilizations, if they qualify for that description, fall within a much lower, even primitive order." With regard to the Native claim that they had possessed the territory in question at the time of Creation, he wrote, "I am satisfied that the . . . witnesses honestly believe everything they said was true and accurate. It was obvious to me, however, that they were recounting matters of faith which have become fact to them. If I do not accept their evidence it will seldom be because I think they are untruthful, but rather because I have a different view of what is fact and what is belief."[13] Then, having ruled the oral traditions of the Natives inadmissible as evidence, he found the Natives could not prove that they had occupied the lands from "time immemorial," "as everyone knows, . . . a legal expression referring to the year 1189 (the beginning of the reign of Richard II), as specified in the Statute of Westminster, 1275."[14]

In so speaking, McEachern betrayed not only an extreme colonialist, ethnocentric bias–"He treats them like wolves. . . . The analogy would be closer to a wolf society than a human society," anthropologist Michael Asch declared[15]–but also his shaky grasp of British history and legal precedent. The year 1189 represents the beginning of the reign of Richard I, not Richard II. Further, he confuses "time immemorial," which simply means a "time when the memory of a human is not to the contrary" with the phrase "time of memory," a term in both Blackstone and Lord Coke meaning "when no man alive hath any proof to the contrary, nor hath any conusance to the contrary."

For their part, the Natives believed that they had met the burden of proof set by McEachern. Miluulak (Alice Jeffrey), hereditary chief of Gitksan, declares:

> Our people have been asked over and over: "How can you substantiate who you are? Who are you to say you have ownership of the territories?" The answer is clear. We have ownership by what we call *Ayook Niiye'e*. It is the law of our grandfathers, and the first law that our people have is called, *Ayook'm Simoquit Gimlahax*, which we call our relationship with the Almighty, who is the grandfather of the heavens. He is the one who breathes life into each and every one of us.
>
> The laws of our grandfathers go so far back in time that you cannot discount them. The song that we sing when a new chief takes his title is called *Limx ooii*. It means for thousands and thousands and thousands of years our people have existed.
>
> When you talk to any of us, and you look at all the symbols that we have, that dates us, telling us how long we have occupied and held our territories. When we count time, it is from the flood onward, which is well over ten thousand years of existence. This more than substantiates our claim above any that other people

would have in regard to our territories. It substantiates our right to rule our lives as we see fit.

When they ask what we feel our basis is in regard to title, I don't think that there is any question. The title is very clear. The ownership has never changed. It is only the definition in the law in regard to ownership that has changed.[16]

John Petoskey, in his essay "Indians and the First Amendment," writes:

> Although the First Amendment prevents governmental interference with the free exercise of religion, this protection has been substantially denied by the United States government in regard to Indian religions based on specific sites. This denial is based not so much on any improper application of Supreme Court First Amendment principles and analysis, although it is that; rather, the denial is rooted in religious ethnocentrism that permeates the relationship between the United States and Indian societies whereby the courts are judging Indian religious claims by standards developed for Judeo-Christian religions.[17]

He is undoubtedly correct concerning the ethnocentrism of the judicial system. After all, there have been fifty cases adjudicated in the federal courts involving sacred sites and religious freedom claims; Natives have lost in all fifty instances. Petoskey errs, however, when he speaks of a "misapplication" of "First Amendment principles and analysis," in that he does not take into account the history and purpose of the free exercise clause. He does not take into account the absence of a concept of the holy or sacred.

Seen in this light, the decisions in *Lyng* and *Smith* and their progeny, however lamentable and objectionable, become comprehensible. To state briefly the facts of each case: In *Lyng*, the Supreme Court refused to block the construction of a timbering road that would have a devastating impact on land considered sacred to the Yurok, Karok, and Tolowa tribes of northwest California; in *Smith*, the high Court upheld denial of unemployment benefits to members of the Native American Church who had been dismissed from their jobs as a result of ritual use of peyote.

In *Lyng*, the Court refused to prohibit the road despite the fact that it was undisputed that it "would cause serious and irreparable damage to the sacred areas which are an integral and necessary part of the belief systems and lifeways of Northwest California Indian peoples."[18] It found a compelling state interest in the building of the road for economic purposes and in the state's ability to control lands it owned. The Court stated flatly, "The Constitution simply does not provide a principle that could justify upholding [the Indians'] legal claims."[19] The majority opinion is shot through with language demonstrating the lack of a concept of the holy.

Even the strong dissent by Justice Brennan, joined by Justices Marshall and Blackmun, which struggled to uphold the Natives' claim, admitted that it is not enough simply to allege that the land in question is held sacred. While the United States Court of Appeals for the 9th Circuit had enjoined construction of the road, it acknowledged the same thing. The dissenting opinion at that lower level accurately presages the Supreme Court decision and squarely addresses the absence of the holy. In addressing a report on the proposed road, commissioned by the U.S. Forest Service, a report that recommended against construction, the dissent declared that the report had applied an "inappropriate definition" of religion. It reads in part:

> The report states, "Because of the particular nature of Indian perceptual experience, as opposed to the particular nature of predominant non-Indian, Western perceptual experience, any division into 'religious' or 'sacred' is in reality an exercise that forces Indian concepts into non-Indian categories, and distorts the original conceptualization in the process." The report then suggests that hunting and fishing are religious activities for Indians. While that may be correct in an anthropological sense, the federal Constitution does not recognize such a broad concept of "religion."[20]

The *Smith* case can be viewed in a similar light, dealing with ritual observance and containing, as it does, language that points up the absence of the holy. The major flaw of the *Smith* decision—and it is indeed a major flaw—is the virtual repeal in religious freedom cases of the compelling state interest test. Under the *Smith* rule, laws that are neutral and of general applicability need not be subjected to heightened scrutiny even if they have significant adverse effects on religion. As envisioned by the Court in *Smith*, the government would have to demonstrate a compelling state interest in a legislative enactment only when it failed to meet the twin tests of neutrality and general applicability. Thus only laws enacted deliberately to suppress or discriminate against a religion would come under this more rigorous test. Such was the case in *Lukumi Babalu Aye*.

The *Smith* rule was all the more startling in that it was gratuitous. As Justice O'Connor said in her concurrence, the same result could be reached by positing a compelling state interest in preventing drug use—or, one supposes, by finding such an interest in keeping at least those who work in drug-rehabilitation centers, as did the persons involved in the case, drug free. Even those, like myself, who considered it essential to restore the compelling state interest test via RFRA, have to admit that generally only poorly drawn laws will be struck down since a compelling interest can be found in almost any instance.

What then must be done? Naming and delineating this lacuna in the jurisprudential system—the absence of the holy—is one thing. To propose a corrective is quite another. Judges fear that if such a concept of sacredness were imported into the law it would be impossible to regulate any conduct no matter how destructive, and that every individual would become a law unto herself or himself.[21] And the freedom to act, unlike the freedom to believe, cannot be absolute.

Prior to *Lyng* and *Smith* some courts applied a test by which they were called upon to determine whether a given practice or site was "central" to a particular Native religious system. This "centrality" approach, however, proved largely unworkable because of the difficulty of the factual determination and because it set so high a standard before legal protection would attach. Anthropologist Deward Walker notes:

> As interpreted by the courts . . . "central" has a meaning best described as indispensable, essential, or requisite. The courts have, therefore, introduced a very high standard that must be met for First Amendment protection of American Indian sacred geography. Under this interpretation of "central," preservation of a specific sacred site can be achieved only if it is deemed to be essential, indispensable, or requisite for the practice of a particular tribal religion. In its applications, this standard goes well beyond the meaning of "infringement" and borders on "extinction." In other words, to receive First Amendment protection, American Indians must demonstrate that a change will not merely infringe but virtually destroy a religious practice or belief. Judgments by courts as to centrality, therefore, are being made in terms of a standard of survival/extinction.[22]

As an alternative to centrality, Walker suggests *integrity* as a standard. "Integrity" means "an unimpaired condition" or "the quality or state of being complete or undivided," "completeness." According to Walker, "Infringement then can be understood as a forced or undesired change in the customary practice of a religion." This test has the virtue of being "more open to factual investigation than a standard of centrality. Determination of whether the integrity of a religious practice has been violated would rest on answers to factual questions." Among the inquiries upon which such a determination might be made, Walker suggests three:

1. Is the affected practice held by members of the group to be an essential part of their religion? or,

2. Are there alternatives to the affected practice acceptable to members of the group? or,

3. Would removal or alteration of the affected practice impair or prevent other essential practices of the religion?[23]

In 1996, the Supreme Court of Canada applied something like Walker's integrity test in the *Van der Peet* case. Dorothy Van der Peet, a Sto:lo Indian, was convicted of selling salmon to a neighbor. Before the Canadian Supreme Court, the issue was whether there was a constitutionally protected aboriginal right to engage in commercial fishing. The High Court found against such a right in *Van der Peet*: "While the court didn't rule out the native commercial fishing right, it has put the onus on natives to clearly prove that the practice previously existed."[24]

Opponents of aboriginal rights quickly heralded *Van der Peet* as placing a limit on the "expansive interpretation" given such rights by the Canadian government and courts.[25] Though the case was unquestionably a loss, Native leaders, in contrast, stated that the court "had finally set a clear test for defining Indian rights that many Indian nations can easily meet."[26] Accounting for these divergent reactions was the failure of non-Native critics to understand the new test articulated by the court and its potential implications. The decision stated that courts must look at both Natives' relationship to the land and the "practices, customs [and] traditions" of a given Native culture. Aboriginal rights are those "practices, customs or traditions" that are "integral to a distinctive culture" and that existed at the time of non-Native settlement. The real hope of the *Van der Peet* decision lies precisely in this language that opponents see as a limit—that practices, customs, or traditions *integral* (that is, "essential to completeness," "constituent") to a distinctive culture will be protected. The approach in *Van Der Peet* is essentially that advocated by Walker. Though admittedly far from perfect, it should nevertheless make it easier to protect cultural and religious traditions that have until now been extremely difficult to vindicate in the courts. While it remains to be seen if courts in the United States will adopt the *Van der Peet* approach, Indian law in Canada and the United States tend to parallel each other broadly, and the case should provide a new arrow in Native legal quivers.[27]

Vine Deloria has suggested that it is a mistake to focus exclusively on First Amendment analysis and issues. He believes that federal/Indian treaties should be enough to protect Native religious traditions through the application of the principle of tribal sovereignty. His advice merits hearing. As resistant as courts may be to treaty and sovereignty claims, they are at least categories, like the aboriginal title of the *Otoe and Missouria* case, the law can apprehend.

I myself believe that ultimately we will be forced always to seek redress from Congress and through the legislative process in curative bills such as RFRA and NAFERA. Elizabeth Cook-Lynn illustrates why this should be so when, citing scholars such as Deloria and Felix Cohen, she states that, for Native Americans, "America's legal theory often violates the basic principles of justice."[28] It should be noted that some of the most significant Native victories, such as the return of Blue Lake to the Taos people, have been accomplished through work in Washington rather than in the courts.

The best that can be hoped for from the courts is a strict application of the compelling state interest test, coupled with the integrity test of *Van der Peet* or possible tests suggested by Justices Brennan, Blackmun, and Souter who, while affirming traditional First Amendment interpretation, extended their reach to grasp, I believe, for some concept of the holy. In their dissents in both *Lyng* and *Smith*, Brennan and Blackmun argued for a centrality test by which courts would be called upon to balance the centrality or indispensability of a practice or site to a Native religious tradition, as interpreted by the Natives themselves, against the claimed state interest opposing it. As noted above, though in itself not free from problems, this, broadly speaking, is the approach of RFRA. For his part, David Souter, in his concurrence in *Lukumi Babalu Aye*, called for courts "to preserve a right to engage in activities necessary to fulfill one's duty to one's God, unless those activities [threaten] the rights of others or the serious needs of the State."[29]

Lacking a concept of the holy, our legal system finally is incapable of comprehending Native religious freedom and land claims. As the colds winds of autumn prepare to blow for yet another year, it continues an open question whether freedom of religion for America's indigenous people will remain, as Justice Blackmun said in his dissent in *Smith*, "merely an unfulfilled and hollow promise."[30]

Author's Notes: Prognostication is more properly the province of pundits rather than professors. It may be true that those who do not know history are condemned to relive it, but history remains an unreliable forecaster of future events. The common law, however, is based on the principle of *stare decisis*. Cases are decided in accordance with precedent. Therefore an examination of past judicial decisions should allow the legal scholar to predict with at least some accuracy how a court will rule in a given instance. This is, of course, a gross oversimplification. There is space for creativity, personal philosophy, and change in any ruling.

Sadly, since the writing of this essay, many of my fears about the future of First Amendment litigation have been realized. On September 25, 1997, the Supreme Court handed down its decision in *City of Boerne v. Flores*. The 6-to-3 decision struck down RFRA as unconstitutional. In so doing, the High Court reaffirmed the rule of *Employment Division v. Smith* and once again consigned the "compelling state interest test" to the judicial recycling bin. Justices O'Connor and Souter, who have made clear their opposition to the *Smith* rule, joined by Justice Stephen Breyer (who was not on the Court at the time of either *Smith* or *Lukumi Babalu Aye*), dissented and called for a reexamination of *Smith*. Ruth Bader Ginsburg, perhaps the most liberal justice, voted with the majority.

Though phrased in terms of separation of powers between Congress and the Court rather than in freedom of religion, the majority opinion has serious implications for First Amendment jurisprudence. Its logic would apply equally to NAFERA, which now seems open to challenge. It could also have a more indirect impact upon a pending suit by non-Native rock climbers who are suing the National Park Service. At issue is the Service's ban on climbing on Wyoming's Devil's Tower (a sacred site known as Bear Lodge to Natives) during the month of June, when it is used by Natives for religious ceremonies. Plaintiffs in that suit contend that the ban violates the First Amendment.

The most troubling aspect of *City of Boerne* is that none of the nine justices, including the dissenters, questioned the major premise underlying the decision. For years it had been settled that in the case of constitutional rights, the Court could set a base level of protection, but Congress could raise the bar. Conservatives rejected this "one-way ratchet," and now they have been vindicated by the majority opinion. Once, the Supreme Court declared that government "follows the best of our traditions" when it "respects the religious nature of our people and accommodates . . . their spiritual needs." Now it appears that call has been rescinded.

Notes

[1] *Lyng v. Northwest Indian Cemetery Association*, 485 U.S. 439 (1988).

[2] *Employment Division v. Smith*, 494 U.S. 872 (1990).

[3] *Church of Lukumi Babalu Aye v. Hialeah*, 113 S. Ct. 2217 (1993).

[4] Jeffrey L. Sheler and Ted Gest, "How Big Is God's Tent?," *U.S. News & World Report* (February 24, 1997), pp. 44-45.

[5] For discussions of the Court and religious liberty in both Native and non-Native contexts, see John R. Wunder, *"Retained by the People": A History of American Indians and the Bill of Rights* (New York: Oxford University Press, 1994), pp. 193-99; and Ronald B. Flowers, *That Godless Court?: Supreme Court Decisions on Church-State Relationships* (Louisville: Westminster/John Knox Press, 1994).

[6] Jace Weaver, *Then to the Rock Let Me Fly: Luther Bohanon and Judicial Activism* (Norman: University of Oklahoma, 1993), p. 138; *Choctaw Nation v. Oklahoma*, 397 U.S. 620 (1970).

[7] Stephen Carter, *The Culture of Disbelief: How American Law and Politics Trivialize Religious Devotion* (New York: BasicBooks, 1993), p. 9.

[8] Vine Deloria, Jr., and Clifford M. Lytle, *American Indians, American Justice* (Austin: University of Texas Press, 1983), p. 131.

[9] James M. Washington, "The Crisis in the Sanctity of Conscience in American Jurisprudence," 42 De Paul L. Rev. 11 (1992); see Rudolf Otto, *The Idea of the Holy* (London: Oxford University Press, 1923).

[10] James Kent, *Commentaries on American Law*, vol. 3 (New York: O. Halsted, 1828), pp. 312-13.

[11] Luther Lee Bohanon, "The Autobiography of Judge Luther L. Bohanon," unpublished manuscript, 1988, p. VI-3; Weaver, p. 47. For a more detailed discussion of the Otoe and Missouria, by a scholar involved in their case on their behalf, see Berlin Basil Chapman, *The Otoes and Missourias: A Study of Indian Removal and the Legal Aftermath* (Oklahoma City: Times Journal Publishing Co., 1965).

[12] Don Monet and Skanu'u (Ardythe Wilson), *Colonialism on Trial: Indigenous Land Rights and the Gitksan and Wet'suwet'en Sovereignty Case* (Philadelphia: New Society Publishers, 1992), p. 188.

[13] Ibid.

[14] Ibid., p. 189.

[15] Ken MacQueen, "A Landmark Ruling Shocks Anthropologists," *Vancouver Sun* (July 13, 1991), p. 1.

[16] Miluulak (Alice Jeffrey), "Remove Not the Landmark," in *Aboriginal Title in British Columbia: Delgam Uukw v. the Queen*, ed. Frank Cassidy (Montreal: Institute for Research on Public Policy, 1992), p. 58. For other statements by the hereditary chiefs, see Gisday Wa and Delgam Uukw, *The Spirit in the Land: Statements of the Gitksan and Wet'suwet'en Hereditary Chiefs in the Supreme Court of British Columbia, 1987-1990* (Gabriola, B.C.: Reflections, 1992).

[17] John Petoskey, "Indians and the First Amendment," in *American Indian Policy in the Twentieth Century*, ed. Vine Deloria, Jr. (Norman: University of Oklahoma Press, 1985), p. 221.

[18] *Lyng*, 485 U.S. at 442.

[19] Id. at 452.

[20] *Northwest Indian Cemetery Protective Association v. Peterson*, 795 F.2d 688, 701 (9th Cir. 1986) (Beezer, C.J., dissenting).

[21] *Reynolds v. United States*, 98 U.S. 145, 166-67 (1879).

[22] Deward E. Walker, Jr., "Protection of American Indian Sacred Geography," in *Handbook of American Indian Religious Freedom*, ed. Christopher Vecsey (New York: Crossroad, 1991), p. 112.

[23] Ibid., pp. 112-13.

[24] Rudy Platiel and Ross Howard, "Indians Don't Have Right to Sell Catch, Court Rules," *Toronto Globe and Mail* (August 22, 1996), p. A1.

[25] Jeffrey Simpson, "Aboriginal Rights Are Different Things to Judges and Politicians," *Toronto Globe and Mail* (September 4, 1996), p. A20.

[26] Platiel and Howard, p. A1.

[27] Ibid., p. A16; Simpson, p. A20; Jace Weaver, "Natives Will Challenge Authority," *Toronto Globe and Mail* (September 7, 1996), p. A21.

[28] Elizabeth Cook-Lynn, "Editor's Editorial," *Wicazo Sa Review* (Spring 1997), p. 7.

[29] *Lukumi*, 113 S.Ct. at 2249 (Souter, J., concurring).

[30] *Smith*, 494 U.S. at 921 (Blackmun, J., dissenting).

Contributors

Betty Louise Bell (Cherokee) is an assistant professor in American culture, English, and women's studies at the University of Michigan, where she also serves as director for the Program in Native American Studies. She has published one novel, *Faces in the Moon*, and is currently co-editor of the Norton Anthology for Native American Literature. She is also working on a study of early Native women writers.

Steven Charleston (Choctaw) is the former Episcopal bishop of Alaska. He is currently serving as chaplain at Trinity College in Hartford, Connecticut.

Viola F. Cordova (Mescalero Apache) has held numerous teaching positions in universities in the United States and Canada, most recently at Lakehead University in Thunder Bay, Ontario. She received the Ph.D. in philosophy from the University of New Mexico.

Diane Glancy (Cherokee) is a professor of English at Macalester College in St. Paul. She is the award-winning author of numerous books of poetry, fiction, and nonfiction.

Donald A. Grinde, Jr. (Yamasee) is director of the ALANA (African American, Latino, Asian American, Native American) Studies program and a professor of history at the University of Vermont. His most recent of numerous books is *The Encyclopedia of Native American Biography* (co-authored with Bruce E. Johansen).

Leana Hicks (Nahua descent/mestizo) is a student at Yale University. She has most recently been involved in research in Costa Rica.

Freda McDonald (Anishinaabe) is a traditional Anishinaabe elder. She currently resides in Thunder Bay, Ontario.

Dennis McPherson (Anishinaabe) is associate professor of philosophy and director of the Program in Indigenous Learning at Lakehead University in Thunder Bay, Ontario. He worked closely with the Royal Commission on Aboriginal People, about which he writes in this volume. He is the author of *Indian from the Inside: A Study in Ethno-Metaphysics* (with J. Douglas Rabb).

Homer Noley (Choctaw) is the director of the Native American center at the School of Theology at Claremont. He is the author of *First White Frost: Native Americans and United Methodism.*

Margaret Sam-Cromarty (Cree) is the author of *James Bay Memoirs: A Cree Woman's Ode to Her Homeland* and several other volumes of poetry. She has held numerous readings and lectured throughout the United States and Canada. She lives a traditional life in Fort George on James Bay, Québec, with her husband, William.

Andrea Smith (Cherokee) received the M.Div. from Union Theological Seminary in New York and is currently a doctoral student in history of consciousness at the University of California, Santa Cruz. She is a founder of the Chicago chapter of Women of All Red Nations. She is the author of the widely anthologized article "For All Those Who Were Indian in a Former Life," dealing with New Age appropriation of Native traditions.

Tweedy Sombrero (Navajo) is pastor of the Garfield Indian United Methodist Church in Phoenix, Arizona, and a doctoral candidate at the School of Theology at Claremont.

George Tinker (Osage) is professor of Native American cultures and religious traditions at the Iliff School of Theology in Denver. He is the author of *Missionary Conquest: The Gospel and Native American Cultural Genocide.*

Jace Weaver (Cherokee) is assistant professor of American studies and religious studies at Yale University and a lawyer. His two most recent books are *That the People Might Live: Native American Literatures and Native American Community* and *Defending Mother Earth: Native American Perspectives on Environmental Justice,* which he edited.

Craig Womack (Creek-Cherokee) teaches in the Native studies department at the University of Lethbridge in Alberta. He is the author of the forthcoming *National Literatures: Making a Return to American Indian Community.* He is also completing a novel, *The Spirit of Resistance.*

Index